Faith Formation of the Laity in Catholic Schools

The Influence of
Virtues and Spirituality Seminars

A volume in
Research on Religion and Education

Series Editors:
Lyndon G. Furst, *Andrews University*
Stephen J. Denig, *Niagara University*

Research on Religion and Education

Lawrence R. Jones and Nancy C. Roberts, Series Editors

*American Evangelicals and Religious Diversity: Subcultural Education,
Theological Boundaries, and the Relativization of Tradition*(2006)
edited by Kevin M. Taylor

*Issues of Governance and Identity in
Catholic Higher Education During the 1960's* (2004)
edited by Anthony J. Dosen

Religion, Education, and Academic Success (2003)
edited by William Jeynes

Faith Formation of the Laity in Catholic Schools

The Influence of Virtues and Spiritulity Seminars

by

Sister Patricia Helene Earl
Marymount University

Information Age Publishing, Inc.
Charlotte, North Carolina • www.infoagepub.com

Library of Congress Cataloging-in-Publication Data

Earl, Patricia Helene.
  Faith formation of the laity in Catholic schools : the influence of virtues and spirituality seminars / by Patricia Helene Earl.
     p. cm. -- (Research on religion and education)
  Includes bibliographical references.
  ISBN 978-1-59311-714-6 (pbk.) -- ISBN 978-1-59311-715-3 (hardcover) 1. Catholic
schools--United States--Faculty. 2. Lay teachers--In-service training--United States. 3. Faith
development. I. Title.
  LC501.E23 2008
  371.071'273--dc22

                                                                        2008021241

Printed in the United States of America

This book is dedicated with eternal gratitude to my mother, Helen Earl, and my aunt, Mae McLaughlin, who provided me with strong personal Catholic values at home and with the gift of Catholic education for 16 years. Their vision and love, while alive, have been the constant inspiration and models for my life and my work.

CONTENTS

PROLOGUE

This book is written to assist all those who work with young people, especially in our Catholic schools and other religiously affiliated programs, in developing students' faith formation by helping them to grow in virtue and in their spirituality. For 10 years, beginning when I was assistant superintendent of schools in the diocese of Arlington, Virginia and continuing now as I direct the Catholic school leadership program at Marymount University in Arlington, I have team-taught a 2-day seminar, "Catholic Virtues: Developing the Inner Life," to educators in the Diocese of Arlington, Virginia which has inspired principals and teachers to develop a virtue of the month program in many of the diocesan schools.

In addition, because of the success of this "virtues seminar" I developed another presentation on developing spirituality, a 4-week program designed to renew and enrich teachers' spirituality so that they could in turn share their faith and provide for the faith formation of their students. This book reflects a study of these two programs. The results of the research helped me to see why they were so successful, and how the seminars influenced the attendees' personal faith formation, their pedagogy in integrating virtue and spirituality into the classroom, and their understanding and appreciation of the mission of Catholic education. These results have been the source of several articles, a presentation at the annual leadership conference sponsored by the Australian Catholic University (2004), and presentations at the annual National Catholic Educational Association convention (2004, 2005, 2006). The specific content of the virtues seminar is found in my book, *Building the Builders: Faith Formation in Virtue*, published by the National Catholic Education Association (2006), Washington, DC.

Based on the assumption that you cannot give what you do not have, and on the notion that catechesis is a life-long process and we are all life-long learners, I hope that this book will be helpful for all those who are called to educate our youth in the knowledge and daily practice of their faith, especially in understanding virtue and putting it into daily practice. Throughout the text, while the research and seminars were designed for the Catholic schools, the outcomes which show the growth in faith formation also suggest that these types of programs in virtue development or character education and spirituality would benefit any school trying to deepen the faith formation of its educators as well as its students by adapting them to the specific faith content. I hope the reader will be as enthused in wanting to renew or develop the faith formation of faculty and students, as I was in discovering the benefits of these programs. Thus renewed, you will be empowered to help your faculty and students come to a deeper and more personal knowledge and love of God through virtuous living.

INTRODUCTION

Faith Formation of the Laity in Catholic Schools: The Influence of Virtues and Spirituality Seminars by Sister Patricia Earl is the third book in the Religion and Education series published by Information Age Publishing. Doctor Earl is a member of the Philadelphia Province of the Immaculate Heart of Mary Sisters and an assistant professor and director of the Catholic School Leadership Program at Marymount University in Arlington Virginia.

The need addressed by this book is a need common to many religious schools, not only of the Catholic tradition, but also the various Protestant, Jewish, and Moslem denominations—how to insure that the laity who are involved in the school are mature and growing in their faith. Faith-based schools, by their very nature, must insure that the students who attend these schools are enriched in faith through their encounters with God and with faith-filled teachers. With declining numbers of ordained clergy and professional religious in the schools, faith-based schools are turning more and more to laity to manage and to teach in these schools.

This decline is acute in Catholic schools. At one time, almost 100% of the teachers in schools were priests or religious brothers and sisters. Since the 1960s, this percentage has declined dramatically. For most of the past 40 years, the lay teachers who were recruited to teach in Catholic schools had been themselves taught by priests and religious sisters and brothers. This is no longer the case. Three new trends have emerged. First, most of the teachers in these schools have experienced only a few, if any, priests, religious sisters or brothers in their own Catholic school training. The second trend is that increasing numbers of Catholic teachers graduated from public schools. The final trend is that some Catholic school teachers are members of other faiths and have had little formal training in the Catholic faith with which they are to enrich their students.

These same patterns are true for teachers in other religious schools. While some teachers may have been taught by members of the clergy, or may have graduated from denominational schools and universities, most have no formal training in spiritual formation. Nor are they prepared to assist children and youth in the development of a spiritual nature. In addition, many teachers and administrators in religiously affiliated schools are graduates from the public sector with no religious education other than what they learned in attendance at religious services within their own faith community. How then do they develop faith in the young people under their care? This book provides one approach to answering that important question.

Dr. Earl is the former assistant superintendent of schools for the Arlington Roman Catholic Diocese. In that capacity, she first developed the virtues seminars, in which principals and teachers were inspired to create a Virtue of the Month program for their students. As lay principals and teachers continued their faith development, they asked her to help them continue their growth in faith through a spirituality seminar. This book documents the development and implementation of the virtues and spirituality seminars.

It is the belief of the editors, one of whom is Catholic and the other is Seventh-day Adventist, that this book will help all people who are responsible for, administer and teach in, or are part of religious-based schools to enhance the faith dimension of their schools. While the setting for the study Dr. Earl conducted was with teachers in Catholic schools, the principles of faith formation she tested have wide applicability to other faith communities. We are pleased to offer this book both to educators in the Catholic schools and to those in other religious schools.

Stephen J. Denig
Lyndon G. Furst

ACKNOWLEDGMENTS

I wish to thank all those who have made this book and its contents possible. First of all, I am grateful to my religious community, the Sisters, Servants of the Immaculate Heart of Mary, Immaculata, Pennsylvania, for the opportunity to serve as assistant superintendent of schools in the Diocese of Arlington and for my advanced study. My experiences in classroom teaching and administration in Catholic schools have provided me with an understanding of Catholic education and ability to respond to educator's requests for guidance in the development of character education and personal spirituality.

I also want to thank those who supported and advised me in my doctoral research at George Mason University, Fairfax, Virginia, Dr. Dennis Dunklee, Dr. Gerald Wallace, and Dr. Joseph Maxwell. Without their approval and guidance, this study and its results might not have continued.

A special word of thanks goes to all of the teachers and principals in the Arlington Diocese (over 500) who have attended these seminars, and especially those who participated in this research study.

I am also grateful to all those at Information Age Publishing, especially George Johnson, Rev. Stephen Denig, and Jerry Furst. It has been a joy to work with them, knowing that they provide so many resources for all of us involved in education.

CHAPTER 1

THE CONTEXT OF CATHOLIC SCHOOLING

Traditionally, Catholic schools in the United States were staffed exclusively by priests, religious sisters, and religious brothers. Today, however, they are predominately staffed by laypersons. This change in teaching staff has inevitably altered, to one degree or another, the essential religious character and culture of Catholic schools. While the religious quite naturally filter all of their teachings through their own religious training and emphasize the mission, spirit, culture, and charism of Catholic education, lay staff often lack the same intensely religious experiences to bring to the teaching/learning environment. In addition to high academic standards, an important attribute of Catholic education is, in fact, the religious, spiritual, values-oriented environment that parents value. To maintain this environment, do the laity need in-service assistance in the overall mission, spirit, culture, and charism of the Catholic schools' religious foundation? To provide this assistance, is there an available model for this training that could be adapted to this purpose? Can this model be adapted to assist any religiously based school with the faith formation of faculty and students?

Faith Formation of the Laity in Catholic Schools: The Influence of Virtues and Spirituality Seminars, pp. 1–11
Copyright © 2008 by Information Age Publishing
All rights of reproduction in any form reserved.

BACKGROUND OF THE PROBLEM

A brief history of Catholic schools in the United States will help to explain the significance of the role and presence of religious sisters, religious brothers, and priests in the establishment and development of U.S. Catholic education. It will show how teacher preparation became significant among the religious, which, in turn, contributed not only to the quality of their preparation, but also to their spiritual formation and ability to integrate the faith into the total curriculum. It will also heighten the importance of maintaining the Catholic identity of these schools as the current period of time shows a steady decline in the present and future presence of religious staff.

BRIEF OVERVIEW OF THE HISTORY OF
CATHOLIC SCHOOLS IN AMERICA

Catholic schools have a long tradition in the United States. They were founded in the United States to assist parents in the faith formation of their children, as well as to provide these children with a solid education that would prepare them for life. It is a story of a social institution that adapted itself to a constantly changing society while upholding its two primary goals; namely, "the preservation of the religious faith of Catholic children and the preparation of these children for productive roles in American society" (Walch, 2003, p. 5). That there are only four major historical surveys of the history of the American Catholic parochial school system written since 1900 makes this one of the most neglected topics in American historiography (Walch, 2003). These include works by James A. Burns, Bernard Kohlbrenner, Harold A. Buetow, and Glen Gabert.

The roots of Catholic education in America can be traced back to the early missions that provided religious education to the Native Americans. The Spanish focused their efforts in the South with their first settlements in Florida in 1565. In 1606, the Franciscans opened a school in what is now St. Augustine, Florida to teach Christian doctrine, reading and writing. Similarly, the French "black robes" started in Canada and gradually established foundations in the Midwest and the South in what are now the cities of Detroit, St. Louis, New Orleans, and Mobile. The Jesuits instructed dedicated Native American students, including Blessed Kateri Tekakwitha (1656-1680), who became a Catholic and instructed children near Montreal. Even though Catholicism was prohibited in many of the English colonies, except Maryland and Pennsylvania, the English priests continued to nurture the faith of the colonists. Though Catholics were a minority, the Jesuits established a preparatory school, Newton Manor, in the late 1600s mainly to instruct boys as potential candidates for seminary study in Europe. They opened a second Catholic school, Bohemia Manor, in 1745 to prepare students to enter the College of St. Omer's in Flanders. Among its first students were John Carroll, who would become the first Catholic bishop in the United States and his cousin, Charles Carroll, one of the signers of the Declaration of Independence (Walch, 2003). In 1718, the Franciscans opened a school for boys and in 1727, the Ursuline Sisters established the first Catholic school for girls in New Orleans (Buetow, 1985).

In the 1770s, state legislatures began to drop restrictions preventing Catholics from becoming citizens and added statutes granting freedom of conscience and religion. Pennsylvania passed these laws in 1776 and Maryland followed eliminating all restrictions on the practice of Catholicism. Protestants and Catholics fought side by side for independence. With the large immigrant population in the late 1700s from Ireland, France, and Germany, many viewed Catholics as foreigners. Bishops relied on parish schools to fulfill "The task of Americanizing these foreign-born Catholics without compromising their faith" (Walch, 2003, p. 16). Catholics in Philadelphia opened the first parochial school, St. Mary's, in 1783. Bishop John Carroll's first pastoral letter in 1792 "emphasized the importance of Christian education as a means of instilling principles that would preserve religious faith" (p. 16). The establishment of Georgetown University in 1789 fulfilled Bishop Carroll's vision for Catholic "college," though the boys who first attended ranged in ages from 10-16. In 1799, the Sisters of the Visitation founded a similar nearby school for girls, Georgetown Visitation Preparatory.

While other Catholic schools continued to open in various major cities, the birth of the Catholic school system is attributed to St. Elizabeth Ann Bayley Seton who began a school in Emmitsburg, Maryland in 1808 for the purpose of educating the daughters of Catholic families (Convey, 1992; Kelly, 1996; McNeil, 1996; Melville, 1951). This daughter of the well known Bayley family in New York, after suffering the loss of her husband, converted to Catholicism. Though shunned by her own family because of her conversion, her vision included the creation of a religious order, the American branch of the Daughters of Charity that became the framework for Catholic schooling for the decades that followed. The Sisters of Charity brought stability and order to the development of Catholic education as they established Catholic schools in Maryland, Pennsylvania, New York, Washington, DC, Ohio, Delaware, and Louisiana. She became the first native-born American saint (Walch, 2003). Soon after, Catholic immigrants built a large number of schools to educate their children in the Catholic faith and to prepare them for life in the United States. Large numbers of non-Catholics also asked to attend these schools, indicating that the schools' programs must have been desirable (Buetow, 1985).

In 1852, the Catholic bishops met in a plenary council to discuss the state of Catholicism in the United States. With increased numbers of Catholics, dioceses, and provinces, American Catholicism was truly national with dioceses from Baltimore in the East to Oregon in the West. The bishops were resolved to support Catholic schools. The number of parish schools in the United States jumped from 1,400 in 1875 to 2,500 in less than a decade (Walch, 2003).

Though the Catholic schools began to flourish in the middle of the nineteenth century, they did so amid a spirit of anti-Catholic bias, where those of other faiths felt that Catholics might weaken the American spirit and divide the country because of their allegiance to the Pope in Rome as head of their church. With increased immigration and growth in the Catholic communities, American Catholics first tried to reform the public schools to rid them of their fundamentalist views. When this failed, they began to open their own schools with the help of religious orders, including the Sisters of Mercy, from Ireland, under Sister Frances Warde, in 1843, and the Sisters, Servants of the Immaculate Heart of Mary, a teaching community organized in 1845 in Michigan by Sister Theresa (Almaide) Duchemin, originally an Oblate Sister of Providence. The success of these schools sparked more bigotry, the formation of groups such as the Know-Nothing Society committed to wiping out "foreign influence, Popery, Jesuitism, and Catholicism" (National Catholic Educational Association [NCEA], 2007), and much violence and prejudice.

In 1884 (Heft, 1991), the bishops of the United States convened the Third Plenary Council of Baltimore and in 1885 established an extensive parochial school system which affirmed the establishment of the first system of parochial school across the nation and the first unified system of Catholic schools with a diocesan school board by Bishop John Neumann of Philadelphia in 1885. "The board was charged with raising funds to support Catholic schools, reviewing Catholic school materials, and planning for the construction of new schools" (Walch, 2003, p. 48). The bishops described a conflict between the Church of God and spirit of the world that was influenced by movements of indifference, naturalism, and materialism that were causing the world to drift from religious truth and adopt a secular outlook on the meaning and purpose of life. The council required that every Catholic church would establish a parochial school within 2 years (Convey, 1992). Though the council failed to realize that not every parish had the economic resources to establish its own school, it had a significant impact on the organizational structure of Catholic education. Though Catholic schools had been administered by their pastors and trustees, the council supported the model of a diocesan school board, begun by Bishop Neumann just weeks before its decrees. The establishment of diocesan school boards in the years 1885-1920 reflected a major step in organizing, standardizing, and controlling parochial schools.

Teacher preparation, at least up to the American Revolution, was almost nonexistent and teacher standards were low in Catholic, as well as other schools (Buetow, 1985). Priest-teachers in Catholic schools for boys were often educated in Europe and unrivaled in academic ability. Scarcity of teachers was a concern for all schools. Catholic schools were more fortunate than others in having groups of religious, dedicated teachers living in community, guided by a Gospel-centered spirituality, who provided their services generously and without consideration of much financial remuneration. In these early days, the teaching sisterhoods were trained by the educated priests. Later, the religious sisters trained their own novices within each congregation of religious sisters. Catholic schools continued to grow, as did the numbers of religious congregations.

A number of other religious orders for women were founded to teach the poor, the immigrant, and the pioneer children in the United States. Among them were the Sisters of Loretto and the Sisters of Charity of Nazareth, founded in 1812 in Kentucky, and a Dominican community, founded in 1822 in Springfield. Mother Mary Elizabeth Lange established a school in Baltimore to serve the poor and in 1831, founded the Oblate Sisters of Providence, serving the African American education at a time when slavery was still strong in parts of the country. A person of mixed racial and ethnic background, an immigrant with gifts of energy, faith, and talent, she "embodied the new American Church (NCEA, 2007). Other European religious communities sent religious sisters to the United States to serve as teachers, as well as nurses and other social service ministries.

> Since the very early days of our nation's history, daughters of this country and immigrants from other lands have joined religious communities, taking their religious calling to the edge of the lonely frontier and into the crowded inner cities. Thousands of diverse young women have fearlessly followed in their footsteps, leaving behind family and the familiar to embrace lives committed to prayer, teaching, healing, and social action. Religious sisters nursed both Confederate and Union soldiers during the Civil War.... Religious sisters participated in the opening of the West, traveling vast distances by horse, wagon, train and boat to minister in remote locations, setting up schools and hospitals and working among native populations on distant reservations. Religious sisters created the largest private school system even known. They financed and administered these institutions.... Their efforts prepared countless immigrant children to enter the mainstream of American life and offered educational opportunities to girls and women that were rare in those days. Religious sisters built colleges, hospitals, orphanages and charitable

institutions that served millions of people; they staffed and managed complex organizations.... As authors, sculptors, painters and musicians, religious sisters contribute to the cultural and spiritual landscape of the nation... while sharing a common focus on prayer and contemplation. (Leadership Conference of Women Religious, 2007, pp. 5-7)

Tens of thousands of religious sisters staffed the parish schools in the nineteenth century. Walch (2003) noted that the parochial school system could not have grown without the contribution of these sister-teachers. However, their success is even greater when one looks at the obstacles that they faced. The first religious sisters who came from Europe often lacked preparation and often lived in poor housing with little food. With a variety of students from different racial and ethnic backgrounds, social standing, and financial standing, the religious sisters also realized that their students and their families had few religious or educational traditions. With so little in common and little on which to build, their task of teaching was even more difficult. "Yet these women accepted their realities as an opportunity from God" (p. 135). In adapting to the New World, religious communities had to adapt to their new conditions, often eliminating the professional training and substituting it with a course in methods and relying on gathering professional experience by learning by doing.

The Civil War divided North and South but diluted religious prejudices. Following the war, Catholic education continued to grow. The Second Baltimore Council calling for parochial schools in 1866, and the Third Baltimore Council in 1884 demanding that all parishes open schools within 2 years. More religious orders were founded. St. Katherine Drexel began the Sisters of the Blessed Sacrament to provide education to the blacks and Native Americans (NCEA, 2007). In the 1995 Harper-Collins Encyclopedia of Catholicism, Thomas Groome wrote that "Throughout history, there is no more compelling instance of Catholic commitment to education than the school system created by the U.S. Catholic community" (NCEA, 2007).

The building of Catholic schools in the Midwest received more tolerance largely due to the size and economic role of the Catholic communities. There was a greater acceptance of the immigrants since they provided cheap and dependable labor. In addition, since there were few public institutions in the 1832s and 1840s, the Catholic social institutions played a major role in urban development and thus, had a positive impact on both the Catholic and non-Catholic populations. However, the debate over the financing of public and private schools was still present. Midwesterners put their energy into building Catholic schools rather than protesting the financial issues. In some Northeastern communities, such as

Boston, public schools prevailed over Catholic; yet, in New York and Philadelphia, "the parish school was a dominant institution in every Catholic neighborhood" (Walch, 2003, p. 52).

Issues related to religious tolerance and practices by Catholics and non-Catholics alike, as well as financial support by the Catholic Church and/or public education funds helped to create three models of parochial education form the post-Civil War period until World War I. Walch (2003) describes four educational choices for Catholic parents. A significant percentage of Catholic parents subscribed to the public school system as a means to insure future prosperity for their children in society. The second group did not want a curriculum totally lacking in religious instruction but they did not want to abandon a public education. Thus, they tried to build good relations with the public school boards to provide "publically supported secular institutions taught by Catholic teachers in parish owned classrooms," with after-school religious instruction (p. 82). A third group of parents did not support formal relations with the public school board but they wanted to follow much of the public school curriculum within the parish school. Finally, the fourth group, a largely immigrant population, did not support any link with the public school system but favored parish schools that also emphasized native language, culture, and religion. Thus, in the last half of the nineteenth century and first quarter of the twentieth century, there was no single model of Catholic education. "The style and substance of Catholic parochial education varied from region to region, diocese to diocese, and even from parish to parish across the United States" (p. 83).

The religious sisters' experience varied across the country depending on the commitment of bishops and parishes in the establishment and operation of parish schools. In some dioceses, they received support from the parish, in others they were totally on their own. Many congregations operated independently with each diocese, negotiating with their pastors, raising their own funds, establishing their own schools, and closing them if there was no support.

However, while the Third Plenary Council had mandated that every parish establish a school, which increased the demand for sister-teachers, it also decreed that teachers should be examined periodically to insure a high quality of Catholic instruction. The council also urged religious communities to establish normal schools for the training of sister-teachers.

In 1902, the Institute of Pedagogy was established in New York City to provide teacher training for teachers in the Archdiocese of New York. Over time, a Religious Sisters College was established near The Catholic University of America first offering summer institutes and then a correspondence school at The Catholic University of America in 1905. It became an official affiliate of The Catholic University of America in 1913.

By 1919, it offered instruction to over 1,800 religious sisters from 151 congregations. Eventually other Catholic colleges offered similar teacher training programs. Some dioceses offered teacher institutes to all teachers in Catholic schools. By 1910, practically all teaching orders had established their own teacher training programs. To offset issues related to faculty preparation and status as educational institutions, many Catholic colleges established education departments and teacher training programs. In 1919, at a meeting of the Catholic Education Association, the superiors of women's religious communities and administrators of Catholic women's colleges agreed that state certification was inevitable. They felt that they could improve the quality of their teaching preparation while also meeting the demand for more teachers every year. The number of sister-teachers who attended summer normal schools increased 176 percent between 1921 and 1926 (Walch, 2003). As the sister-teachers professional training increased from what had been provided in the earliest days,

> What was never compromised, however, was the leadership role played by women religious in parochial education from the mid-nineteenth century on. In fact, it would not be difficult to make the case that sister-teachers were the single most important element in the Catholic educational establishment.... The responsibilities of sister-teachers for the spiritual and educational life of the American church were extraordinary. (pp. 150-151)

Efforts to establish national professional standards were largely unsuccessful until the 1920s when state legislatures began to require certification of private school teachers. Before this time, there was little interest in these standards by bishops, communities of women religious or parish pastors because more importance was first placed on cultivating religious vocations. With the limited time available to train the applicant in the vocation of religious life, limited attention was often given to teacher training.

> With only a limited amount of time for the education of novices, congregations focused on character formation and general intellectual development;.... Of greatest importance to every congregation of religious sisters was to inspire in every novice a sense of community tradition and commitment to the rule of the founder of the order.... Young novices ... were assigned to parishes with high percentages of experienced teachers. It was the veteran sister-teachers who trained the novices in the ways of the Catholic classroom. In the manner of a craft, the master teachers trained their apprentices. (Walch, 2003, pp. 136-137)

This craft system approach was a major from of teacher training until teacher certification grew in importance in the 1930s and 1940s. It was popular because it was economical, allowed more time for spiritual formation and development of the religious vocation for the novice, and allowed the religious orders to get more religious sisters into the schools. With the growing demand for Catholic education, there never seemed to be enough vocations to meet the demand for sister-teachers.

The religious sisters taught successive generations the basic beliefs of the faith, grounded them in Christian living, and gave them a sense of responsibility to maintain a Christian atmosphere in their homes and in future generations of children. Walch (2003) concludes that while the number of immigrants contributed to the growth of the American Catholic Church, the work of the sister-teachers in nurturing a life-long faith in numerous generations of American-born Catholics was equally important in the expansion of the Catholic population.

After the turn of the century, the U.S. Office of Education recognized the importance of Catholic parochial schools in the educational life of the nation.

> "The most impressive religious fact in the United States today," began one chapter in the *Report of the U.S. Commissioner of Education for 1903*, "is the system of Catholic free parochial schools. Not less than one million children are being educated in these schools. This great educational work is being carried out without any financial aid from the state" (Walch, 2003, p. 100)

Walch describes this as a turning point in the history of Catholic education. "For the first time, the federal government officially took notice of the nation's second school system. Catholic education had come of age" (p. 100).

At the same time that the number of schools rapidly increased to try to keep up with the rising number of students, there was little national or diocesan coordination. There was a growing need for organizations and procedures to add some centralization to school planning and supervision at the diocesan level. In 1905, E. F. Gibbons, the superintendent of schools in Buffalo, New York recognized the need for this organization to foster communication among teachers, support the Americanization of ethnic schools, and demonstrate the uniform quality of parochial education to parents who were hesitant about enrolling their children. By 1910, over 55% of American dioceses had schools boards, and 17% of these dioceses had superintendents. By 1930, the percentage of diocesan superintendents almost quadrupled and all American bishops recognized the need for more order in the administration of parochial schools (Walch, 2003).

During the early part of the twentieth century, Catholic educators also established national organizations to promote communication among teachers, administrators, and bishops on issues affecting parochial schools. The Catholic Education Association was founded in 1903 as a national forum for educational ideas and became the National Catholic Education Association in 1928. The Education Department of the

National Catholic Welfare Conference was started in 1919 to look at issues related to government involvement while also representing the Church hierarchy in one unified voice on education (Walch, 2003). By 1930, Catholic education "was more efficient, more structured, and more ordered than it had been thirty years earlier" (p. 117).

Up until the 1950s, Catholic schools were almost entirely staffed by priests, religious sisters, and religious brothers. Statistically, the U.S. Catholic school system reached its peak in 1964 (Groome, 1998). There were over 13,000 schools with 5.6 million students. Until the mid-1960s, priests, religious brothers, and religious sisters made up 95% of the faculty and staff of U.S. Catholic schools. These religious, sisters, brothers, and priests, "have engaged in Catholic educational purposing" (Cook, 2001, p. vi). They have made it possible for teachers and students to contribute to and receive satisfaction and achievement as they have directed their efforts to the fulfillment of their school's Catholic purpose. The devotion of religious priests, religious sisters, and religious brothers has often inspired teachers and students so that the school's Catholic identity became identified with the generous and self-less devotion of these men and women religious (Cook, 2001; Jacobs, 1996). A Catholic school was essentially a school that was predominantly administered and staffed by religious. The presence of religious, with their faith and spirituality developed through their formation or preparation for this vocation, was the distinguishing mark of a Catholic school.

However, by the mid-1990s (Cook, 2001), lay people made up 95% of the faculty and staff of U.S. Catholic schools. The number of religious sisters, religious brothers, and priests has steadily declined, while the percentage of lay men and women committed to the Catholic Church's educational apostolate has substantially increased. Recent statistics from the National Catholic Education Association (NCEA, 2002) report that in 2001-2002 full-time equivalent professional staff numbered 155,658: laity 94.2%, religious/clergy 5.8%: lay women: 75.0%; lay men: 19.2%; religious sisters: 4.4%; religious brothers 0.07%; priests 0.07%. While the generosity of the laity to respond to God's call to serve is valuable for the Catholic schools, there is concern that the laity will receive the formation needed to preserve and perfect the identity of the Catholic school (Cook, 2001).

This Catholic identity is centered on a set of beliefs that give each school a moral purpose. Walch (2003) cites a recent study by Bryk, Lee, and Holland (1993), *Catholic Schools and the Common Good*, which identifies hallmarks of successful Catholic schools which he believes could be adapted to any school, public or religiously based. These include decentralization, a shared set of beliefs, size, and academics. Decentralization describes the Catholic school system which is controlled by a superintendent and diocesan board of education, but which the day to day administration and funding are administered at the local level. Parents have greater involvement working with their particular school rather than a general system-wise administrative body. In a Catholic school, parents, faculty, and students share a set of beliefs that also provide a moral purpose for the school and a code of conduct. The smaller size of most Catholic schools allows for more interaction and communication since it is easier for parents and faculty to know each other, faculty often have more than one role in the school, and there is a greater ability for educators to be role models for the students. Finally, academics are vitally important in Catholic schools. Limited in size and resources, they focus more on the basics and are less drawn to follow passing and untested fads. Students are, therefore, prepared well in mathematics and literary skills, as well as other core subjects, and future success in higher educational levels.

While each of these qualities is important, two of the hallmarks seem to support this research and resulting programs in cultivating virtue and spirituality; namely, sharing a common set of beliefs and because of size, serving more effectively as role models. They highlight why the research and programs suggested throughout this book could be adapted and become valuable resources for any faith-based school. While the study and my own research are focused on Catholic schools and faith formation in the Catholic tradition, the results of the study support the importance of sharing a common set of beliefs, beliefs which can be cultivated through the study of one's faith, development of a spiritual relationship with God, and promotion of sound moral behavior or virtue which thus, produces a shared code of conduct which focuses on the dignity of and respect for the human person made in God's image. That faculty can serve as role models makes it even more important that they too are formed in their faith so that they witness and model their faith as they interact with their students. This points again to the importance of faith formation, and highlights the general concept which can be adapted according to the specific doctrinal beliefs that form the heart of any faith-based school.

The next chapter will begin to look at some research to assist the laity in their own faith formation so that they can continue to share this with their students, preserving the Catholic identity while promoting academic excellence and thus, continue to fulfill the mission of Catholic education. While the research was done in Catholic schools and within the doctrinal beliefs of the Catholic faith, this could easily be adapted for any faith-based school, especially since virtuous living is recognized as valuable in all faiths, even if not always presented in the same doctrinal context as in a Catholic school, and developing a relationship with one's God is at the heart of any religious faith, even if the means of developing that spirituality vary.

CHAPTER 2

CURRENT ISSUES OF STAFFING THE CATHOLIC SCHOOL

This book documents the results of research which was prompted by two major real-world concerns regarding Catholic schools in the United States. The first centered on maintaining the Catholic identity of the Catholic schools, and the second centered on the growing interest in character education.

First, the increasing decline in religious vocations is a concern for the Catholic schools. Founded not only to provide a well-rounded education for students, but also a sound formation in the Gospel values of Jesus Christ and the doctrinal teachings of the Catholic Church, the Catholic schools were predominantly staffed by religious sisters, religious brothers, and priests. Through their respective formation programs, they have been well formed and trained in the principles of the Catholic faith. In addition, religious communities have traditionally been built around certain charisms. These, in turn, have inspired the individual spirituality of the members. Though Catholic schools traditionally provide an excellent academic education, it is the formation of students' spiritual life through the Catholic faith and following the example of Christ that have made the Catholic school unique and distinct. With fewer religious to staff the schools, is there a way to preserve the charism of the Catholic school so that

Faith Formation of the Laity in Catholic Schools: The Influence of Virtues and Spirituality Seminars, pp. 13–20
Copyright © 2008 by Information Age Publishing
All rights of reproduction in any form reserved.

it can continue to provide for the total development of students on all levels, including their spiritual formation? Catholic schools are flourishing, but the hope for future success cannot rest on history or past reputation. It will depend on the laity to sustain the academic quality and continue to instill a spirit of faith and value rooted in Christ. Yet, there is concern. In spite of academic and pedagogical preparation, will the laity have the needed faith formation to keep the true Catholic identity alive? These same concerns are found in any school that tries to sustain the academic quality while trying to instill a spirit of faith rooted in the founder of its faith. Thus, the same question applied to the Catholic school could also be asked of any religious school; namely, in spite of academic and pedagogical preparation, will the laity have the needed faith formation to keep their religious identity alive?

Second, in an age that sees increasing violence and lack of self-esteem and respect for the dignity of humanity, there has been a growing interest in looking for ways to develop character, to promote sound values, and to foster a deeper sense of morality. The founders of our democracy maintained that moral education was fundamental for the success of a democratic society (Lickona, 1991). Character education was integrated into curriculum. Along with discipline and good example, schools instructed children in patriotism, hard work, honesty, and courage among other virtues.

William Bennett (1993, 1999), former Chairman of the National Endowment for the Humanities and Secretary of Education under President Reagan, has renewed awareness of moral truths in literature with his collection and commentary on virtues, as well as guide for parents seeking to educate the whole child. While focusing on skills and knowledge, good elementary schools should transmit to each generation "our 'common culture,' the things that bind Americans together as one people" (Bennett, 1999, p. 11). This "common culture" includes the knowledge, ideas, and understanding of who we are. It is found in our historical documents, including the Declaration of Independence and the Constitution; in principles, such as believing that all men are created equal; and in past events, such as the landing of the *Mayflower* at Plymouth and the *Eagle* on the moon. It is found in stories that introduce children to our common legacy. For Bennett (1999), "Teaching cultural literacy is part of the effort of raising good citizens" (p. 12). Schools assist parents in the development of character in their children and recognize that intellect and character are partners in the formation of youth. Good habits, virtues, and seeking the good are vital for the future of society.

Yet today, signs of a decline in fostering self-discipline, moral choices, and respect are evident. Drugs, sex, and alcohol increasingly tempt children at early ages. With an alarming rise in youth violence (Lickona,

1991), society is more aware that children are changing, not just in the violent extremes of teenagers, but in the speech and actions of younger children. Broken families, lack of supervision, poor parenting, greed, materialism, and a media culture that can stunt moral judgment seem to be fostering an "ethical illiteracy" (p. 5) where basic elements of moral knowledge seem to be disappearing. For educators seeking to assist parents in the total development of their children in an age that reflects a decline in moral values and standards, it is important to look for ways to promote good values, moral principles, and ethical standards in the formation of our children and the moral health of the nation.

The decline in religious vocations and interest in trying to preserve the Catholic identity of our schools and the decline in moral values and interest in trying to instill them in our children are two separate issues. However, they may be complementary issues. When the bishops met at the Third Plenary Council of Baltimore in 1884, they were concerned about the rise of secularism, materialism, and the decline of moral values. This prompted them to mandate a system of Catholic schools in order to spread the faith, as well as to prepare all students who attended to take their place in the world with dignity and respect. Perhaps if today's church can maintain the Catholic school, in spite of declining religious, it can continue to contribute to the character development and moral stamina of society. Perhaps if any faith denomination can maintain its religious schools, it can continue to contribute to the character development and moral stamina of society.

SIGNIFICANCE OF THE PROBLEM

This study begins to address the issue of how to preserve the Catholic identity of our Catholic schools at a time when the numbers of religious sisters, religious brothers, and priests still continue to decline. If the laity comprises 95% of the faculty and staff in the Catholic schools, then they will need to assume the responsibility for the continued development of the Catholic identity of these schools.

Numerous church documents written by the hierarchy of the Catholic Church identify the purpose of the Catholic school. The National Catholic Educational Association is exploring issues of history, heritage, and culture in the Catholic schools (Cook, 2001; Jacobs, 1996). These are helpful in trying to describe and clarify the Catholic identity of the Catholic schools.

With fewer religious on staff to model and mentor the laity, how can we teach the laity and what should we teach them to enable them to continue to build a Catholic system of education? My own 13 years of experience as assistant superintendent of schools for the Arlington Diocese working with teaching personnel have made me aware of the increasing number of teachers who are coming to our Catholic schools for the first time, without ever having attended a Catholic school as a student. Many of these teachers not only need to be taught the church teachings or doctrine, but also need to understand the purpose and identity of a Catholic school. Those in administration in Catholic education have an obligation to share not only the Catholic faith and sound pedagogical methodology, but also in some degree the spiritual formation that the religious sisters, religious brothers, and priests received. My experience has shown me that those who generously come to teach in a Catholic school are also eager to learn about the faith and are searching to understand their own spirituality. A philosophy of Catholic education seeks to educate the whole child intellectually, physically, emotionally, socially, and spiritually. One must know the subject in order to teach it, regardless of what the subject may be. Similarly, if teachers are to continue to educate the whole child, including the spiritual dimension, then they too must be growing and developing their own spirituality. Otherwise, the Catholic school system risks losing an essential component of its identity. The core values and teachings that identify each religious faith are at the heart of its identity. Thus, teachers who are called to educate students within any specific faith, must not only know some of the doctrine of that faith, but must be growing and developing their own spirituality within their respective religions. Otherwise, they too risk losing their own identity.

There seems to be an increase in the literature related to identifying this Catholic identity and to raising this as a significant issue for Catholic schools. Our Sunday Visitor Publishers created a 2-day program and a 2-day follow-up, primarily designed for principals, to assist them in their understanding of Church issues, and the qualities that contribute to the Catholic identity of the school. The National Catholic Educational Association created a program, Shepherding the Shepherds (National Catholic Educational Association, n.d.), as well as one on promoting Catholic identity to assist principals in learning how to be the spiritual leaders of their schools. However, research needs to be done in the area of spiritual formation of the lay faculty and staff to assist them in their spiritual formation. Certainly, the demands of their daily lives would prevent them from obtaining the more concentrated spiritual formation which priests, religious sisters, and religious brothers receive. However, since Catholic schools in the past were almost entirely staffed by these religious, and the Catholic school was identified by the presence of a particular religious community, are we to assume that if religious vocations decline, that Catholic education will also decline? The generosity and support of the laity to staff the schools, and the ongoing desire of parents to select this type of education for their children seem to provide the foundation for the continued existence of Catholic schools. However, we need to share the foundation, the faith, and the formation from our history and experience in order to continue to create the Catholic culture of these schools. The same may be said of any faith-based school which must share the foundation from its history, its faith, and the formation growing out of that history and experience with its faculty and its students.

In addition to providing for the spiritual formation of the laity who staff Catholic schools, diocesan offices, and principals need to be concerned with the character education of students. This issue is not unique to the Catholic schools but is a challenge for all schools. With a rise in secularism and materialism and a seeming collapse of the family, all schools must try to teach children good values (Lickona, 1991). It is possible that whatever we can do to maintain the identity or heart of the Catholic school or any school built upon a particular faith may assist us in fulfilling our purpose to form faith-filled and moral citizens who are prepared to contribute to the continued growth and development of society.

SPECIFIC PROBLEM

As indicated, there are two major real-world problems or concerns that prompted this study. While the research is gathered from Catholic schools, the responses could reflect any school that advocates the importance of faith in God, developing ones spirituality, and acting in a virtuous manner toward others. The reader could substitute his/her religion each time the word "Catholic" appears.

From the study, the first real-world problem or concern centers around maintaining the Catholic identity of the Catholic schools, and the second centers around the growing interest in character education. Specifically, with the decline in the number of religious staffing our Catholic schools and the increased role of the laity, what can we do to assist the laity in their formation so that the purpose, spirit, culture, and charism of the Catholic school are maintained and Catholic schools can continue to grow and provide for the total development, including spirituality and character education, of the students who attend?

Responding to the interest in spirituality that emerged during Catholic diocesan school board meetings several years ago, I created a series of seminars for teachers. The first was a 4-week series on basic elements of spirituality. The second was a 2-day summer seminar on virtues for the classroom. Both seminars were well received and I continue to offer them regularly each year locally and in other parts of the United States as well. Since the number of teachers attending continues to increase, and since I receive ongoing feedback from teachers who have attended, I wondered if these seminars could have an impact on the lay teachers' understanding of Catholic schools. Based on my own formation as a religious sister, I have tried to capture a few of the elements that were part of my formation and build my seminars around these elements of basic spirituality and moral development. If Catholic schools have traditionally been associated with the priests, religious sisters, and religious brothers, who had some type of lengthy spiritual formation, and if I have tried to create a mini-formation through these seminars, can these seminars or similar types of programs contribute to the issues of Catholic identity and character education?

RESEARCH GOALS

The primary goal of this study was to pursue research that could impact leadership in Catholic education and educational leadership in general. Most immediately, the research interests of this author resulted from personal experience in working with educational personnel (K-12) in the Catholic schools, and the desire to impact the character education of children, primarily by showing some particular needs for staff development for educators. This personal experience convinced the author that, only to the degree that our educators understand and continue to develop their own character formation, could they truly motivate, model, and inspire children.

The continued growth and existence of Catholic schools is particularly important to the author, especially in a period where there are fewer vocations to religious life. Catholic schools began through the work of these men and women. Their contributions are primary to the Catholic identity of the schools. A major problem exists to maintain this Catholic identity in spite of fewer religious and more lay staff. What did these religious men and women contribute to education, and especially character education of children? How did they learn their charisms and goals, and what and how did they pass these on to their students? What theories of learning were/are involved? What concepts of literacy can be applied to character education, both for the student-learner and the adult-learner/teacher? What impact could this discovery have not only on Catholic education, but also on character education in the non-Catholic sector? If qualities and concepts and charisms can be identified, what principles of learning can be extracted and applied to any school setting with modification?

Most of these problems, topics and theories could be approached primarily through qualitative methods of research that go beyond the limits of this study. First, a study of written documents from the archives of some religious communities could determine original qualities or methods of instruction. Then, interviews could be conducted with some of these religious as well as lay teachers to look for parallels and consistency over time. Case studies could show the effectiveness of methods. In addition, some quantitative approaches to collecting data could assist in quantifying and objectifying results.

This current study focused on selected case studies to show the effectiveness of methods. Specifically, lay teachers who attended the seminars provided information and insights from their perspective on how these seminars have influenced them and what impact, if any, these seminars have had on their understanding or perception of Catholic schools. By determining that these seminars had a positive influence on teachers and their understanding of Catholic schools, it would then be feasible to go back in subsequent studies and look at religious communities. By trying to capture elements of their formation that they considered essential to the Catholic school, and then creating additional seminars for teacher formation, this could impact the continued Catholic identity of our Catholic schools. If the spirituality and virtue seminars have influenced teachers' ability to provide for the character education of students, this could be helpful not only for the Catholic schools, but also for any school system. The heart of this inquiry and the various research questions are concerned with the future and with teacher formation, either to maintain the mission or purpose of Catholic education, or to develop the character education of students that underlies these questions. Understanding the type of influence and the depth of impact that the seminars have had on these teachers could help to determine if and how one can transmit the moral values of a culture or the Catholic mission of a school system in order to ensure the continued existence of each.

RESEARCH QUESTIONS

The research questions for this study were developed to explore the issues of Catholic identity and character education. These questions provided the foundation for this study. The research questions were:

1. What sorts of significant experiences do these virtue/spirituality seminars produce and how do they affect the participants?
2. In what specific ways have the seminars been reflected in participants' teaching or influenced their thinking about their teaching pedagogy?
3. How do participants, upon completion of the seminars, define character education and articulate whether or not a relationship exists between the seminars and character education?

4. Is there an impact on lay teachers' perceptions of Catholic educa-
    tion as a result of participation in the seminars?

However, these questions could be adapted by other religious schools so
that the value of these faith formation programs could apply equally to
these schools.

The next chapter will explore the concept of faith formation though
some of the literature that has been developed by those who support its
value and the need for all people to develop and grow in their own faith
formation. This will reinforce the importance of educators in faith based
schools to assist students in their faith formation as well. Finally, after
looking at some general principles of faith formation across a variety of
religions, faith formation will be examined from the perspective of Catholic literature.

CHAPTER 3

THE VALUE OF
FAITH FORMATION

The concept of faith formation can be applied to any religious denomination regardless of its origin. While this study focused primarily on the faith formation of lay teachers in Catholic schools, there is a growing body of knowledge on faith formation in general. A brief look at some of this literature will help to establish the importance of this topic for any religiously based school suggesting that the content and outcomes of this study may be adapted to suit the specific doctrines.

HISTORICAL OVERVIEW OF FAITH AND
PRAYER IN THE UNITED STATES

Faith and religion have played an important role from the earliest days of the colonization of our country and the quest for religious freedom sought by so many immigrants. During the period from 1640-1750, how to teach Christianity and convey moral values challenged New England. The Puritans needed a guide to educate and instruct their children on the need for prayer and strong morals. *The New England Primer* (1690), the most popular book in the New World after the Bible, combined a study of the alphabet with the Bible, catechism, and prayer. It was an integral tool in the education of youth into the nineteenth century and had a profound

Faith Formation of the Laity in Catholic Schools: The Influence of Virtues and Spirituality Seminars, pp. 21–36
Copyright © 2008 by Information Age Publishing
All rights of reproduction in any form reserved.

impact on the character of early America. "Integrating prayer and spirituality with practical learning became the perfect formula" (Moore, 2005, p. 42). *The New England Primer Improved* or *An Essay and Pleasant Guide to the Art of Reading: The Assembly's Shorter Catechism* continued to be popular and prayer and piety focused more on death, the fires of hell and original sin than on developing the child's devotion to God. *Family Prayers* encouraged parents to assume responsibility for insuring regularity in the children's prayer which was viewed as the way to build a virtuous life. As families traveled west and were distanced from their churches, the Bible and prayer books helped to maintain spiritual devotions.

In the late nineteenth century, Catholic and Jews brought their own prayer cultures with centuries of ritual and religious practices. Parochial schools began to emerge among Catholic, Jewish, and some Protestant congregations (Moore, 2005). The McGuffey's Readers, created by a Presbyterian minister, William Holmes McGuffey, were a basic foundation in public education. Referring directly to God and prayer, as well as poetry, grammar, and printing, the reader was "an educational model that taught students moral lessons through the popular literature of the day as well as through his personal insights on how to lead a proper Christian life, including plenty of prayer" (Moore, 2005, p. 199). From 1885-1900, prayer continued to mature in content and "grew even more deeply embedded, becoming an inextricable part of the country's presence in the world stage" (Moore, 2005, p. 240).

A world of creativity, invention, and entrepreneurship emerged at the turn of the twentieth century. This age of intellectualism and advances in science and technology led many to believe that humans could control and surmount the obstacles of life. As a result, this "Age of Unbelief" saw many American turn "away from the tenets of organized religion to probe for themselves the true essence of universal spirituality" (Moore, 2005, p. 242). For some prayer was their only spiritual outlet; while others found it difficult to try to define universal truths. In 1902, William James, brother of Henry James, wrote *The Varieties of Religious Experience*, to show how individual religious experience was the basis for spiritual life. As a proponent of pragmatism, he tried to analyze prayer, religion, and human beings. "He helped to make religion and even mystical experiences more acceptable by mingling science and religion in profoundly novel ways" (Moore, 2005, p. 244).

While academics seemed to be more popular than religion, religion continued to be important on college campuses. Hymn books and music appropriate to the religious traditions of schools were printed for colleges, including Harvard, Rutgers, and the U.S. Military Academy at West Point. Though chapel services were not required in many places, "chapel" remained the "spiritual heartbeat of most college campuses" (Moore, 2005, p. 244).

This was also a time of transformation. The large number of Catholic and Jewish immigrants from Europe, as well as a strong Protestant movement in rural American and some urban areas, influenced our country. The Pentecostal Movement and Revival Movements were begun with such famous individuals as William Ashley "Billy" Sunday taking the lead.

With this time of great awakening in the shadow of the Industrial Revolution, the emphasis shifted personal sin to the social sins of poverty, crime, prejudice and ignorance. A Congregationalist minister, Rev. Charles Sheldon first asked the question which has become popular again in our time, "What would Jesus do?" in his book, *In His Steps*. Rev. Walter Rauschenbusch's *Prayers of the Social Awakening* revealed the social problems of the time in its invocations according to social groups, classes, and causes (Moore, 2005).

As America's churches tried to reach out to potential membership, the idea of "muscular Christianity" (Moore, 2005, p. 257) became increasingly popular. "They believed that men strong in body and mind could overcome the world's ills and forge a promising future" (Moore, 2005, p. 257). The YMCA promoted "God in the gym" (Moore, 2005, p. 258). Prayer remained the heart of this muscular Christianity. Both President Theodore Roosevelt and President Howard Taft were strong supporters of this movement.

During World War I, America's churches and synagogues supported the troops, publishing and providing them with devotional materials including prayers, Bible readings, and hymns. The Lutheran Church printed a prayer book with numerous devotions, such as, "For the Success of Our Arms" and "Against the Enemies of our Nation." The Chaplain's Aide Association of the Catholic Church published military missals for Mass and a prayer book, *A Rule for Life*. Through the Bishop White Prayer Book Society, the Episcopalians distributed the *Book of Common Prayer* (Moore, 2005, p. 261). The prayer effort during the war inspired Americans to support the U.S. Treasury Department by purchasing savings stamps, thrift stamps and bonds. It inspired patriotic and religious songs as well.

The 1920s and 1930s saw a growth in the arts. These were considered by some to be "reflective decades in U.S. history. Not only were Americans defining themselves a global players and expressing themselves creatively, if not dynamically through the arts and humanities, they were also experiencing the realities of economic despair and vulnerability" (Moore, 2005, p. 298) following the Great Depression. While this seemed to be a time of spiritual void, it was temporary.

Prayer sustained the troops in World War II. "Reflecting on the mysteries of God and their own role in a very changed world order, many Americans adopted prayer as a means to help them thrive, if not survive, in the face of extraordinary challenges" (Moore, 2005, p. 322). Margaret Mead, the twentieth century anthropologist, advocated prayer and sacred rites as "a critical stabilizing force in society" (as cited in Moore, 2005, p. 366). "She believed that time-honored prayer practices intertwined throughout daily life and within the American calendar could offset the tendency toward being 'alienated from our own culture' "(p. 366). The psychologist, Karl Mennger, believed that prayer was essential in human development. "In accepting personal responsibility, owning up to individual failings, and then surrendering to the healing nature of payer, man and women could find a very real and effective means to deal with everyday life" (pp. 366-367). He believed that "pride and political correctness had superseded the examination of conscience and consequent search for forgiveness" (p. 367). Even now in the twenty-first century, Internet use shows that people are looking for spiritual support. Science and medicine have shown that prayer seems to have a positive effect on physical and mental health. *How?*

From this brief historical overview of the role of prayer throughout the development of the United Sates, the importance of prayer, moral growth, and conscience formation have shown to be important regardless of the specific religious beliefs. Thus, faith formation plays a significant role in any religion. Authors from various religious backgrounds have contributed to our further understanding of the meaning and value of faith formation.

FAITH DEVELOPMENT THEORIES

Robert Morneau (1995) provides a valuable understanding of faith and religion, which also highlights the reality that faith formation is important for all those who hold a set of beliefs in any particular faith. He speaks of the relationship that exists among images, attitudes, and behavior. There is the power and beauty of images which help to form our attitudes, and our attitudes, in turn, play a major role in forming our behavior. Referring to a definition from Avery Dulles, he states: "faith is the radical conviction that God's redeeming love surrounds and sustains us." In trying to show the relationship between poetry and faith, poetry is a use of words which are concrete and not abstract, … a way of trying to in some way take our deepest yearnings and aspirations and find form and shape for those. Beauty is faith and poetry coming together. Poetry grows from images. We need faith and we need pictures. We need to visualize and try to see that faith is really important. A story that goes into the imagination helps to convey faith, its meaning and its value at a totally different level than theological investigations. We need pictures to help us beside theology to understand the mystery of God and to plan our life. Stories change our lives because a story shapes our emotions, guides our education, energizes our actions, and anoints our sufferings. Stories are powerful and Morneau (1995) cautions that we need to be careful of the stories we read because they can change our lives, both for better or for worse. Thus, we need to be selective in the pictures we see and the images that we allow to fill us. In relation to reading, music, and art, we need to select only the best "when it gets into your bloodstream, it cannot get out and will stay with us for fifty years or more."

Morneau (1995) also states that an image carries an experience in a compressed form, for example, the message of love conveyed in seeing a wedding ring on someone's hand or a rainbow. History suggests that each age appeals to its most impressive technology as a metaphor, a symbol, an image for the cosmos and even for God. So God in the Industrial Age was more of a Big Machine that kept things going.

Failure of the imagination results in boredom about life and alienated relationships. There is an inability to see others in his or her wholeness. When the imagination fails, doctrines become ossified, witness and proclamation become wooden, doxologies and liturgies become empty and ethics becomes legalistic. We loose enthusiasm and everything is by rote and there is a failure to have life. It is the imagination challenges us to vitality and to the fullness of life. It enables the believing community to discern possibility, to see options for life, for goodness, for meaningful living and avoid being fatalistic. Imagination helps us to receive newness and healing within our life and we need healing and newness for our journey of faith and life. Imagination gives us flexibility and it robs us of contentment because if our imaginations are alive with visions of what cannot yet be seen, we cannot be content with what we are because there is more that the Lord invites us to do and to become. We have the ability of visioning of what is not yet there, we have images of hope.

There is also a dark side of the imagination where it is undisciplined and uncontrolled. Purity of the mind, of speech and of action is necessary and imagination that is linked to the Lord gives us that possibility. If the imagination breaks down or is absent, then our lives are threatened. When we wish, hope, fear, believe or plan, our imagination shows us possibilities. It may be productive or unproductive and can being us closer to the truth about ourselves or carry us away from who we really are. It can make our actual experience richer or poorer, make us neurotic and frustrated or realistic. Thus, we need to keep our imaginations based on reality and guide our decisions and our world view and view of God.

The principle of osmosis operates on a variety of levels of our lives and reminds us on how the world around us shapes our lives.

Faith deals with reality, core values, deep commitments that lead to destinies within our life. Symbols, images, metaphors transform horizons of our life and integrate our perceptions of reality. A symbol will alter our scale of values and reorient our loyalties, aspirations, and attachments in a manner far exceeding the power of abstract conceptual thought. The symbols and images get into out system. So for example, one will remember a song or picture more than all the words of a sermon.

People without deep faith live with no center and no heart and thus, one can only expect violent confusion, injustice and chaos. Without faith we have no center and no heart. All Christians believe through the prism of the cross, the image that defines us, points us to the mystery of God's love and the tragedy of personal and collective sin. There can be no theology without a story, no abstract concept of the kingdom without an image to support it. We cannot live by a disembodied faith, we need the *incarnation* and our faith must be incarnated in concrete actions. Actions speak louder than words. We cannot live with a disembodied faith; it must lead us to action.

An ounce of faith is worth all the theology ever written. Faith is not theology. Theology is a study and reflection on a religious faith in coherent systematic language and faith is an experience of God. There can be great theologians who have no faith and some who have great faith, who cannot articulate a sentence. Faith is given not to images or idolatry but to reality. It is about mystery where we do not have full comprehension. Faith cannot comprehend the mystery but we need analogy, metaphor and symbol to try to communicate it.

The contemporary crisis of faith in our society is largely a crisis of religious imagination, a crisis of images that really point to the truth of life. Images lead to attitudes which lead to behaviors. Morneau (1995) concludes his talk with one central image—the heart—I will give you a brand new heart and offers a prayer that all may have a pure heart to see Him, a humble to hear to hear Him, a heart of love to serve Him, and a heart of faith to abide in the mystery of our God.

Morneau's (1995) discussion of image, faith, and religion helps to create a broad concept of faith formation, what it is and how it occurs. It serves as a foundation to see that what this book proposes as a means for faith formation can be adapted for doctrine and content and applied to other religious schools but its underlying message can apply to faith formation for all. The study suggests that for us to share the faith with our students, we must first have a deeper understanding of its meaning and value for us personally. Then the images and activities that we use to teach our students will be rich in meaning.

Bruce Powers (1982) defines faith as the interpretation of the way persons have experienced life. It is a way of knowing the unknown, trusting the unknown. With its various degrees of understanding, it is a way of knowing the existence of God, Jesus as personal redeemer, and Holy Spirit as the presence of God infusing life and empowering church. Powers shows its development through five stages or interwoven phases of life including nurturing (age 0-6), when parents and teachers nurture, indoctrination (ages 7-18) into the content of faith, reality testing (ages 19-27) moving from idealism into realistic life experiences, making choices (ages 28-35) when we recognize that our choices direct our lives and have consequences, and active devotion (ages 36+), when we live our convictions.

John Westerhoff (1976) presents four stages of faith development. The first is *experienced faith* which is received from those who nurture us. It molds and influences our lives and the core of our faith during the impressionable stages of life. Affiliative faith describes the next stage in which we assume the characteristics and values of those who support us and may identify with a particular faith. The third phase is that of *searching faith* in which we may question and experiment with different religious interpretations and recognize that our faith has been formed by others rather than our own personal beliefs. Finally, the fourth stage is *owned faith* which is a conversion experience in which we assume responsibility for beliefs and practices. Later in 1980, Westerhoff revised his description of stages, seeming to combine his first two stages so as to include only three: *affiliative faith*, *searching faith*, and finally, *mature faith*. In this third stage we are guided not by the community but by our own relationship with God. We feel a sense of belonging but can also challenge the community when guided by conscience. We recognize that we continue to grow in our interaction with others who share our faith. Thus, he affirms that adults too need to be concerned with continued growth in faith and recognize that the core of mature faith rests in a childlike faith.

James Fowler (1991) suggested seven stages in his theory about faith development. *Primal faith* (infancy) with its trusting relationship with parents or others lays the foundation for later faith with basic rituals of care, interchange and mutuality. In the *intuitive-projective faith* (early childhood), lasting faith images are created through stories and symbols that stimulate the imagination and feelings. Moral emotions and standards and awareness of taboos begin to emerge though not controlled by logical thinking. Representations of God begin to develop based on the child's experience of family adults. In the *mythic-literal faith* stage (elementary school through adolescence), logical thinking develops to establish some order and distinguish real from fantasy. Children can begin to understand meaning and life through stories. In the *synthetic-conventional faith* stage (middle adolescence), the child can rely on abstract ideas and concepts to search for meaning and patterns, show concern about the future relationships, identity and work, and recognize a personal and loving relationship with God. The fifth stage, *individuative-reflective faith* stage (young adult) questions, examines, and reclaims values and beliefs. The young person makes conscious choices about identity and commitment. In the Conjunctive Faith stage (midlife and older), the adult integrates opposites in life and appreciates symbol and story from one's personal life and that of others. There is a hunger for deeper relationships to the reality understood through symbols, and biblical narrative helps to reform and reshape life, giving it meaning. Finally, in the final stage, Universalizing Faith, the person is rooted in a oneness with the power of being or God. They are less self-centered and more focused on overcoming violence, oppression, and other social ills with an awareness of the love and justice and the reality of the kingdom of God.

The idea of developing various stages of faith development is often related to various theories on the development of the human person with reference given to Piaget, Kohlberg, and Erikson. As a result, a number of other faith development theories exist (Stephens, 1996; Peck, 1993). It is interesting to note that the stages cross over a variety of religions and that one can enter a stage and slip back into an earlier stage, move quickly through a stage, or retain vestiges of earlier stages.

More recently, Fowler (2004) describes the origin of his faith development theory, tracing it back not only to his Methodist minister father and Quaker mother and his studies at the Harvard Divinity School, but also to the influence of Kohlberg, Piaget, and experience with Jesuit theology and the spiritual exercises of St. Ignatius. Fowler notes that while those who first used faith development theory were Catholic religious educators who wished to strengthen the moral development of students, Protestants had a mixed evaluation of it. The strongest support came from faith traditions that emphasized the rational potential of people and communities who were properly socialized and able to use their moral reason, especially Unitarian Universalists. United Methodists, liberal Baptists, Episcopalians, Disciples of Christ, and Reform Jews recognized stages of development as useful for teaching but expressed caution that because of the fallen nature of humanity, rationality was prone to self-deception and moral complacency. They spoke of the need for repentance, reliance on the guidance of the Holy Spirit, ongoing redemption, and offsetting the self-focused anxiousness underlying proneness to sin. Fowler personally felt Lutherans, Presbyterians, and Orthodox Jews were more cautious about the value of faith development theory in religious education and formation. Fowler believes that what separates those who subscribe to the faith development theory from those who have reservations is the "effort to define faith in a functional and structural form that can be inclusive of the dynamics of faith in many traditions" (¶ 31). Those who support the theory with its focus on different levels of cognitive, moral and emotional operations find the stage theory helpful in addressing readiness and teaching methodology. The "scaffolding that the theory offers is also helpful in shaping the educational aims involved in teaching and exploring faith traditions" (¶ 31). Fowler asserts that the structuring power of the contents of religious faith traditions—teachings, scriptures, practices, and ethical orientations, with their substance and power—are never to be ignored in the use of faith development theory. It should never be the primary goal of religious education simply to precipitate and encourage stage advancement. Rather, paying attention to stage and stage advancement is important in helping us shape our teaching and involvement with members of religious traditions (¶ 32). The theory serves as a model, based on research, "that spiritual nurture and approaches to ministry that embrace education … have much to offer" (¶ 33). He believes that in today's society the fundamental tasks of formation and shaping practices should be at the front of faith formation development. "This is the time for a faithful, courageous, and insistent renewal of a religious education for leadership that, in the power of God's Spirit, draws us toward a global faith and ethics" (¶ 42).

FAITH FORMATION AND PRACTICES

Looking at various proposals related to faith development theory, what are some of the current tasks and shaping practices to promote faith formation? Wineland (2005) asserts that we must first live our faith and not just confess it. It is more than simple belief; it includes a sense of trust. It is at the same time something we have, we believe, we do, and we cannot fully understand. Each of us has a faith story, each of us is a faith story and we are simultaneously teacher and student. When we teach, we also learn from the student. Each of us is also made in the image of God.

Veverka (2004) believes that there is an intrinsic relationship between educating for religious identity and responsible pluralism. Just as people need a sense of belonging, a sense of home, they also need to explore and be enriched by a sense of the other. There is no generic religion because we find God through certain images and symbols, stories and traditions. Our religious traditions are our unique story over time, "the accumulated wisdom of a people bound together by common memories and hopes that shape the religious and moral imaginations of its members" (¶ 5). However, religious identity is not static, but a dynamic process through which religious meaning is in interpreted according to changing times and challenges. It is both historical in its roots and traditions and ongoing in how to live in a relationship with God now at this time and place. Religious identity is nurtured in communities where the members that sense of identity and purpose. However, we live in a pluralistic society. Our culture often challenges this religious commitment and the roots can be shallow. Yet, we benefit from the richness and diversity of others. Veverka reminds us that "For Christians and Jews, educating for religious identity requires attention to pluralism because the shape of our traditions has the imprint of the other on our respective histories" (¶ 19). Encountering the other not only enriches my own self-understanding, but the relationship is "in some sense constitutive of that identity" (¶ 19). Religious practices nurture a particular religious tradition. However, they also serve as a meeting ground for others to explore the boundaries that separate and the bonds that unite each religious tradition. Thus, as the reader explores this study which focused on faith formation in Catholic schools, it will hopefully be an opportunity to discover bonds that unite all together as well as boundaries that provide the unique richness of each religious tradition.

Yust (2004) suggests that while faith is a given, faithfulness is cultivated by children and adults living together in a relationship with God. Adults need to be consciously aware of the messages that they give to children. In a world that seemingly places less emphasis on compassion, respect, and meaning, adults need to create a spiritual world for their children so that the children can see the relationships and the tensions between their local community and their religious community. One way to do this is through storytelling about the faith which can help to link the abstract language of belief and symbol with daily experience. Thus, children can be bicultural and bilingual. Linking back to the idea of faith development theory, she shows how religious language contributes to faith formation, relying on age appropriate and developmentally appropriate reasoning, metaphors and symbols to capture attention, and concrete detail to make it personal. Yust emphasizes the need for prayer and silence, noting that children are capable of using silence to get in touch with their spirit and with God. She describes a variety of ways of praying including mediation and centering prayer, praise, petition, thanksgiving, confession, and using art, music and poetry as well. She believes that spiritual awareness "has to be activated or it may remain dormant for long periods, even most of a lifetime" (p. 122). This requires reflection, imagination and religious knowledge. Spirituality must be developed both inwardly in developing one's relationship with oneself and with God as well as outwardly in service to others. Adults have a vital role to play in this nurturing process of faith formation. However, in order to share this with their children, they too must learn to balance both their inward and outward spiritual journey.

The idea of using literature to establish relevancy between religious content and everyday life for children is reinforced by Edgington (2002) in his discussion about character education. Character education is a fast growing school reform movement of high priority to parents in the United States. Relating character education to cultivating virtue or core values on which society depends for its continuation, it includes values such as honesty, courtesy, respect, responsibility, and compassion. While the desire to teach it exists, teachers are not sure how to teach it. Recalling the early days of United States history and the *New England Primer* and others books mentioned earlier in this book, Edgington recalls the use of literature in values instruction from the last. Literature blended with practical modes of instruction in values is a powerful mode of character instruction.

In addition to raising questions about the priority of character education, cultural changes are affecting faith formation today. Horrell (2004) refers to a "re-thinking and re-imagining of the Dynamics of Educating for the Development of a Sense of Christian Identity" (¶ 6). Dynamics traditionally involves nurturing and conversion. In many Christian faith communities, children and adults are nurtured gradually so that they come to understand the doctrines and practices of their faith as a foundation for their relationship with God and their personal sense of identity within their faith. Today with single parent and blended families, with a variety of cultural and faith options, there is a growing trend for the individual to construct their own faith identity from structures that give meaning and value.

Horrell (2004) also notes a shift from religious belief toward the importance of spiritual experiences and religious practices. As a result, past Christian faith formation consisted largely of learning the doctrines, prayers and rituals of a particular Christian view of the world. One gradually embraced a common framework of meaning and value that provided security and applied to all life issues. Today, in place of world views, diversity, pluralism, multiculturalism, rapid changes, and unprecedented situations have diverted the postmodern world from established guides and faith communities to a search for spiritual experiences and religious practices that lead one beyond anxieties and discomforts to draw from a wider variety of religious traditions and connect with the inner self, the world, and God. Thus, religious education places more emphasis on viewing differences and connecting spirituality with a diversity of beliefs. There is also a renewed sense of the value of Christian witness, challenging people to look at the way faith affects all aspects of their daily lives.

However, there is also a growing loss of the deep symbols such as tradition, moral obligation, and hope leading to more violence and threat to life. It is important to focus on centering attention on those aspects of life where the symbols are still important and striving to recover these deep symbols by rethinking and reembodying them for the present. Hope which has been culturally diminished must be recovered to connect people to one another and to a transcendent source of meaning. As a result, Horrell (2004) notes some of the modern approaches to building faith communities where faith formation attempts to explore or reassert the deep symbols of Christian faith as the foundation for personal and social identity in a fragmented world where meaning and value are trivialized. Thus, Horell (2004) suggests that "religious educators need to be people of hope in order to foster hope" (¶ 44). This includes hope in the church, hope in Christian symbols and practices, hope in our youth and hope in us.

Fortosis (2001) offers a theory for spiritual formation formulated from an evangelical Protestant perspective, identifying its major components through scriptural references to the Apostle Peter. There are three stages: formative integration, responsible consistency, and self-transcendent wholeness. In the first stage are new Christians as well as those who do not mature in their faith. The second stage includes those who take responsibility and are consistent in their spirituality and Christian experience. The final stage is rare and characterized as a supernatural walk with God, a deep and peaceful intimacy with God through good times and bad.

Matthaei (2004) suggests the need to provide new processes of growth in faith and spiritual formation in light of the U.S. culture and in light of a Methodist movement. Faith formation is described as "participation in God's work of inviting persons into relationship with God, self, others, and creation" (¶ 3) and it can be achieved by an "intentional" process within a specific tradition. The purpose of faith formation is to deepen one's relationship with God and the witness to this relationship through word and action. Mathaei uses the concept of ecology not in relation to humanity and creation but in relation to faith formation as an intimate with God and others that helps us to know ourselves and who we are called to be. Through creation, people are part of God's communion and are related to creation, but are separated from full communion by sin. We need to respond to God's gift of life by cultivating our relationship with God and creation to restore full communion with God, the goal of faith formation. The Methodist concept of community relied on the importance of community to provide relationships, structures and practices to help to deepen this relationship with God. Matthaei proposes an intentional ecology of faith formation "as an interconnected, interdependent, and interacting complex of relationships, structures, and practices that nurture faith in a communion of the faithful" (¶ 13). In this model, teachers, preachers, and leaders are the models of a faith-filled life in trying to be faithful through life's various opportunities and challenges. They nurture and encourage others to respond to God's grace. Worship is essential as the community instructs and nurtures knowledge and practice of the faith. "Faithful living grows out of participation in the liturgy of the faith community" (¶ 34). The story of one's faith becomes the story of each person and forms the individual so that living the story provides meaning for life.

Having looked at the broad concept of faith formation, one can see that it has value across religious denominations. Though this review has looked at predominantly Christian faith formation, parallel research exists in other denominations, including African (Haitch & Miller, 2006), Muslim (Patel, 2003), Jewish (Schwartz, 2001; and Westerman, 2005), and Orthodox (Unsworth, 2000). Before looking at educational theory to support faith formation, the next section will focus on some of the Catholic Church documents on faith formation since the actual study focused on the Catholic school.

Church Documents on Catholic Spirituality and Catholic Schools

Vatican Council II's *Declaration on Christian Education* (Pope Paul VI, 1965) showed that education is an important concern of the Church, which

> has the duty of proclaiming the way of salvation to all men, of revealing the life of Christ to those who believe, and of assisting them with unremitting care.... The Church, ..., is under an obligation, therefore, to provide for its children an education by virtue of which their whole lives may be inspired by the spirit of Christ. (No. 8, p. 730)

The Catholic school holds a prominent place in this process. Through the educational process, it nurtures the intellect, develops a capacity for sound judgment, and introduces students to their cultural heritage. It fosters values and prepares its students for professional life. Its multicultural diversity promotes understanding and forms the center for activity and growth for all members of its community. Like other schools, the Catholic school pursues cultural goals and the natural development of its students. However, the Catholic school also seeks to create an atmosphere enlivened by the Gospel spirit of freedom and charity. It strives to help adolescents in their personal development, as well as their spiritual development. It seeks to link human culture to the message of salvation so that all knowledge acquired about the world, humanity, and life will be illumined by faith.

The U.S. Catholic Bishops in their 1972 document, *To Teach as Jesus Did*, affirmed that the Catholic school is distinguished by the integration of religious truths and values with life. The bishops note the importance of this in light of the current "trends and pressures to compartmentalize life and learning and to isolate the religious dimension of existence from other areas of human life" (No. 105, p. 29).

The Congregation for Catholic Education (1988) promulgated *The Religious Dimension of Education in a Catholic School*. Among the six goals for the Catholic school, three are related to the purpose of the school:

- Defines the schools identity: in particular, the Gospel values which are its inspiration must be explicitly mentioned;
- Gives a precise description of the pedagogical, educational and cultural aims of the school;
- Presents the course content, along with the values that are to be transmitted through these courses (pp. 52-53).

In addition, the Congregation stablished criteria to assist in the educational objective so that the cultural, pedagogical, social, civil, and political aspects of school life would be integrated. Some of these criteria included fidelity to the Gospel proclaimed, respect by the Church, rigor and respect in the study of culture, the autonomy of human knowledge and the rules of the various disciplines, adapting the educational process to the particular circumstances of students and families, and sharing responsibility with the Church. The Congregation stressed the importance of the religious dimension of the school to strengthen the formation process. Some of the conditions to create a supportive climate included agreement with the educational goals, cooperation in achieving the goals, interpersonal relationships based on love and Christian freedom, individual daily witness to Gospel values, and incentive for students to strive for the highest level of formation possible.

The Congregation (1988) stressed the importance of the "climate", which, "if it is not present, then there is little left which can make the school Catholic" (No. 26, p. 13). This climate should be noticed as soon as one enters a Catholic school as though one had entered a new environment, permeated by a Gospel spirit of love evident in a Christian way of thought and life and the presence of Christ. The crucifix alone does not create the climate, but the people, who, by word and example, make the spirit of Jesus present and active (Keating, 1990). Instruction in religious truths and values is integral but is not simply one additional subject. It should be "the underlying reality in which the student's experiences of learning and living achieve their coherence and their deepest meaning" (U.S. Catholic Bishops, 1972, No. 103, p. 29). The Catholic school must motivate the student to come to the faith, to integrate it into life, and to accept and appreciate its values (Keating, 1990).

The Declaration on Christian Education (Pope Paul VI, 1965) addressed the role of the teacher, viewed as a vocation, requiring special qualities of mind and heart, careful preparation, and readiness to accept new ideas and to adapt to the old. The teaching vocation is esteemed since the teacher helps parents in carrying out their duties and acts in the name of the community by undertaking this career. Teachers in Catholic schools, as in any school, should be prepared with appropriate qualifications, as well as adequate religious and secular learning. Skilled in the art of education, they should also "bear testimony by their lives and by their teaching to the one Teacher, who is Christ" (No. 8, p. 733). They should also work cooperatively with parents. *The Declaration on Christian Education* also affirmed its gratitude to the priests, Religious, and laity who "in a spirit of evangelical dedication have devoted themselves to the all important work of education" (No. 8, p. 737).

The spirituality of the teacher is a vital teaching force, especially when matched by the parents' spirituality (Keating, 1990). Real formation occurs when parents and teachers together show the child how to grow and develop in faith. The aim of catechesis is to develop understanding of the mystery of Christ in the light of God's word. Saying "yes" to Christ involves accepting God's word, but then endeavoring to know it better (John Paul II, 1979). The task of the catechist is to explain the truths of faith and Christian morality and to encourage the practice of virtue (Pius X, 1905). Formation, therefore, must be a part of and complement to the professional formation of the Catholic school teacher (Sacred Congregation for Catholic Education, 1982). The goals of this religious formation must be personal sanctification and apostolic mission, two inseparable elements in a Christian vocation. It requires a human and well-rounded formation, as well as a formation in spirituality and doctrine (Congregation for the Clergy, 1997).

Religious have had a powerful impact on the ministry of Catholic education and the entire Catholic community (Keating, 1990). The Congregation for Catholic Education (1988) stated:

> These men and women have dedicated themselves to the service of the students without thought of personal gain, because they are convinced that it is really the Lord whom they are serving…. The strength and gentleness of their total dedication to God enlightens their work, and students gradually come to appreciate the value of this witness. They come to love these educators who seem to have the gift of eternal spiritual youth, and it is an affection which endures long after students leave the school. (No. 35, pp. 16-17)

In an age of diminishing religious, the laity are assuming a greater role in Catholic education: "The lay teacher has emerged as the dedicated professional who can fully exemplify the ecclesial vocation described by the Holy Father. This has been one of the great gifts and joys of the postcouncilor Church" (Keating, 1990, p. 16). The culture of Roman

Catholicism offers a unique vision about human existence and configuration of core commitment enabling members to bring that vision to reality. The vision and core commitments distinguish Catholics, their experience of God and their spiritual imagination. Authentic Catholic schools provide members with an experience that springs from this Catholic vision, transmits the commitments, and captures the spiritual imagination. This Catholic school culture is a Catholic school way of life (Cook, 2001). The Catholic school principal and teacher are the architects of this Catholic culture. Cook has proposed seven building blocks to promote the Catholic culture of the Catholic school: identify and integrate core religious beliefs and values using the school's mission statement, honor heroes and heroines who exemplify Gospel values, create and display a symbol reflecting Gospel values, rediscover the school's religious and historical heritage, and socialize faculty and staff to Gospel values and religious mission (p. 98).

In addition to literature on principles of educational leadership, literacy, and teacher formation, it was important to include literature related to Catholic education to establish the credibility of the seminars and their value for Catholic education and the faith formation of the laity. The Church documents revealed primarily the goal or purpose of Catholic education and the importance of the formation of teachers in Catholic schools. The Church documents established the guidelines or goals for the formation of the laity in Catholic schools and established the need for committed teachers, both informed about and formed in their faith. The former relates to their doctrinal knowledge; the latter relates to their own spiritual development in relation to Christ.

The next chapter will provide an overview of important theory related to educational leadership, emergent literacy and the scaffolding principle that supports learning, caring, moral education, character education, and spirituality. Looking at this variety of literature will establish the validity of creating programs designed to strengthen the faith formation, whatever the faith, of those who teach and administer so that they can pass this on to their students, and to give credibility to creating a program centered on either developing virtue or spirituality in both the teacher and the student. All of these theories can be applied to any religious school and would have meaning and provide pedagogy, especially for those in the education field.

CHAPTER 4

THEORETICAL FOUNDATIONS OF FAITH FORMATION

The United Church of Canada describes faith formation as:

> holistic. It takes into account the whole person—thinking, feeling, loving, hurting, imaginative, and creative. God is encountered in the church, the cultural community, and the created world from which participants come. Experience of the heart—mystery, wonder and awe—are as important as rational expressions through doctrine, dogma, and creeds in forming faith. Faith formation in the church happens, not just through the practice of spiritual disciplines, important as these continue to be, but through full participation in the life, ministry, and mission of the church as it engages with its cultural community. (United Church of Canada, 2000)

This statement highlights the two major real-world problems or concerns that prompted this study and shows that the issues of this study, though focused on Catholic schools, are shared among various religious denominations. The first concern centered on maintaining the Catholic identity of the Catholic schools, and the second centered on the growing interest in character education. A review of relevant theory and literature served as a foundation for this study.

Faith Formation of the Laity in Catholic Schools: The Influence of Virtues and Spirituality Seminars, pp. 37–62
Copyright © 2008 by Information Age Publishing
All rights of reproduction in any form reserved.

THEORY

Relevant theory, both Catholic and non-Catholic, related to the real-world problems of maintaining and developing the Catholic identity of Catholic schools and the growing interest in character education focused on education leadership, literacy, and teacher formation. These theories serve to establish a foundation to show the need for the spirituality/virtues seminars, a model of how learning occurs, and the value of these seminars in teacher preparation. A brief review of some basic elements of education leadership establishes the existence of spiritual leadership as a basic component of the role of the Catholic school principal. Recognizing this role of the Catholic school principal as the spiritual leader, who must nurture the spiritual formation of both faculty and students, helps to establish the importance of creating seminars to nurture the spirituality of the teachers within the Catholic school. A brief review of some major theories of literacy, emergent literacy, scaffolding, and storybook reading establishes some basic principles of literacy and learning that could serve as a model of how learning takes place. These principles of learning help to establish how spiritual formation and character development can be developed through the spirituality/virtues seminars. Finally, a brief review of some issues related to teacher formation considers how literacy and staff development may be intertwined. Focusing on the theory that a teacher's own personal development may be an important part of teacher preparation helps to establish the value of the spirituality/virtues seminars not only for the catholic school but for any religious school. Thus, the theory related to education leadership, literacy, and teacher formation serves as a foundation to establish the need for the seminars, a model of learning, and the value that these seminars could have.

Educational Leadership

Among the various roles assumed by a principal, Hughes and Ubben (1984, p. 4) identify five major areas in which the effective principal functions: school-community relations, staff personnel development, pupil personnel development, educational program development, and business and building management. The roles of instructional and managerial leader are two key components. Hersey (n.d.) emphasizes 12 tasks most needed by a principal: problem analysis, judgment, organizational ability, decisiveness, leadership, sensitivity, range of interests, personal motivation, stress tolerance, educational values, oral communication, and written communication. Lipham (as cited in Kimbrough & Burkett, 1990) contends that there are two major functions that a principal must perform; namely, management and leadership. These two functions are intermingled and separate. Management duties refer to the efficient running of the school, while leadership duties are more creative and motivational (Kimbrough & Burkett, 1990, pp. 30-31). Instructional leadership is also vital in order to assist the faculty in defining educational purpose. Instructional leadership tasks (pp. 117-121) include reaching agreement on instructional goals, making decisions about the nature of curriculum content, organizing leadership experiences for learning, improving the instructional program, evaluating the school's performance, and maintaining an orderly climate.

Sergiovanni (1984) maintains that the competent school principal must provide a school environment that is characterized by three forces: managerial, relational, and educational. The managerial force refers to the ability of a principal to use the needed skills to establish an orderly school where students and staff can rationally pursue learning. The relational force refers to the ability of a principal to build a human environment of cordiality, respect, and cooperation among students and staff. The educational force refers to the ability of the principal to establish a learning community that is aware of the state-of-the-art knowledge related to the functions of teaching and learning. These qualities create school competence. School excellence is created when two additional forces are evident: symbolic and cultural. The symbolic force refers to the ability of the principal to assume the role of "chief" and model goals and behaviors that signal a vision to others of what has meaning and value. The cultural force refers to the ability of the principal to articulate the purposes and values of the school in order to create a meaning-filled experience for staff and students.

While Sergiovanni's (1984) remarks could apply to any school, his vocabulary is familiar to Catholic school leaders: "School culture includes values, symbols, beliefs, and shared meanings of parents, students, teachers, and others conceived as a group or community. Culture governs what is of worth for this group and how members should think, feel, and behave" (p. 9). The Catholic faith, as do other religious traditions, provides principles, norms, customs, traditions, and common meanings that enliven Sergiovanni's terms.

> From the first moment that a student sets foot in a Catholic school, he or she ought to have the impression of entering a new environment, one illuminated by the light of faith, and having its own unique characteristics … everyone should be aware of the living presence of Jesus … [his] inspiration must be translated from the ideal to the real. The Gospel spirit should be evident in a Christian Way of thought and life which permeates all facets of the educational program. (Congregation for Catholic Education, 1988, No. 25)

taking up Leadership & challenges

The Catholic school leader applies these forces of leadership to meet the challenges of nurturing spiritual growth and formation. It can be assumed that the Catholic school must possess the qualities associated with competence. However, to be excellent, the Catholic school leader must accept the challenge of articulating a Christian vision and the development of spiritually self-aware and motivated Christian individuals (Muccigrosso, 1994).

In order to assist Catholic dioceses in developing Catholic school leaders, a committee was formed in 1991 of persons associated with the United States Catholic Conference (USCC) Department of Education, the Chief Administrations of Catholic Education of the National Catholic Educational Association (CACE/NCEA), and the National Catholic Graduate Educational Leadership Programs (NCGELP) of Catholic Colleges and Universities (Ciriello, 1994). The fruits of this committee were a set of competencies encompassing the knowledge and skills expected of a Catholic school administrator who was well prepared. These expectations were related to three leadership roles: educational, managerial, and spiritual. Building upon the solid foundation provided by educational and managerial expertise, the Catholic school principal must also foster the spiritual and faith development of all members of the Catholic school community (Muccigrosso, 1994). Spiritual leadership is central to the identity of the Catholic school. The Catholic school principal must foster both the religious and academic mission of the Catholic school. The Catholic school principal guides the spiritual formation of faculty and students, which involves "establishing and nurturing a real relationship to Jesus and the Father in the Holy Spirit, through a vigorous sacramental life, prayer, study, and serving others" (National Conference of Catholic Bishops, 1979, No. 173). As any principal, the Catholic school principal also monitors the teaching and learning process in all subject areas.

faith leadership

If Catholic schools are to continue to be distinguished by their strong faith communities and not become private schools characterized as schools of academic excellence and a religious memory, attention must be given to faith leadership and how it is being developed in school leadership (Wallace, 1998). The faith leader may be one who has no doubts about the school's identity and influence of the Catholic mission on the school (Buetow, 1985). The faith leader is able to build a community of faith around a vision of the Church that is shared by all members of the community (Gorman, 1989). The role of the faith leader may be divided into two parts: the spiritual attributes that a person brings to the job through a personal faith experience, and the pastoral competencies to create a prayer environment, develop a sense of community service, witness to the faith, and integrate the Gospel message into the curriculum (Drahmann & Stenger, 1989).

Literature related to educational leadership identified a variety of responsibilities associated with any school leadership role. Some researchers identified these responsibilities as management and leadership, or managerial, relational, and educational. To these qualities associated with school competence, Sergiovanni (1984) added the importance of symbolic and cultural forces to distinguish schools of excellence from schools of competence. Building on the value of developing school culture, the Catholic school leader, as well as the leader of any religious school, can apply these symbolic and cultural forces of leadership to meet the challenges of nurturing spiritual growth and formation of faculty, as well as students. The literature on educational leadership served as foundation for identifying the spiritual leadership that should be a part of the Catholic school. Recognizing that the Catholic school leader must nurture the spiritual formation of both faculty and students helped to establish the importance of creating seminars to nurture the spirituality of teachers within the Catholic schools. Thus, this literature served as a foundation for the need and importance of providing seminars related to spirituality and virtue.

Literacy

Since this study focused on the issues of Catholic identity and character education, selected theories related to learning provided insight not only into the ways in which children learn, but also into the ways that adults learn. The latter was important in the actual design of the virtue and spirituality seminars for teachers; the former may be important if teachers are to teach about Catholic identity and character, or spirituality and faith formation.

Family Literacy

Family literacy is an important area of research in literacy if one views the family as a foundation for learning (Purcell-Gates, 2000). Research supports the positive relationship between the home environment, IQ, and language development in the child (Leseman & deJong, 1998; Purcell-Gates, 2000; Snow, Nathan, & Perlmann, 1985; Strickland & Morrow, 1989; Sulzby & Edwards, 1993; Sulzby & Teale, 1991; Yaden, 2000). A focus on home practices has led to research on literate practices, such as storybook reading within the family and the home as a primary source for a deeper understanding of language and literacy development (Purcell-Gates, 2000). Using stories to highlight various virtues is one primary way that teachers were encouraged to help to form students in their faith.

Emergent Literacy and Scaffolding

Another significant theory is emergent literacy (Strickland & Morrow, 1989; Sulzby, 1994; Sulzby & Teale, 1991; Teale & Sulzby, 1996; Teale & Sulzby, 1986; and Yaden, Rowe, & MacGillivray, 2000). Sulzby and Teale (1991) offer a definition of this area as behaviors in reading and writing that precede and develop into conventional literacy. Children are somehow innately predisposed to become literate and all adults must do is provide an environment rich in literacy artifacts and activities. Almost every study reviewed for this project cited the work of these researchers. In their research, they examined "emergent literacy" for insights on children's literacy learning, what they do with literacy, what they know about reading and writing, and what would be the implications for classroom teaching strategies. Among their contributions, Sulzby and Teale (1996) note that for most people in a literate society, learning to read and write begins early in life. The functions of literacy are an integral part of the learning process that takes place. Reading and writing develop concurrently and are interrelated in young children's reading experiences. Children learn through active engagement, constructing understanding of how the written language works. Children and parents interact through print.

Storybook reading is a socially created, interactive activity; that is, it is more than the reader's oral rendering of the text. The language of the adult and the child surrounds the author's words. The participants cooperate and seek to negotiate meaning by using verbal and nonverbal means. The adult supports the child's performance through successive engagements. Gradually, the adult transfers more and more autonomy to the child (Sulzby & Teale, 1991). Based on this "scaffolding" concept, reading aloud is an act of construction. Language and the accompanying social interaction are integral to the influence of storybook reading on literacy development. Storybook reading is typically routinized in dialogic cycles. Routines create predictable outcomes, which allow children to participate, serving to scaffold the activity and helping the children to complete the task beyond their capabilities. The child also develops expectations of the kinds of language in books, and later independent re-enactments and decoding skills. These patterns of storybook reading change over time with the child's age, knowledge, and experience. From these interactive readings, children's independent, not-yet-conventional readings emerge. A wide range of parental storybook interactions shows success over time in typically developing children with a wide range of developmental behaviors.

The role of routine in language acquisition, and the evidence of routine in the mother-child interaction during picture book reading were additional research topics. Snow, Nathan, and Perlmann (1985) conclude that mothers used individualized styles and adapted to the child's growth, as the child became more competent. Children with many book experiences may develop a generalized sense of story or expectations of the nature of the narrative and may learn specific expressions and informative content from recurrent reading. Some children can switch to the adult reader role and become more dominant in selecting the conversational topics, as they become familiar with the topic. Thus, the elements of routine and specific signs of growth and adaptation resulting from repetition were a significant theme to support the importance of home reading for preschool children for these and other researchers (Galda, 1984).

A brief review of some major theories of literacy, emergent literacy, scaffolding, and storybook reading established some basic principles of literacy and learning that could serve as a model of how learning takes place. These principles of learning helped to establish how spiritual formation and character development can be developed through the spirituality/virtues seminars.

Catholic education acknowledges that parents are the primary educators of their children. To provide for consistency and transition from home to school, literature related to family literacy provided a starting point for reviewing basic practices of literacy. Since Bennett (1993) speaks of "moral literacy," understanding some key principles associated with literacy established a link between the learning process and the acquisition of spirituality and virtue.

From this perspective, as the author and presenter of the seminars, I formed a relationship with the participants similar to that found between a parent and child where emergent literacy (Strickland & Morrow, 1989; Sulzby, 1994; Sulzby & Teale, 1991; Sulzby & Teale, 1996; Teale & Sulzby 1986; and Yaden, Rowe, & MacGillivray, 2000) occurs. Sulzby and Teale (1991) offer a definition of this area as behaviors in reading and writing that precede and develop into conventional literacy. Teale and Sulzby (1996) note that the functions of literacy are an integral part of the learning process that takes place. Children learn through active engagement, constructing understanding of how the written language works.

In addition to finding a similarity between the influence of the seminars on teaching pedagogy and Emergent Literacy, the concept of "scaffolding" (Sulzby & Teale, 1991) described a link between what and how these teachers were taught and what and how they, in turn, chose to teach these religious truths, elements of prayer and spirituality, and virtue and right conduct to their students. Sulzby and Teale (1991) explain "scaffolding" in relation to storybook reading. The language of the adult and the child surrounds the author's words. The participants cooperate and seek to negotiate meaning by using verbal and nonverbal means. The adult supports the child's performance through successive engagements. Gradually, the adult transfers more and more autonomy to the child (Sulzby &

Teale, 1991). Based on this "scaffolding" concept, reading aloud is an act of construction. Language and the accompanying social interaction are an integral part of the influence of storybook reading on literacy development. Thus, through cooperation, interaction and routine, the scaffold is built so that gradually, the adult reader does less and the child begins to do more and more of the reading, gradually becoming independent.

I used this model of learning and acquisition of literacy in designing the seminars, hoping that by teaching, guiding, and experience, and repeating that each week or in each seminar session, the participants would become more assured and confident and able to teach their students what they had been taught. If the opening premise was, "You cannot give what you do not have" then by the end, the author hoped to be able to say, "But you can give what you do have." Many participants commented about copying or modeling teaching methods, as well as perceptions of listening, and attitudes of patience and calm. In addition, they repeated these same things with their students. Thus, the "emergent literacy" and "scaffolding" provided good models of learning, both in incorporating them into the author's plans, and in listening to how participants followed this same model in their plans.

Research on Teacher Formation

Doyle (1990) describes teacher education research as "a loosely coordinated set of experiences designed to establish and maintain a talented teaching force" (p. 3). Against this definition, Doyle identifies five major themes or paradigms for the teacher; namely, "Good Employee," "Junior Professor," "Fully Functioning Person," "Innovator," and "Reflective Professional." Each of these is a model for teaching. Yet, combined together, they create a set of stages in which teacher education moved from seeking to prepare teachers in practices at one end to fostering the reflective capacities of observation, analysis, interpretation, and decision making at the other end, with knowledge, personal development, and proactive innovation in the middle.

Doyle (1990) also writes about future research in teacher education. He states that the study of teaching practices "shifts ... to an explanation of how a practice works and what meaning it has to teachers and students in a particular context" (p. 20). As a framework for the study of teachers' knowledge, context and thought must be combined. The purpose is to understand how meanings are constructed in classroom settings.

In their study, the Santa Barbara Classroom Discourse Group (1994) proposes a broader understanding of literacy:

As members of a group accomplish the events of everyday life, they construct a model or models of literate action that define the boundaries of
what counts as literacy in their particular group. In turn, this model serves
as a frame for future interactions, which in turn modify the model. (p. 146)

Their definition of literacy shows how literacy was defined, redefined,
constructed, and reconstructed with a group so that "the outcome of this
process is not a single definition of literacy, but an understanding of the
multiplicity of literacies individuals face as they become members of ever-
expanding groups and communities" (p. 147). They conclude that "like
their students, the teachers were influenced by the opportunities they
have to learn new ways of being teachers and engaging students in learning" (p. 148). In addition, they conclude that issues of literacy and professional development are intertwined: "As teachers ... explore ways their
students learned to be literate, they extended, modified, and refined their
own knowledge and views of literacy" (p. 149).

Feiman-Nemser (1990) explored alternative approaches to teacher
preparation. Her notion of reflective teacher education resembles Doyle's
(1990). In describing a "Personal Orientation" approach, Feiman-Nemser
states: "The teacher's own personal development is a central part of
teacher preparation" (p. 225). She proposes three types of future research
in teacher education: program studies, implementation studies, and
impact studies. Program studies examine programs as educational inter-
ventions. Implementation studies examine factors that promote the success or failure of various programmatic reforms. Impact studies explore
the effects of particular program components and learning opportunities
on teachers' ideas and practices.

The literature related to teacher formation established the need for
research in this area, particularly to learn how various practices work and
how meanings are constructed in classroom settings. The Santa Barbara
Classroom Discourse Group (1994) provided a broader understanding of
literacy enabling the author to look at the seminars as a means for developing the moral literacy that Bennett (1993) describes. Finally, Feiman-
Nemser (1990) provided a theory to support the importance and value of
assisting teachers with their spiritual growth since "personal development
is a central part of teacher preparation" (p. 225).

Literacy and Caring
In order to establish a foundation for a study that centered on Catholic
identity of the Catholic schools and the general growing interest in
character education, the author reviewed additional literature on the
importance of caring as an aspect of literacy, moral and ethical education,
character education, and spirituality. A review of literature related to caring

as an aspect of literacy not only helps to create the atmosphere for learning but also supports the premise that a teacher's personal development is important to professional development. The concept of caring is essential to character education and spiritual formation since the caring teacher seems to be able to teach more effectively. If the caring teacher teaches how to care, then it may be possible to show that the moral, virtuous, character educated and spiritual teacher may teach others to be moral, virtuous, strong in character, and spiritual. Since spiritual leadership is important to the Catholic school or any religious school, and since one of the seminars is a spirituality seminar, it was important to include some review of literature on spirituality. Thus, a review of literature related to literacy and caring, character education, and spirituality served as a foundation for the content and purpose of the spirituality/virtues seminars.

In addition to recognizing the value of storybook reading as an aide to the language and literacy development of a child, each of the reviewed studies on this topic seems to be part of one continuous developing commentary on the importance of the parent or significant caregiver in the storybook event. All of the studies cited seem to lead to a general conclusion that frequency of reading is very important. The more experience a child has, the more he/she benefits. However, quantity is not the only ingredient. Quality is even more significant. How a parent interacts with the child, the types of questions that engage and encourage the child's curiosity, the motivation and cooperation that a parent fosters, and the enthusiasm and modeling for the enjoyment and love of books are vitally important. Successful home experiences seem to balance an informal and natural interaction with the direction needed to focus children's attention on the picture, page, or topic in the storybook event.

In considering the importance of caring to education, Sergiovanni (2000) believes that teaching is a profession founded on both methods and mastery of a discipline. "To teach is to profess something, and professing requires standing for certain virtues that include making a public commitment to serve ideas and people. Caring is the cornerstone of this commitment" (p. 35). Sergiovanni's statement summarizes the findings of several other researchers (Arlin, 1999; Elbaz, 1992; Noddings, 1984, 1988, 1991, 1993a, 1999) to demonstrate the importance of caring. Schools should be centers of care that promote human development and respond to human needs. Both teaching and caring depend on cultivating special relationships between and among teachers and students. Teaching may be equated with caring; caring may be equated with teaching. Thus, the relationship between teaching and caring is an important one to consider.

In his review of competencies of caring, Sergiovanni (2000) develops his theory about caring as the cornerstone of the commitment needed for teaching. This commitment includes a sense of being there for the other person and a sense of compassion. Caring and serving for him are the foundation anchors for the profession of teaching. He believes that every pedagogical action shows how one is oriented to children, either living up or failing to live up to teaching responsibilities. Sergiovanni gives three life world conditions of pedagogy:

> loving care for the child; hope for the child; and responsibility for the child —all of which provide a moral basis for the practice of teaching. These conditions are at the center, driving the more instrumental system world conditions needed to make schools academically, socially, and developmentally effective places for all of our students. (p. 36)

Thus, he believes that service to people, ideas, and caring are the professional virtues that contribute and provide substance for school character. Professionalism and character need to be intertwined. With care as the cornerstone and character a goal for education, teachers are concerned about maintaining and nurturing higher levels of competency, while paying attention to caring and community building. Sergiovanni seems convinced that competence alone is not a sufficient goal for education. Competence and care need to join together in the practice of teaching.

While Sergiovanni (2000) seems to encompass the notion of caring and the foundation for moral education within his study, Noddings (1984) views caring as essentially a feminine quality or approach to ethics as well as moral education. In her work, Noddings first examines what she considers basic elements of caring. These include: to be in a state of mental suffering or engrossment, a burdened state of anxiety, fear or solicitude about someone or something, and to be charged with the protection, welfare or maintenance of someone or something. Noddings also believes that caring helps one to grow and become a full person, echoing the whole child concept in a Catholic philosophy of education, and a holistic approach noted by the United Church of Canada.

Within this understanding of caring, Noddings (1984) believes that care requires action by the one who cares as well as engrossment in the "one caring." The action could include both observable acts and acts of commitment, perhaps only seen by the one performing them. Yet, this indirect caring raises the question of how this would be conveyed to the one being "cared for." Similarly, the engrossment and what is done would depend on a variety of conditions viewed through both the eyes of the one caring and the one cared for. However, the fundamental aspect of caring is the displacement of interest from the individual's reality to the reality of the other. The individual goes beyond self to see the other's reality as a possibility, and thus, must act to eliminate the intolerable, reduce the pain, or fill the need of the other; "when the other's reality becomes a possibility for me, I care" (p. 14). Noddings believes that "This caring for self, for the ethical self, can emerge only from a caring for others" (p. 14). Thus, the link between caring and ethical caring seems to emerge.

Noddings (1984, 1988, 1991, 1993) also is able to distinguish two separate but related roles in a caring relationship: the one caring and the one cared for. She notes that whatever one does in life, one is either the one caring or the one cared for. A teacher is one caring, who is engrossed in the cared for and receives the other completely and nonselectively for the interval of caring. While holding to one's own ethical ideal, the teacher starts from a position of respect or regard for the projects of the other. In asking questions, the teacher receives not only answers but also the individual student. Valuing what the student says, right or wrong, the teacher probes for clarification, interpretation, and the involvement of the cared for. The student is more important than the subject matter. The one caring is not necessarily permissive but can lead, persuade and coax toward examination of school subjects. Noddings (1984) views the task of the teacher as influencing and receiving the student while also looking at the subject matter with the student. She states, "Apprehending the other's reality, feeling what he feels as nearly as possible, is the essential part of caring from the view of the one-caring" (p. 16).

However, to be in a caring relationship both the one caring and the one cared for must contribute appropriately. The one caring offers something that is received by and completed in the one cared for, who, in turn, looks for something that tells of the regard of the one caring. There is a sense of disposability or readiness to spend oneself or be available or present to the cared for. This engrossment is a desire for the other's well being. Caring (Noddings, 1984) is reactive, responsive, and receptive. The one caring listens, takes pleasure or pain in what is recounted, and warms and comforts. The one cared for sees concern, delight, and interest in the eyes, and senses the warmth of the verbal and body language of the other. Noddings believes that no act is as important as the attitude of the one caring. The one cared for "feels not so much that he has been given something as that something has been added to him" (p. 20). Yet, the response from the one cared for is essential to the relation. Gratitude, direct acknowledgment, spontaneous delight and happy growth are responses from the cared for that show the caring has been received. Noddings suggests that there is a need for relation and caring in teaching. If the student rarely responds, is negative or denies the effort of the teacher, then the caring could become a burden. This, she states, has implications for schools looking for ways to offer support to this caring ethic and to caring individuals. The ethic of caring itself suggests that this should be done.

To care is to act, not according to a fixed rule, but with affection and regard (Noddings, 1984). Therefore, actions may vary, being predictable in a global sense but unpredictable in detail. The one caring may act to please the cared for. However, this should be for the person's own sake and not with the expectation of a grateful response to generosity. Noddings notes that there could be conflict between what the cared for wants and what the one caring thinks is best. The one caring would display behavior, conditioned not by rigid principles but by broadly defined ethics that responds to situations with regard for human affections, weaknesses, and anxieties. For Noddings, this is not a prescription or set of conditions for behavior but a sense of being enlightened about the questions to raise in situations and where to find the answers. Neither did she reduce ethics to a need for human judgment. Instead, Noddings proposes an ethic that not only recognizes human judgment in fact and feeling but could also allow for conditions where judgment, in the logical and empirical sense, could be put aside in favor of faith and commitment. She notes concern that if institutions shift to abstract problem solving, and shift from the cared for to the problem, there could be increased focus on self-interest, and satisfying the requirements for care taking. Noddings feels this could give rise to the disappearance of being present in interactions with the cared for.

Larrivee (2000) maintains that the foundation of a caring learning community begins with the teacher who bonds with students and nurtures thoughtful interactions among students. She discusses four fundamentals of a caring community: respect, authenticity, thoughtfulness, and emotional integrity. Teachers who cultivate respect are concerned with the dignity and worth of the individual, with acceptance and listening, with establishing trust, and with understanding differences and perspectives. Teachers who cultivate authenticity are real and "walk the talk" of their students, are truthful and validate their students' rights to feelings, are able to cultivate a safe classroom where mistakes are allowed, and are attentive to appropriate self-disclosure with students. Teachers who cultivate thoughtfulness stress mutual consideration and the emotional well being of all, tolerance and acceptance of classmates, and cooperation and collaboration. Teachers who cultivate emotional integrity communicate with emotional honesty, deal with the present moment, validate students' rights to express feelings, challenge students to accountability, and provide students with feedback.

All of the research related to caring and education supported the idea that caring is essential for education. It is an essential quality for the committed teacher. It builds the rapport needed between teacher and student. It provides motivation for the student, not only to learn, but also to become a caring individual.

The concept of caring was significant to this study. The research supported the concepts of emergent literacy and scaffolding in learning how to care. This supported the idea that if caring could emerge as a result of scaffolding, then other character qualities could potentially develop in the same manner.

However, it also supported the importance of caring in the learning process and in developing a good self-concept. The research created a foundation for recognizing the importance of caring as a component of character education. In addition, the study examined the influence of the seminars on teachers' understanding of the mission of Catholic education. If a valuable component of education includes care, then it is even more important in a school that professes to be rooted in the Gospel values of Christ. The importance of caring in education established the importance of looking for signs of caring, especially in teachers' interaction with students. Any evidence of teachers' growth in caring because of attending the seminars could increase the importance of the seminars in fostering this caring manner. This could be important in establishing the importance of caring in a character education program in any school, and especially a school with a Catholic mission or religious foundation.

Moral or Ethical Education

For Noddings (1984), ethics is the philosophical study of morality. A personal ethic is something explicable with rules, ideals, and experiences that guide and justify one's conduct. She uses "ethical" and "moral" interchangeably and assumes "to behave ethically is to behave under the guidance of an acceptable and justifiable account of what it means to be moral. To behave ethically is not to behave in conformity with just any description of morality" (p. 27). She expresses belief in an irremovable subjective core and a longing for goodness that provide the universality and stability for a definition of morality. She believes her ethic of caring is a form of caring that is natural and accessible to all, and states that much of her proposal for an ethic of caring can be found in Christianity.

In a later study, Noddings (1988) develops the idea of caring as a moral orientation to teaching and the aim of education. Providing a brief history of a growing interest in character education in the schools, she contrasts her understanding of traditional ethics with her ethics of caring. Where the former emphasizes duty as the motivation for action, the latter emphasizes acts done out of love or a natural inclination. One calls on duty or obligation only when love fails. For Noddings, the primary concern for ethical agents is the relation itself, not only what happens physically to others in the relation, but also how they might feel and respond to the act under consideration. This natural caring is the source of ethical caring that energizes both the giver and the receiver. Ethical caring is its servant.

Recalling her earlier study (1984) where she equated the ethical and the moral, Noddings (1988) develops her concept of moral education. For her, it involves modeling, dialoguing, practice, and confirmation. Moral education involves modeling. To encourage responsible self-affirmation in students who are interested in academic subjects and who will develop into fully moral persons, teachers need to treat students with respect and consideration and encourage this same respect in them. Thus, teaching moments can be caring moments for Noddings.

Moral education involves dialogue. There needs to be openness between teacher and student, so that neither is tempted to draw conclusions at the outset of their interaction. There must be a mutual search for enlightenment, responsible choices, and solutions to problems that show signs of reciprocity. Noddings strongly believes that time is essential in order for teachers and students to know each other well. This will also help them to develop a mutual trust.

Moral education involves practice. Service opportunities need to be provided both inside and outside of the classroom. Students need to be encouraged to support one another, to be given opportunities for peer interaction. It is important that the quality of the interaction be as important as the academic outcome.

Finally, moral education involves confirmation. Included here would be looking for a worthy motive for a seemingly unworthy act, and attributing the best possible motive consonant with reality to the cared for. The one caring would thus reveal an attainable image of the cared for that is perhaps better than that of his or her manipulated acts. Noddings believes that what we reveal to the individual of self as being ethical and intellectual has the power to nurture or destroy the individual's ethical ideal. Noddings affirms how important it is for the teacher or the one caring to nurture the student's ethical ideal. Thus, by conducting education from a moral perspective, the teacher could attempt to enhance the moral sense of the student.

Noddings (1993) affirms that the heart of moral education is ordinary conversation. To be valuable for moral education, conversation should possess three qualities. First, the adults must be reasonably good people. They should be people who try to be good, who consider the effects of their actions on others, and who respond to the suffering of others with compassion and concern. Second, adults need to care for children and enjoy their company. They can show this through their expression, and through the opportunities they provide to their children to explore and debate, as well as to correct and discuss things of moral interest as they arise. Third, they should place the person over the topic in importance. Thus, through a partnership with their students, education could be less a debate with students and more a conversation between partners who like each other and enjoy each other's company. Once a relation is established, there is less possibility of violence, and compromise is a possible solution to conflict. Sometimes, there may be no resolution, and both parties may remain committed to their perspectives. Yet, even if they can maintain a regard and respect for the other with a pledge of no harm, "a great moral victory has been won" (p. 116). Noddings suggests that respect leaves one open to learning and exploring. It is a preparation for a moral life that is rooted in openness, friendliness, trust, and caring. This takes time and parents and teachers need to talk with and listen to children, enjoy each other's company, and show by what they say and do that it is possible to live appreciatively and non-violently. However, Noddings also concludes that this is not a guarantee that all children will become good people and suggests the supplement of religious instruction.

Schaps, Battistich, and Solomon (1997) also describes the elements of a caring community and shows how it is essential for character education. He proposes that when children's needs for belonging, autonomy and competence are met through membership in a school community, they are likely to be affectively bonded with and committed to the school. They are more likely to identify and behave in accord with its goals and values. Thus, if schools are to foster long-term learning and growth, Schaps et al. maintains that schools must provide opportunities for membership in a caring community of learners and important, challenging, and engaging learning opportunities. If students feel that they are valued as contributing members of a group, then they are more likely to be dedicated to the shared purposes of helping and supporting each other as they work, grow, and learn together.

Elbaz (1992) also addresses this moral dimension of teaching, noting Noddings concept of caring (1984, 1991) as a moral orientation to teaching. Suggesting that more has been written on the cognitive aspects of teacher thinking, Elbaz identifies three qualities to characterize the moral dimension of teachers' knowledge; namely, hope, attentiveness, and caring. Stories are viewed as an essential feature of teacher thought and a carrier of moral import. Thus, Elbaz draws several conclusions from research based on teachers' narratives to highlight the importance of moral knowledge amid the emphasis on technological knowledge. After developing the themes of hope and attentiveness as part of the moral voice in teaching, Elbaz describes the caring teacher as one who cares for the differences and the uniqueness of each child and recognizes variability in attitudes, abilities, experience, disposition and need.

Bennett (1993) maintains that moral education not only involves rules and precepts, but also explicit instruction, exhortation, and training.

Moral education must provide training in good habits and affirm the importance of moral example. There is the need for moral literacy, where teachers explain and model good moral practices or virtues (Bennett, Finn, & Cribb, 1999). In his introduction to *The Book of Virtues*, Bennett (1993) discusses the importance of stories in the task of the moral education of youth and in the development of fundamental character traits that he calls virtues. Similar to the theme of The Santa Barbara Discourse Group (1994), he suggests that the teaching of stories engages us in a renewal that can welcome children to a common world of shared ideas, to a community of moral persons. Bennett states:

> Along with precept, habit, and example, there is also the need for what we might call moral literacy…. The purpose of this book is to show parents, students, and children what virtues look like, what they are in practice, how to recognize them, and how they work. (p. 11)

Gardner (1999) did not capture the essence of the moral domain as an instance of human intelligence. For him,

> the central component in the moral realm or domain is a sense of personal agency and personal stake, a realization that one has an irreducible role with respect to other people and that one's behaviors toward others must reflect results of contextualized analysis and the exercise of one's will…. "Morality" is then properly a statement about personality, individuality, will, character—and in the happiest cases, about the highest realization of human nature. (p. 77)

Coles (1986) examines moral thinking and how it is shaped by influences outside the home. He also examines the issue of moral conduct (1997) as it develops in response to the way a child is treated at home or in school, a response to moral experiences as they take place in a family or a classroom. Moral intelligence (1997) is acquired and grows not only by memorization of rules and regulations but also "as a consequence of learning how to be with others, how to behave in this world, a learning prompted by taking to heart what we have seen and heard" (p. 5). The child witnesses adult morality or lack thereof, looks for cues about how to behave, and finds them in parents and teachers. Life's experiences, as well as stories (Coles, 1989), provide nourishment for the moral imagination,

> that "place" in our heads, our thinking and daydreaming, our wandering and worrying lives, where we ponder the meaning of our lives and, too, the world's ethical challenges; and where we try to decide what we ought or ought not to do, and why, and how we ought to get on with people, and for what overall moral, religious, spiritual, practical reasons. (Coles, 1997, p. 7)

Research on moral or ethical education outside of Catholic literature is important to support the value of moral education for any student.

In addition, since Bennett (1993) identified his collection of stories on virtue with the importance of "moral literacy," the reviewed literature supported a broader view of literacy. Noddings (1984, 1988) identified caring as a moral orientation to teaching and the aim of education. Her components of moral education included modeling, dialogue, practice, and confirmation which supported the methodology used within the seminars.

In addition, Noddings (1993) developed the idea that ordinary conversation served as the heart of moral education. One of the definitions of prayer cited in the seminars was the idea that prayer is conversation with God and the oxygen of the soul. From a secular perspective, if conversation could serve as the heart of moral education, then from a religious perspective, conversation with God through prayer could provide the religious foundation for moral education in a Catholic school or any faith-based school. This increased the probable value of the spirituality seminars, which explored developing that personal relationship with God, and the virtue seminars, which explored developing virtue and moral behavior.

Coles' research (1986) on moral thinking, moral development, and moral intelligence stressed the need for this development and the importance of giving witness or learning from others' behaviors. This supported the purpose and methods of both seminars to assist teachers in teaching others to be moral and virtuous. It provided the foundation for doing additional research on character education that is associated with moral knowing, feeling, and behavior (Lickona, 1991).

Character Education

Character education has been a part of American education since colonial times (Burrett & Rusnak, 1993). The *Hornbook* (1896) contained the Lord's Prayer. *The New England Primer* (1805) taught skills necessary for a "proper life and eternal salvation." The preface of the *McGuffey Reader* (1836) notes: "Careful attention is paid to develop the character of each student through selected stories." Both public and private/parochial schools emphasized the importance of achieving socialization goals through the schools. Burrett and Rusnak cite six principles for implementing what they call the integrated character education approach:

1. Character education is part of every subject, not just another subject.

2. The school and community are vital partners in the character education of youth.
3. A positive classroom environment supports character education.
4. Empowered teachers are in the best position to carry out the goals of character education.
5. Character education is encouraged through administrative policy and practice.
6. Character education is action education (p. 18).

Based on Aristotle's definition of character as right conduct in relation to others and to oneself, Lickona (1991) offers a way of thinking about character that is appropriate for values education:

> Character consists of *operative values,* values in action. We progress in our character as a value becomes a virtue, a reliable inner disposition to respond to situations in a morally good way. (pp. 50-51)

Lickona (1993) notes three reasons for the renewed interest in character education. With the decline of the family, traditionally the child's primary moral teacher, a moral vacuum is being created. There are troubling trends affecting today's youth; namely, poor parenting, wrong types of role models, sex, violence, and materialism portrayed in the media, and peer group pressures. As a result, Lickona notes a number of trends including rising youth violence, dishonesty, and growing disrespect for authority. As a result of this moral decline, Lickona believes that adults are making an effort to teach moral values to youth because they have an objective worth and a claim on our collective conscience.

Throughout many of his works, Lickona (1976, 1991, 1992, 1993) addresses several basic questions that he considers to be important to character education: (a) Why should we teach good character? (b) What values should we teach? (c) What is good character? (d) What strategies can we develop to do this? In response to the first question, he identifies several reasons why schools should make a commitment to teaching moral values and developing good character, in addition to focusing on academic achievement. These are rooted in the premise that character is both the ultimate measure of an individual and of a nation (Lickona, 1991, pp. 20-22). This is a challenge that parents and educators face, and working together as allies should be an important part of character education. In response to the second question, he provides guidance for schools about how to choose values, defines a "moral value" and its relationship to religion, and highlights two values as a foundation; namely, respect and responsibility (Lickona, 1991, pp. 36-48). In response to the third question, he identifies three major components of good character; namely, moral knowing, moral feeling, and moral action.

> Good character consists of knowing the good, desiring, the good, and doing the good – habits of the mind, habits of the heart, and habits of action. All three are necessary for leading a moral life; all three make up moral maturity. (p. 51)

Within each of these components, he delineates several goals to be targeted and achieved through character education. He also proposes that a psychology of character needs to pay attention to environment (Lickona, 1991, pp. 49-63). Finally, Lickona proposes a comprehensive approach to values and character education. He describes nine classroom strategies and three school wide strategies to assist in creating a character education program. For Lickona, a complete values education must touch both the mind and the heart if these actions of good character are to become real.

Lickona's (1991) approach to teaching values education is centered on respect and responsibility and is influenced by these key ideas: (a) historically, education has both helped people to become smart and to become good; (b) "good" can be described in moral values that affirm the dignity of humanity, of the individual and of society; (c) respect and responsibility are two universal values; (d) respect involves showing regard for the value of someone or something and responsibility is the active part of this morality; (e) educating for respect and responsibility is educating for character; and (f) schools hoping to build character must have a comprehensive approach to values education that uses all phases of school life to foster character development. This goal of character education requires actions and strategies that need to be implemented in each classroom by teachers and in each school across the curriculum.

> Every interaction, whether part of the academic curriculum or the human curriculum of rules, roles, and relationships, has the potential to affect a child's values and character for good or for ill. The question is not whether to do values education but whether to do it well. (p. 70)

Respect and responsibility are the two primary values in Lickona's (1991) education program. They promote the good character of the individual and of the community and "constitute the core of a universal, public morality" (p. 43). They are so fundamental that Lickona labels them as "the 'fourth and fifth R's' that schools not only may but also must teach if they are to develop ethically literate persons who can take their place as responsible citizens of society" (p. 43). A host of other moral values stem from respect and responsibility.

Respect and responsibility provide the moral content that Lickona (1991) believes should be taught in a democracy. However, schools also need to understand the concept of character and make a commitment to developing it within their students. Thus, Lickona's psychology of character with its various components is essential. Otherwise, moral education of literacy is reduced to a list of dos and don'ts and lacks the purpose of being integrated into this total character development.

Lickona's work (1976, 1991, 1992, 1993) on character education provides his insight on the basic elements of good character, especially, respect and responsibility. It also provides a program of how to implement character education within the classroom, the school, and the community in general. Lickona's methods provided a framework in the design of the virtue seminar and a foundation for exploring the meaning and value of any virtue, as well as for integrating virtue throughout the school community.

Spirituality

Today, society, in general, has an increased interest in spirituality. Contemporary magazines, such as *Ladies Home Journal* (1998), *Modern Maturity* (2000), *America* (2000), and *Educational Leadership* (1993) show that the quest for spirituality is not only a Catholic or even Christian idea but one that could be associated with any particular religion, as well as within a secular society. People are longing for the sacred, even those who have rejected institutional religion (Halford, 1999). Webster (1965) defines "spirituality" as "sensitivity or attachment to spiritual values" and "the quality or state of being spiritual." The word, "spirit" is defined as "an animating or vital principle held to give life."

All forms of spirituality seem to have a common thread, "the quest of the human spirit for something that is above us, that is bigger, deeper, 'more than' the ordinary surface reality of life" (Guinan, 1998, p. 1). Both Hebrew and Christian Scripture have a concrete meaning of "spirit." Whether the Hebrew *ruach* or the Greek *pneuma*, the basic meaning is "wind/breath" (Merkel, 1998). Christian spirituality could be broadly defined as "our life in the Spirit of God" or "the art of letting God's spirit fill us, work in us, guide us" (Guinan, 1998, p. 2). It deals with the whole person, body and soul, thoughts and feelings, hopes and fears, living in and with the power of the Holy Spirit. It deals with the whole life of the whole person, calling the individual to live life to the fullest. The call and challenge of the spiritual life is intended for all people.

There are different styles of spirituality including Christian and non-Christian forms. Some of the major Christian forms are drawn from the writings of St. Benedict, St. Francis, St. Dominic, St. Theresa (Aumann, 1985). Many authors have written on spirituality outlining principles of prayer, discernment, asceticism, direction, silence, solitude, reading, meditation, journal writing, contemplation, and service to guide a person's growth in the spiritual life (Keating, 1987; Morneau, 1996; Muto, 1984; Van Kaam & Muto, 1978). Growth in the spiritual life occurs within the individual. It cannot be seen or measured. From a religious perspective, "Spirituality is true if it emerges from the context of living in the daily situation as God's will for me. This everydayness, commonplace as it is, is the truest measure of the spiritual life" (Van Kaam & Muto, 1978, p. 20). Growing in the spiritual life means becoming more aware of being rooted in God and depending on Him for every breath, thought, and action. The anonymous author of the ancient *Cloud of Unknowing* (fourteenth century) speaks of the spiritual life as one of longing, looking ahead to achieve union with God. In general, "Whenever a meaningful community of life exists—a sense of identity, a sharing of joy and pain, of questioning and challenge, of searching and growing—we can legitimately discern a style of Christina spirituality" (Guinan, 1998, p. 3). However, because each person is unique, "our response to God's call will be as unique as each person, each child of God, who has ever lived" (p. 4). Spirituality in the Catholic tradition is nurtured by Scripture, sacraments, prayer, and the presence of others.

Philosophers have viewed education as a spiritual vocation with its foundation being the educator's own spirituality (Groome, 1998). "Spirituality" is a core principle of Groome's approach to education:

> Our spiritual propensity arises from the deepest core of human being. It permeates who we are. It is a longing that allures us, through the depths of oneself, to experience glorious Mystery and ultimate Meaning as the backdrop of our lives and to enter into conscious relationship with the Ground of our Being—with God. (p. 323)

For Groome, every teacher and parent has a call or vocation to be a "humanizing educator, to teach with a spiritual vision" (p. 37). This calling (*vocatus*) is heard within one's being and comes from beyond one's self. As a result, philosophers, including Plato and Aristotle, "have understood educator as a spiritual vocation, implying that its surest foundation is the educator's own spirituality" (p. 37).

Groome (1998) defines "spirituality" as "the animating and defining human principle that is the very life of God in humankind" (p. 325). He proposes that all educators can engage learners as spiritual beings. His ongoing process throughout his study includes this spiritual development as an integral part of any curriculum. He advocates the importance of this spiritual dimension in the life of the educator and provides strategies to assist the educator's development, as well as strategies to use in teaching the learner. In addition, religious schools should "overtly nurture the spirituality of their students" (p. 354) throughout the curriculum. However, Groome also maintains that public schools can create environments to educate students as spiritual beings: "if teachers permeate the school and classroom with three more R's—Respect, Responsibility, and Reverence—the ethos may be far more likely to care for souls, without ever using religious language" (p. 355). Groome broadens the value of respect and responsibility (Lickona, 1991) and links these two qualities with reverence, which seeks to recognize the deepest truth about anything. This underlying spirituality accounts for the breadth of Groome's humanizing and holistic vision, educating not only for character (Lickona, 1991), but also educating for life. For Groome, the purpose of education is to assist learners to become fully alive human beings who can help to create a society to serve the common good of all. The purpose and process of educating are inspired and synonymous with a spiritual vision, especially given the nature of what educators can affect at the heart's core of learners, and if they try to educate for life for all. Groome believes that the ultimate goal of this education enables people to become fully alive human beings and to fulfill their ultimate human vocation with a horizon that stretches to the Transcendent. Reflective of the value of caring in education as developed earlier, Groome believes that a humanizing education seems more likely for educators who have an abiding faith in the worth of their vocation, the potential of their learners, and in Gracious Mystery. Groome uses the term "Gracious Mystery" to refer to God who is a mystery to humanity, infinitely good and loving, and known by faith enlightened by reason. In addition, faith in a religiously held conviction makes it more possible for that conviction to become a source of educators' commitment in their educating. United by this spiritual vision, drawing from a variety of "depth structures," and providing the practical guidance to make this vision a reality in the educator's soul, style, and space, Groome develops his total vision of "educating for life for all."

Palmer (1999) notes that the fear of spirituality has had negative effects on education: "The price is a school system that alienates and dulls us, that graduates young people who have had no mentoring in the questions that both enliven and vex the human spirit" (p. 6). Schools need to explore the spiritual dimension of teaching, learning, and living. "Spiritual," for Palmer, is not associated with specific creeds or faith traditions, but rather

> the ancient and abiding human quest for connectedness with something
> larger and more trustworthy than our egos – with our own souls, with one

another, with the worlds of history and nature, with the invisible winds of the spirit, with the mystery of being alive. (p. 6)

While the spiritual questions may be associated with God, they are also the everyday questions that drive the search for meaning in life, for the gifts and needs, for trust, for understanding suffering and fear, and for questions about death. Failure to ask these questions may lead to technical triviality, cultural banality, and a desperate cry for meaning. Spirituality (Palmer, 1999), like integrated character education (Burrett & Rusnak, 1993), is not something that needs to be added-on to be included in the curriculum. Palmer believes spirituality is at the heart of every subject just waiting to be brought to light. Any subject being taught should be connected to the learner's life so that the classroom can almost become a "spiritual garden" (Suhor, 1999, p. 15). Like the use of storybook reading in the development of emergent literacy discussed earlier in this review:

we can evoke the spirituality of any discipline by teaching in ways that allow the "big story" told by the discipline to intersect with the "little story" of the student's life. Doing so not only brings up personal possibilities for connectedness but also helps students learn the discipline more deeply. (Palmer, 1999, p. 9)

In an interview (Halford, 1999), Noddings equates educating for belief or unbelief with educating for religious and spiritual literacy. She distinguishes between spirituality and religion: "Spirituality is an attitude or a way of life that recognizes something we might call spirit. Religion is a specific way of exercising that spirituality and usually requires an institutional affiliation. Spirituality does not require an institutional connection" (Halford, 1999, p. 29). Noddings believes that without violating the U.S. Constitution, teachers can address spirituality in their classrooms. They could restore sacred art and music in schools, acknowledging its importance to people and highlighting rituals and ceremonies in which people delight. The stories behind the sacred art and music could also be discussed. She believes that administrators need to open up avenues of discourse and learn enough about spirituality and religion so that they know not only what educators can't do, but also so that they see how much they can do. Spirituality can be recognized in ordinary schools by seeing it in everyday poetry, music, biography, and conversation, even just slowing down periodically to let students look out the window and reflect or talk about a morning sunrise. Schools should have gardens so students can capture the wonder of nature and life.

Hellwig (1998) believes that spirituality must try to be in harmony with the source and meaning of our being in contemplation and in action. Christian spirituality seeks this harmony in a continuing discipleship with

Jesus of Nazareth. With discipleship or apprenticeship, "Christian life is a continual learning from and empowerment by the person of Jesus of Nazareth" (p. 7). She proposes that a Christian spirituality for the future would have four characteristics:

- It needs to be thoughtful and discerning.
- It is called to be countercultural and community building.
- It ought to be open to uncertainty and attuned to an unending process of learning.
- It is called to be practical in the public and private sphere, and ecumenical in seeking allies and inspiration wherever they may be found (p. 8).

The foundations or dimensions of Christian spirituality are catechesis, community, liturgy, and service (Rite of Christian Initiation of Adults, [RCIA], (1986, No. 75). Through the student-teacher relationship, the spirituality can operate in a practical way to permeate the school culture in the Catholic school (Shimabukuoa, 1998). This practical spirituality implies an interior synthesis within the teacher. This continuous spiritual process must become visible through effective interaction with others and the teacher must have great skill in behavioral areas, such as, self-esteem, authentic caring, humility, and communication skills. This is consistent with Groome's (1996) belief that the educator's mission is "to inform, form, and transform" [students] "with the meaning and ethic of Christian faith" (p. 118).

Since spirituality was the topic for one of the seminars, a broad review provided an overview of the meaning and development of spirituality, rather than on gaining knowledge about various forms of spirituality. The literature revealed an interest in spirituality as ancient as Plato and Aristotle and as contemporary as some of today's popular magazines.

Thomas Groome (1998) stressed not only the respect and responsibility of character education (Lickona, 1991), but also the importance of reverence. This inspired his work written from primarily a Catholic perspective. However, he also provided sections in which he showed how his program could be applied to any learning situation, both at home and in school. He stressed the concept of educator as a spiritual vocation, and stressed the importance of the educator's spirituality, as well as the role of engaging learners as spiritual beings. His work, though primarily focused on Catholic education, also showed how he believed any teacher could "educate for life." His work influenced the development of the spirituality seminar sharing his vision of the importance of developing the spirituality of teacher and learner.

The literature of Hellwig (1998) and Morris (1998) provided a Christian approach to spirituality and a model for growth in spirituality that mirrors the RCIA in the Catholic Church. These were important for creating and assessing the spirituality seminar for the Catholic school.

Having reviewed literature on faith formation in general, some of the literature written by Catholic Church leaders in order to establish an understanding of the role and value of the Catholic school from the perspective of the Catholic Church, and some general literature related to educational leadership, literacy, pedagogy, and character education, the next chapter will describe how the seminars were first set up and delivered within the Catholic school system and show how the stories were collected from those who attended the seminars.

CHAPTER 5

FAITH FORMATION
RESEARCH DESIGN

Since the research for this study focused on the spirituality/virtues semi-nars as taught to Catholic school teachers and as an influence on the lay teachers' understanding of Catholic education, it is important to look at some of the literature written by Catholic Church leaders in order to establish an understanding of the role and value of the Catholic school from the perspective of the Catholic Church.

Since the Third Plenary Council in Baltimore in 1884, the Catholic Church has repeatedly expressed its commitment to Catholic education in all forms. This section begins by examining selected Church documents that establish the purpose of the Catholic school, the vocation of the teacher called to teach in the Catholic school, and issues related to the pedagogy and content of material essential to maintain a Catholic school. These form the foundation for some proposed pillars for maintaining the Catholic culture.

RESEARCH DESIGN

This study was a qualitative interview study that explored the influence that a series of virtue and spirituality seminars have had on a group of lay teachers' perceptions of the Catholic school. Where the virtue seminar

---

Faith Formation of the Laity in Catholic Schools: The Influence of Virtues and Spirituality Seminars, pp. 63–70

refreshes the adult learners' knowledge and provides activities to take to the classroom, the spirituality seminar focuses more on the faith formation of the adult learner. This study was retrospective, allowing teachers who have attended one or both of these seminars within a 5-year period, to reflect on these studies and their influence both immediately and over time.

Sampling

The sample (see Table 5.1) included 15 lay teachers within the Arlington Diocese who had participated in the virtue and spirituality seminars that I created. A Diocese (*Catechism of the Catholic Church*, 1992, No. 833) refers to a community of Christian faithful in communion of faith and sacraments with their bishop who is appointed by the Roman Catholic Pontiff. Each diocese has its own system of Catholic schools and churches. In order to capture a variety of perceptions from the participants, the sample included teachers who had attended both the spirituality and the virtues seminars. Though some principals attended, only teachers were interviewed in order to preserve the integrity of the sample and to focus on the influences of these seminars on teachers and their classes. Criteria for sampling also included a representative distribution of samples from the most recent seminars to the original seminars in 1997-98, as well as across the various grade levels.

The spirituality seminar that was studied is a program that I created to provide teachers in the Catholic schools with some basic tips on what spirituality is and how it can be developed. It was designed to give the teachers a background for spirituality based on the Bible, Catholic Church documents, and the *Catechism of the Catholic Church* (1992). It also provides an understanding of what spirituality is, an overview of different forms of spirituality, and the importance of prayer as the key or food for the spiritual life. Each session also provides opportunities for various prayer experiences.

The virtue seminar that was studied is a program that I created to provide teachers in the Catholic schools with a basic understanding of virtue and how to develop it in the classroom with their students. This seminar was designed to give teachers a theological background or basic knowledge about the Sacrament of Baptism, grace, virtue, theological virtues, moral virtues, conscience formation, commandments, natural law, and moral development, as well as a variety of teaching strategies and resources to use in the classroom with students of various ages.

Interviews with those who have attended both seminars allowed the opportunity to see the influence that one seminar had on the teachers'

Table 5.1. Summary Information of Participants

Name	Age	Religion	Yrs. Taught	Yrs. Teaching in Catholic School	Attendance in Catholic School	Grades Taught
Rose	34	RC	1	1	8 elementary	4
Mary	63	RC	28	8	16+	6th-8th
Laura	52	RC	4	4	16+	Art K-8
Natalie	53	Prot.	13	4	0	PK-3
Angel	61	RC	17	16	16	1
Alice	60	RC	26	25	14	K
Dolores	50	RC	21	21	K-5	P. E K-8
						7th, 8th
Lucy	53	RC	13	10	0	3
Elizabeth	51	RC	18	8	K-8	K-1
Rebecca	42	RC	12	6	Catholic Coll.	1, 3, 4, 5, 7
						Librarian
Jeannice	36	RC	12	9	K-8	University
						3, 5, 6
Katherine	56	RC	18	12	14	3rd-8th
						Librarian
Monica	51	RC	27	27	Catholic Coll.	6th-8th
Donna	46	RC	13	13	0	4th-8th
		convert				
Cecilia	50	RC	9	9	16+	K, 2, 5,
						Resource
						Resource

perceptions of the second seminar, as well as to see if attendance at the combined seminars produced any variations in the teachers' perceptions. Within these groups, the sample also included teachers who attended seminars at various times to determine whether the immediate influence of the seminars changes over time, in what ways this may occur, and how it may influence teachers' perceptions of Catholic schools and any result- ing behaviors. Since teachers from all elementary grade levels have attended, the sample included teacher representation across the grade levels. The group did not include male teachers or high school teachers. Out of the 300 teachers who have attended both seminars, less than 1% was male and less than 1% taught on the high school level. Thus, I tried to create a sample that was representative of all of the teachers who attended both seminars within the selected diocese.

A survey was created and sent to every third person from the 300 who attended both seminars over the 5-year period, thus, initially creating a random sample. The survey asked for volunteers for the interviews, and reinforced the initial perception that the seminars were received well. From the 100 surveys mailed, 25% were returned because the teachers had moved. All of the remaining teachers returned their surveys, though 25 offered a favorable written response but declined a taped interview. From the 50 remaining responses to the random surveys, participants were purposefully selected for the research sample from among those who had voluntccrcd to be interviewed to create a sample of teachers that reflected all elementary grades from kindergarten through eighth grade, and to include some special areas, such as art, library, and resource. The sample was representative, in gender and grade level taught, of the entire group that had attended the seminars. Given the small sample, the goal of the research was to provide a generalized question to be answered by a particular sample of the population (Maxwell, 1996, p. 54).

RESEARCH RELATIONSHIP

The research relationship is "often conceptualized as gaining entry to the setting, or establishing rapport with your participants" (Maxwell, 1996, p. 66). As the major instrument for gathering and measuring information in this study, the researcher/author's relationship with the participants potentially could have influenced the rapport and the information that was shared. Since each of the participants had attended one or more seminars, the rapport necessary to gain entry into the interviewees' thinking and perceptions was already established, thus enabling one "to ethically learn the things you need to learn in order to validly answer your research questions" (p. 66). Rapport, an important aide to the research partnership that needs to be established between the interviewer and the respondent, was easily established and maintained.

Research Context

Most of the interviews took place in each teacher's classroom at a time that was convenient for each teacher. This natural setting of the classroom provided an opportunity to look for tangible signs or symbols that could be a part of these teachers' perception of a Catholic school. It also allowed these interviewees to be in their own comfortable environments. The settings were free of distractions from participants' regular responsibilities to students and quiet to facilitate their comfort and openness. Each hour long audio taped interview provided sufficient time for the respondents to share their experiences and to tell their stories.

DATA ANALYSIS

Data analysis for this study incorporated two main approaches to provide a more thorough analysis. Case-focused analysis dealt with individual respondents' experiences related to the seminars and how they perceived they had been influenced by them. Issue-focused analysis dealt with the collective issues revealed by the respondents (Weiss, 1994).

Case-Focused Analysis

Case-focused analysis "make[s] the reader aware of the respondents' experience within the context of their lives: this is what it is like to be this person in this situation" (Weiss, 1994, p. 168). The purpose of the case-focused analysis was to develop an understanding of each respondent's experience of the virtue and/or spirituality seminar, and of their perceptions of the influences that these seminars had on them, on their teaching, and on their understanding of Catholic schools. This resulted in some generalizations after all cases had been analyzed.

Riessman (1993) recommends beginning with the structure of the narrative: "to avoid the tendency to read a narrative simply for content, and the equally dangerous tendency to read it as evidence for a prior theory" (p. 61). Looking at the organization, and asking why the informant develops the tale a particular way with the interviewer allows the researcher to start from the inside and move outward. The researcher looks for meanings encoded in "the form of the talk" (p. 61) and expands outward, identifying "propositions that make the talk sensible" (p. 61). Riessman believes that "individuals' narratives are situated in particular interactions but also in social, cultural, and institutional discourses which must be brought to bear to interpret them" (p. 61). "Contextualizing analysis" (Maxwell, 1996, p. 79) attempts to understand the data within the context of the interviewee's narrative. It links data rather than fracturing it. The case-focused analysis is not be concerned with "relationships of similarity that can be used to sort data into categories independently of context but instead looks for relationships that connect statements and events within a context into a coherent whole" (p. 79). This analysis helped to capture the Catholic atmosphere and culture as each respondent perceived it and to view from within each context, their perceptions of the influence of the seminars on character development and on the respondents' understanding of the Catholic school.

Issue-Focused Analysis

Issue-focused analysis focuses on what can be learned about specific issues, events or processes from any and all of the respondents (Weiss, 1994). It "is likely to move from discussion of issues within one area of discussion to discussion of issues within another, with each area logically connected to the others" (p. 154). Issue-focused analysis was done through coding, sorting, local integration, and inclusive integration (Weiss, 1994). Codings "link what the respondent says in his or her interview to the concepts and categories that will appear in the report" (p. 154). After sorting the coded data, local integration attempted to organize and summarize the coded material in order to develop theories: "Here is what is said in this area, and this is what I believe it to mean" (p. 158). Inclusive integration brought all of the isolated areas of analysis from the local integration and knit them into one story (Weiss, 1994).

Coding and Sorting

Coding, the main categorizing strategy in qualitative research, fractures the data and rearranges it into categories in order to compare data between and within categories and to aid in the development of theoretical concepts (Maxwell, 1996). Sorting places the data into broader themes and issues. Initial coding categories were created from the research questions, theory grounded in the research literature, and three earlier pilot studies related to teachers' perceptions of the Catholic identity of the Catholic school and teachers' preparations in the areas of religion and spirituality. Additional codes were developed as the analysis progressed. Later codes, "often called emic categories" (p. 79), were taken from the concepts of the people studied.

Local Integration

Local integration organized the coded data so that theories could be developed. This part of the analysis assisted in the development of hypotheses related to the significance of experiences in the virtues and/or spirituality seminars, how the seminars personally affected or influenced the participants, any relationship between these seminars and character education, and the influence or impact these virtue and/or spirituality seminars had on the lay participants' thinking in regard to Catholic education. This step helped to identify what was said in each relevant category and then to assign meaning. "Minitheories" (Weiss, 1994, p. 159) were developed by combining the sorted data and by developing some type of display, such as a table or matrix (Maxwell, 1996).

Initially, one table used rows to list the participants and columns for each of the major hypothesis in order to collate data that was pertinent to these specific issues. Thus, reading across a row allowed an understanding of each participant's perceptions, while reading down a column revealed the combined perceptions of the group in order to create each hypothesis and to discuss each as a minitheory.

Validity Issues

Validity refers to "the correctness or credibility of a description, conclusion, explanation, interpretation, or other sort of account" (Maxwell, 1996, p. 87). Researcher bias is an important issue to consider in relation to the validity of any study. Other validity threats for this study could have included threats to description, interpretation, and theory (Maxwell, 1996). Description was concerned with the accuracy of what one saw or heard and the risk of inaccuracy. Interpretation was concerned with understanding the respondents' perspectives and the meanings attached to their words and actions and the risk of imposing one's own framework or meaning. Theory was concerned with paying attention to all data, explanations, and understandings of the issues being studied and the risk of not collecting or paying attention to discrepant data or not considering the alternative explanations or understandings of the issues.

Key validity questions (Miles & Huberman, 1994, p. 278) for consideration were:

1. Do the findings make sense?
2. Are they credible to the people studied and the readers?
3. Do we have an authentic portrait of what we are viewing?

These questions helped to ensure greater internal validity. The participants were volunteers drawn from those who attended the seminars and expressed a willingness to be interviewed. Keeping the questions open-ended, and using member checks to explain any discrepant data or contradictions as they occurred within the interviews helped to create internal validity..

To address the validity threat of accurate description, each of the interviews was audio taped and reviewed as soon as possible after the interviews in order to capture one's impressions resulting from nonverbal communication, while still fresh. A third person transcribed the tapes as soon as possible after each interview. Listening to the interviews in their entirety before and after their transcription minimized the risk of inaccurate interpretation or description. This increased the accuracy of recall. A peer check on random interviews increased the validity of accuracy in description.

To address the threat of imposing personal views or framework on the interpretation, interview questions were open-ended to give the participants the opportunity to express themselves freely without giving information that they believed one wanted to hear. Using member checks verified understanding of the participants words and meanings.

To address the validity threat of not collecting or paying attention to discrepant data, open-ended questions and probing did create the potential for discrepant data to emerge. However, because the research questions were directed to determining what influence these seminars had, any discrepant data was considered as valuable as the anticipated outcomes.

Generalization

External validity or generalizability refers to the validity or transferability of "a conclusion beyond that setting or group" (Maxwell, 1996, p. 97). The issue of external validity raises the question of whether the findings from this study can be applied to other people, Catholic schools or dioceses, other religion courses, or other faith-based schools with similar programs. The size of the study and the limitation of the content taught make this questionable. However, while the findings may not apply to the general population, one hopes that this study will produce implications that, with further study, could have significance in the area of teacher formation and character education, not only for Catholic schools throughout the country, but also for other schools as well.

Having considered the Catholic dimension, the creation of the seminars which frame the study, and some of its research design, the next chapter examines some of the vocabulary that is specific to the Catholic faith so that all who read the future chapters will have a similar understanding of some of the basic terminology and principles with which the participants tell their stories.

CHAPTER 6

A GUIDE TO BASIC CATHOLIC DOCTRINE

In addition to serving as instructional and managerial leaders of their schools, principals in Catholic schools also serve as spiritual leaders. Sergiovanni (2006) cites studies, done by Augenstein (1989) and Augenstein and Konnert (1991), which define:

> The role requirements of the religious dimension as knowing about and making available church documents and other religious sources, providing for spiritual development, being a leader of prayer, creating an environment for religious education, integrating gospel values and other religious principals into the curriculum, and providing services to the parish and civic community. Other types of Christian schools, as well as Jewish schools and Muslim schools, would have similar lists of added roles, responsibilities, and proficiencies that reflect their uniqueness. (p. 35)

Since this study was done in relation to Catholic schools and much of the description relies on terms and doctrine that are common to a Catholic culture, this chapter will briefly clarify some of the Catholic terminology used throughout this book. What follows is not meant to encompass all that the Catholic Church teaches but to provide an introduction and review so that the reader of any faith will be able to appreciate both the content and the context of this study and its results.

Faith Formation of the Laity in Catholic Schools: The Influence of Virtues and Spirituality Seminars, pp. 71–79
Copyright © 2008 by Information Age Publishing

For ease in reviewing various terms, they are organized first according to the following categories: terms associated with Catholic schools, terms associated with the Catholic faith, and other general terms. See Table 6.1 for an alphabetical list of the included terms. To simplify our understanding of terms, those that are general will be discussed first, followed by those that have specific meaning in the Catholic faith, and finally, those that relate to Catholic education.

GENERAL TERMS

Throughout this book, the word, *faith* has been used in relation to the Catholic faith as well as all religious beliefs. It is used broadly to describe a particular set of religious beliefs. A person with faith is one who shares in these beliefs and to have faith in the context of this book is to have a belief in God and to believe in His teachings, using our reason to understand and yet aware of our inability to prove these beliefs in a concrete sensible manner.

Theology in the broad sense is the study of God and our beliefs about Him. Each religious denomination may develop its specific understanding of God and how their faith serves them as a guide through life. The specific set of major and most important beliefs of a particular religion are *doctrines* of that faith.

In addition to the value of studying about one's faith, we come to know God through *prayer* and *meditation*. Prayer may be described as talking to God, conversation with God, or the lifting of one's mind and heart to God. There are four major types of prayer; namely, one adores or praises God for His goodness and His many gifts, one acknowledges or expresses contrition for one's failings, weaknesses, sin, and need for God's forgiveness, one expresses gratitude or thanks to God for life and all that God has given, and one asks or petitions God for one's needs as in supplication. These four words, "adoration," "contrition," "thanksgiving," and "supplication" are often remembers in the simple word "ACTS." One form of prayer is meditation which may take a variety of forms but in a general religious sense involves quiet reflection about God and oneself in relation to Him, perhaps beginning with sacred reading, reflecting on the meaning of these words, how they apply to one's life or speak to the heart, and coming to some conclusion that may lead to a change of heart. It is a form of giving praise and thanks to God and coming to know Him more completely.

Prayer is vital for a person to develop spiritually. Just as one needs food and oxygen for the life of the body, one needs prayer for the life of the soul. If one is spiritual, one is often described as holy, religious, concerned with the divine. The ancient philosophers, Plato and Aristotle,

Table 6.2. List of Catholic Terms

Catholic School Terms	*Catholic Faith Terms*	*Other Terms*
Diocesan Catholic schools	Beatitudes	character
Jesus time	Cardinal virtues	Charism
		Doctrine
Parish school/Parochial school	Centering prayer	Faith in general
Prayer corner	Commandments	Meditation
Private school	Diocese	Morality
Religion certification	First Holy Communion	Pope John Paul II Cultural Center
Religion curriculum coordinator	Franciscans	Prayer
Virtue of the Month Program	Grace	retreat
	Jesuits	Spirituality
	Liturgy of the Hours	Theology
	Marian prayers	Virtue
	Mary, Mother of Jesus Christ	
	Mass	
	Memorare	
	Moral Virtues	
	Parish and parishioners	
	Pontiff/Pope	
	Prayer to St. Michael	
	Rosary	
	Sacraments	
	Sacrament of Penance (or Reconciliation)	
	Theological virtues	
	Vespers	

spoke of the soul as the animating principle of life, the life-giving spirit. Thus, when one speaks of *spirituality*, one is talking about focusing on the development of this life-giving spirit or soul. While today's society uses the term broadly to speak of seeking quiet and developing the inner self, from a religious perspective, one cultivates one's spirituality when one spends time in prayer and meditation to come to know God and oneself in relation to Him. One becomes whole as one develops both the body and soul.

As the soul gives life to the body, so the human person is called to use the God-given gifts of intellect and free will to come to a deeper knowledge and love of God, and to learn to choose to live according to the law of God which is written within the heart and is the foundation for one's guide, the conscience. As one learns to make good choices, one performs good acts. When these good acts are repeated, they become habits. A person who tries to perform these good acts is described as a person of *virtue*. The person who acts regularly in a virtuous manner is considered to be a person of good *character*. The virtuous person, the one of good character, is, therefore, a moral person. *Morality* describes the condition of being a moral person and the study of what constitutes these good and moral actions. When a person manifests a certain set of virtues, one often identifies these as the person's *charism*. Similarly, a group or an institution that continues to manifest these characteristics is often described as possessing this charism.

Finally, in looking at general terms used in this book, the word *retreat* occurs frequently. While the term today has many secular meanings that often refer to an organization taking time away to work on plans or goals, retreat here describes a religious experience. It means a time that a person sets apart to pray, to study, to attend conferences, and mainly to spend time with God in order to reflect on one's relationship with God and to renew one's commitment to Him and to building a life that reflects His goodness, His image and likeness. It may be for a few hours, a day, a weekend, a week or even longer, depending on one's vocation and opportunity for this experience.

The last term included in this general list is the *Pope John Paul II Cultural Center*. This is a museum in Washington, DC that hosts a major exhibit of history and memorabilia of this Pope, as well as a movie of his life. There are not only changeable displays but also a whole floor of hands-on activities that teach children and adults about a variety of topics related to the Catholic Church.

This brings us to the second area of terms for discussion; namely, those that relate specifically to the Catholic Church. The purpose of giving meaning to these terms is to give all who read this book a common understanding of their meaning. All definitions for this section are taken from the *Catechism of the Catholic Church* (1994). Though the discussion of the general terms moved from faith and doctrine to prayer, virtue and morality, the terms in Table 6.1 will be grouped in a similar manner according to the "four pillars" of the *Catechism of the Catholic Church* (CCC). These describe the four main sections of this document; namely, "The

Profession of Faith" or the creed, "The Celebration of the Christian Mystery" of the sacraments and the Mass, "Life in Christ" or morality, commandments, and beatitudes, and "Christian Prayer" or what it is, how one prayers, and the Lord's Prayer.

Beginning with "The Profession of Faith" or the creed in the Catholic Church, the purpose of looking at these terms is not to provide a catechesis of the Catholic religion but rather to clarify terms used throughout this book. Thus, what follows is not a look at our full creed or set of beliefs but only those that are being used here.

However, we say in the words of the creed that "We believe in Jesus Christ, His only Son, Our Lord, who was conceived by the Holy Spirit, born of the Virgin Mary" Thus, *Mary, Mother of Jesus Christ* is mentioned throughout the text. Chosen to be the Mother of Christ, Mary is a perfect example of how we are called to follow the will of God. As the Mother of God, she is called to be the Mother of all believers, the Mother of the Church (CCC 963). Devotion to Mary is an important part of the Catholic faith since through her "Yes" to God's will, Jesus Christ, the Son of God became man and entered into this world that we might be saved. One way in which we express our devotion to Mary is through a variety of prayers in which we invoke her help. These are called *Marian Prayers*. We believe that she is able to intercede for us to her Son to help us in this life. One special prayer of intercession is the *Memorare*.

Another special prayer to honor Mary is the *Rosary*, which includes a brief reflection on Mary and the life of Jesus from the time when the angel Gabriel appeared to her to ask her to be the Mother of God through Jesus life on earth, his passion and death, as well as his Resurrection and ascension into heaven, the coming of the Holy Spirit to found the Church, and Mary's entrance into heaven and coronation as Queen of heaven and earth. The prayer is made up of four sets of mysteries, the Joyful mysteries which treat of Jesus' coming and youth, the luminous mysteries which tell of his life on earth, the sorrowful mysteries which tell of his passion and death, and the glorious mysteries which tell of his Resurrection, the events of the early Church, and Mary's place in heaven. Each of these sets of mysteries contains five specific mysteries on which one reflects while praying five sets of an Our Father, 10 Hail Marys, and one Glory Be on a set of beads, also called a *rosary*.

In our creed or set of major beliefs, we also profess our belief in the "apostolic Church." This suggests that the Church was "built on the foundation of the Apostles, the witnesses chosen and sent on mission by Christ himself" and that "she continues to be taught, sanctified, and guided by the apostles until Christ's return, through their successors in pastoral office: the college of bishops, assisted by priests in union with the successor of Peter, the Church's supreme pastor" (CCC 857). This successor of Peter, the *Pope* or *Pontiff* is the head of the Roman Catholic Church.

The whole Roman Catholic Church is divided into smaller geographical areas around the world. The "particular church" which is the *diocese* "refers to a community of the Christian faithful in communion of faith and sacraments with their bishop ordained in apostolic succession" (CCC 833). Within each diocese, there are individual churches called *parishes*. "A parish is a definite community of the Christian faithful," the *parishioners*, established within a diocese (CCC 2179). "The pastoral care of the parish is entrusted to a pastor as its own shepherd under the authority of the diocesan bishop" (CCC 2179).

The Church's members are composed of those ordained to the priesthood, those embracing the consecrated life, and the lay members, who may be single or married. Those who enter the consecrated life consecrate their lives to God and profess vows of chastity, poverty, and obedience in a stable state of life recognized by the Church (CCC 914). Examples of religious groups mentioned by those interviewed in this book include the *Franciscans*, founded by St. Francis of Assisi and the *Jesuits* founded by St. Ignatius of Loyola.

This brings us to another set of terms associated with the "The Celebration of the Christian Mystery." "The parish initiates the Christian people into the ordinary expression of the liturgical life: it gathers them together in this celebration" (CCC 2179). The central act of this public worship of the Church is the *Mass*, the liturgical celebration of the Eucharist. This representation of Jesus' Last Supper and His sacrifice on Calvary involves both the liturgy of the Word, with Scripture readings, homily and general petitions of prayer and the liturgy of the Eucharist with the presentation of the brad and wine to be consecrated into Jesus' body and blood and received in communion. "The liturgy of the Word and the liturgy of the Eucharist together form one single act of worship" (CCC 1346).

"The whole liturgical life of the Church revolves around the Eucharistic sacrifice and the sacraments" (CCC 1113). The *sacraments* are signs of grace, instituted by Christ and entrusted to the Church, by which divine life is given to us. They bear fruit in those who receive them and strengthen their faith (CCC 1131-1134). For Roman Catholics, there are seven sacraments which celebrate various stages of one's spiritual life with Christ in the Church. They include sacraments to initiate the recipient through various stages into the Church; namely, Baptism, Eucharist, and Confirmation. There are sacraments of healing which strengthen the individual spiritually and often physically; namely, Penance and Sacrament of the sick. There are also sacraments of vocation; namely, Matrimony and Holy Orders. When a person first receives the Sacrament of the

Eucharist, this is called *First Holy Communion*. The forgiveness of sins committed after Baptism is conferred by the *Sacrament of Penance or Reconciliation.*

The mystery of Christ which we celebrate in the Eucharist "permeates and transfigures the time of each day through the celebration of the *Liturgy of the Hours*, the divine office" (CCC 1174). This prayer of the Psalms, meditation on the Word of God, and canticles and blessings which are prayed at various hours of the day by clergy, religious, and lay people is like an extension of the Eucharistic celebration. It does not exclude but in a complementary way "calls forth the various devotions of the People of God, especially adoration and worship of the Blessed Sacrament" (CCC 1174-1178), which is Jesus present in the Eucharist. *Vespers* is a part of the Liturgy of the Hours that is prayed in the late afternoon.

Continuing our use of the *Catechism of the Catholic Church* as a guide for discussion of terms used in this book and that are specific to the Roman Catholic Church, the third pillar of section focuses on "Life in Christ." Virtue was defined earlier as an habitual good act or "an habitual and firm disposition to do good" (CCC 1803). Though there are many virtues, the term, *Theological Virtues* refers specifically to the virtues of faith, hope, and charity which are divine in origin. They relate directly to God. They come from God or are infused by God and they lead the individual back to God. It is through God's *grace*, the gift of his life in our souls, that we recognize and develop these virtues. The *Moral Virtues* are prudence, justice, fortitude, and temperance. They play a pivotal role in our moral development and are also known as Cardinal Virtues.

To guide us in our moral development, God gave to Moses the *Ten Commandments*. This series of 10 directives basically guide us in how we should show our love for God and our love for neighbor. Jesus preached the eight *beatitudes* in his Sermon on the Mount (Matthew 5). These guides are a central proclamation of Jesus' preaching and they shed light on the characteristics of Christian life. They "present a sort of veiled interior biography of Jesus, a kind of portrait of his figure" (Benedict XVI, 2007, p. 74). They fulfill God's promises to Abraham and teach us about the final goal of eternal life, the Kingdom of heaven, rest in God (CCC 1725-1726).

> The Beatitudes display the mystery of Christ himself, and they call us into communion with him ... the Beatitudes are also a roadmap for the Church, which recognizes in them the model of what she herself should be. They are directions for discipleship, directions that concern every individual. (Benedict XVI, 2007, p. 74)

The last section of terms relates to "Christian Prayer." Throughout the stories of the teachers in this study, various prayer forms have been mentioned. Thus, *meditation and contemplation* describe some of these prayer experiences of those interviewed. Throughout the study, no distinction was made to clarify forms and the terms were used interchangeably without getting into specific variations. One particular prayer that a teacher mentioned was the *St. Michael the Archangel Prayer.* This is a traditional prayer in the Church offered to invoke the help of St. Michael the Archangel, who is known for having driven Satan and the fallen angels out of heaven. It asks for his protection in all times of trial and temptation.

The final set of terms used in this book is those that relate to Catholic schools, especially in the United States. They are divided into three types: those related to the organization of Catholic schools, those related to religious education, and those that describe some classroom activities. *Diocesan Catholic schools* are those Catholic schools that are affiliated with a diocese and follow its prescribed policies and procedures. These may be schools that are part of a parish, known as *parochial or parish schools,* or they may be owned and operated by a religious order or private group, known then as *private Catholic schools.*

Within any Catholic school, there is some type of religion curriculum, just as there are curriculum guides for all subjects taught in a school. Usually a member of the faculty is chosen by the principal to be the **religion** *curriculum coordinator.* As with any curriculum coordinator, this person works with the principal to see that curriculum guidelines are followed and works with the teachers of religion to assist them in how to implement the guidelines. Usually in the United States, most dioceses require that teachers of religion have *religion certification,* usually in addition to grade level or subject certification in their field. The requirements differ among dioceses as to teacher preparation and knowledge of Religion content.

In a Catholic school, while academic excellence is a priority, growth in the knowledge of our faith, a loving relationship with Jesus Christ and development of moral principles are at the core of a Catholic school. Prayer is important and students are taught how to pray and how important prayer is in their relationship with Christ.

Many Catholic schools, including those staffed by my own religious community, encourage teachers to have a *prayer corner* in their classrooms. This may be a table placed in a particular corner of the classroom with a Bible, religious articles, a rosary, symbols of the particular season of the Church year, stories of the saints or any materials that will inspire a few moments for quiet prayer. It is a way of teaching students the importance of making time and space for God in their lives. *Jesus Time* is a term used in some of the interviews that teachers of lower grades use to describe the religion period of the day to show little ones thy they have religion class.

The *virtue of the month* describes a way of crating a program to foster virtue in students. In this type of program, the school identifies a series of virtues that they deem important for the school and then they dedicate a month to each virtue with a variety of activities to help children practice that virtue. Activities include Bible stories, other stories, music, identification of well known persons who practiced that virtue, as well as home and school suggestions for the practice of that virtue. The virtue of the month is a major component of the virtue seminars that I created.

Having considered some of the key Catholic concepts and terms used freely by the participants, the next chapter outlines some of the content and methodology used in the actual virtue and spirituality seminars.

CHAPTER 7

OVERVIEW OF THE VIRTUE AND SPIRITUALITY SEMINARS

In today's society, we see the increasing influence of secularism, material-ism, consumerism, and relativism. Our young people face many challenges in learning how to make good moral choices and how to give witness to their faith and the importance of Jesus Christ in giving meaning to their lives. Faith formation of your young people is at the heart of any religiously based school. In our Catholic schools, Christ is the heart of the school. While our schools must strive for academic excellence to prepare students for their future role in society, our first responsibility is to help them to grow and develop a knowledge of our faith, a deep and personal relation-ship with Jesus Christ, and a sensitivity and awareness of reaching out to serve others in need whether in our families, our Church, our communi-ties, or the world. In our Catholic schools, students study about our Catholic doctrine and history. However, they are also encouraged to grow in a relationship with Christ through prayer and to model Christ in their actions and moral choices. Any faith-based school would probably promote the same goals—knowledge of its beliefs, personal relationship with Christ and actions witnessing to Christ in daily living. In order for our students to grow and develop in their faith formation, they need to be taught by adults who are also continuing to grow and develop their own faith formation.

There is an old saying that "you cannot give what you do not have." Given the history of Catholic schools and the past dependence on the

Faith Formation of the Laity in Catholic Schools: The Influence of Virtues and Spirituality Seminars, pp. 81–95
Copyright © 2008 by Information Age Publishing
81

guidance of religious priests, religious brothers, and religious sisters, it is important that one thinks about the faith formation of administrators and teachers as well as that of the students. The virtue seminar and the spirituality seminar were developed from this perspective. In the next sections, a brief overview of each of these seminars will be offered not only to serve as background for understanding the stories told by teachers who attended the seminars, but also to encourage the reader to think about creating similar programs appropriate for any school that wants to nurture religion and faith in its faculty as well as its students.

VIRTUE SEMINAR

We have already seen that much has been written on faith formation as well as character education. There are countless books and manuals filled with creative ideas and for classroom activities and morality based stories to foster good character. However, if we assume that a poster or an activity or even a story by itself will nurture virtue, we are missing what I believe is essential to developing virtue. Our days, whether as educators or students, are filled with many activities. While it is possible to have fun working on practicing moral actions, discussing stories, creating projects, or doing bulletin boards that emphasize virtue, we need to root these activities in something more than a school rule or directive from the principal. Furthermore, we need to raise the conscious awareness of our teachers that this is not just another thing to do or anther directive to implement for then our students perceive the limited application of the activity. In our Catholic schools, as well as other faith-based schools, we can reflect back on Genesis which reminds us that God made us in His image and likeness. From a Christian perspective, based on baptism, we can say that we have received the Holy Spirit and that Christ is present in each of us. Instead of promoting good character as a nice social thing to do, from a religious perspective, we can build on these ideas of being made in God's image and being a dwelling for the Holy Spirit as our reason for showing respect or cultivating virtue.

The virtue seminar is a 2-day program that I created in 1997 when I was assistant superintendent of schools for the Arlington Diocese. In response to a request for this type of program, the virtue seminar had as one if its goals the creation of a school-wide program to encourage students to develop and grow in virtue. However, I firmly believed and still do that there need to be more than a "make and take" session of activities. We needed to find creative ways to teach our students on all levels the meaning and value of virtue in their lives. Acting in a virtuous manner is not just something to study in a religion class but needs to be a lifetime pattern or way of living. Thus, I decided that we first need to renew or in many cases introduce teachers to a simple understanding of the value and meaning of virtue first for themselves in their own lives and then as an important part of their mission in the school to model and teach to their students, whether or not they taught a formal Religion class.

What follows is an overview of some of the content presented to teachers in the virtue seminar. It is includes some basic doctrine and teachings of the Roman Catholic religion. However, readers of other faiths could easily adapt the content to fit their own theology. The important thing is to think about what are the basic elements of theology that we need to know as adults to reawaken our value for virtue so that thus inspired, we may pass this teaching on to out students age appropriately with a renewed sense of enthusiasm that will motivate and encourage them as well.

The virtue seminar has generally been presented over 2 days. The room is filled with ideas for bulletin boards, collections of stories that relate virtue on various age levels, samples of virtue based videos, and samples of commercial materials that provide many activities for teacher and student to foster character. Mention is made of these throughout the seminar, and participants are engaged in sample activities that could be done with various age level students. Samples of student work are also displayed. The content is presented through a multi-media approach. Lectures are interspersed with PowerPoint, video clips, and music CDs. Participants are given ample opportunity to discuss ideas that they use or that others in their schools use.

However, the major presentations during the first day and a half focus on enriching the participants with an understanding of various aspects of the seminar's major theme, "Called in Baptism to the image of Christ through the practice of virtue." Figures 7.1a and 7.1b present a general summary of the 2-day seminar.

The first topic is a presentation on the call received in baptism. This call is God's invitation to each of us to grow in holiness. The concept of holiness is first defined with a reference to Sacred Scripture:

> For this reason, I remind you to stir into flame the gift of God that you have through the imposition of my hands. For God did not give us a spirit of cowardice but rather of power and love and self-control. He saved us and called us to a holy life, not according to our works but according to our own design and the grace bestowed on us in Christ Jesus before time began, but now made manifest through the appearance of our savior Christ Jesus, who destroyed death and brought life and immortality to light through the gospel. (2 Timothy 1: 6-7, 9-10)

Day 1

8:45 A.M.	- Registration
9:00 A.M.	- Welcome, Opening Prayer, and Overview
9:15 A.M.	- Ice breaker
9:30 A.M.	- Virtue and Grace: Answering our Baptismal Call
	– Sister Patricia Helene, I.H.M.
10:15 A.M.	- Break
10:30 A.M.	- Virtue and Grace: Made in God's Image
	– Sister Patricia Helene, I.H.M.
11:15 A.M.	- Activity
11:30 P.M.	- Lunch Break
12:15 P.M.	- Virtue: The Foundation of Conscience
	– Sister Mary of the Sacred Heart, I.H.M.
1:45 P.M.	- Break
2:00 P.M.	- Activities
2:30 P.M.	- Closing Prayer
3:00 P.M.	- Departure

Figure 7.1a.   Catholic virtues: Nurturing the inner life.

A brief overview of documents from Vatican Council II, various Church documents, the *Catechism of the Catholic Church* (CCC, 1992), and the *National Directory for Catechesis* (2005) further emphasizes the meaning of the call to holiness. It also shows that the teacher in a Catholic school must teach the integration of faith and life through word and example in sharing the meaning of this baptismal call age appropriately with students.

With a renewed understanding of the importance of baptism, the concept of grace is reviewed. "Grace is God's gift to help us respond to his call. It is God himself giving himself to us" (Earl, 2006, p. 15). Thus, the

Day 2

8:45 A.M.	- Registration
9:00 A.M.	- Opening Prayer and Recap Day 1
9:15 A.M.	- The Theological and Virtues
	- Sister Patricia Helene, I.H.M.
10:30 A.M.	- Break
10:45 A.M.	- Catholic Leadership
	– Sister Mary of the Sacred Heart, I.H.M.
12:00 P.M.	- Lunch Break
12:45 P.M.	- Virtue in Practice: Activities
	– Sister Patricia Helene, I.H.M.
1:45 P.M.	- Virtue in Practice: Activities
	- Sister Mary of the Sacred Heart, I.H.M.
2:45 P.M.	- Called to Be Disciples of Christ: Go Forth
3:00 P.M.	- Departure

Figure 7.2b.   Catholic virtues: Nurturing the inner life.

idea of living as the image of God is discussed, going back to its reference in the Book of Genesis. The CCC (1992) describes this gift:

> Grace is favor, free and undeserved help that God gives us to respond to his call to become children of God, adopted sons, partakers of the divine nature, and eternal life. Grace is a participation in the life of God. It introduces us into the intimacy of the Trinitarian life. (CCC 1996-1997)

Various types of grace as found in Catholic teaching are discussed including sanctifying grace, sacramental grace, actual grace, and charisms.

After reflecting on our baptismal call as God's invitation to develop and grow in his image and likeness through God's gift of grace, nurtured through reading of Scripture and prayer, and strengthened as we receive the sacraments and perform good works, we look at the practice of virtue "through which we grow in God's image and likeness and respond to our baptismal call" (Earl, 2006, p. 18). We examine virtue on both a natural and a supernatural level and then take a close look at the theological virtues of faith, hope and charity, and the moral or cardinal virtues of prudence, justice, fortitude, and temperance. God calls us in baptism and we respond through his grace by practicing the virtues, thus, fulfilling the covenant that God established with us. More detail on these concepts as well as prayer, personal reflection, topics for discussion, and related activities are found in a thorough explanation of the virtue seminar in *Building the Builders: Faith Formation in Virtue* (Earl, 2006).

Our baptismal call is also a call to conversion to grow in our ability to make good moral choices that guide us to live and promote Gospel values. As adults, we need to be able to distinguish between right and wrong and choose virtue over vice. As educators whether parent, administrator or teacher, we need to be able to teach this to our students. Thus, the next major segment of the virtue seminar provides a look at moral development and conscience formation. Especially in today's society which so often promotes violence, drugs, sexual promiscuity, materialism, isolation, self-indulgence and so many other negative choices through lyrics, commercials, movies, TV, and Internet to name a few, we need to continue to form our own consciences and guide our young people in their conscience formation so that they can distinguish what is morally right from what is temporarily satisfying but ultimately empty and often morally wrong. The images that surround us influence how we think, what we value, how we choose, and who we become.

Once we are aware of the multiple influences in our lives, we recognize the value of conscience. It is "God's voice within us that guides us to do good and avoid evil" (Earl, 2006, p. 34). Again a look at Scripture with the Old Testament stories of Adam and Eve and Cain and Abel, the New Testament story of the Good Samaritan and several documents of the Roman Catholic Church serves as the foundation for the presentation on moral development and conscience formation. Education of the conscience is a life-long task for all of us. It is essential as educators that we are well prepared in our understanding of conscience formation so that we can assist our students to grow in their own conscience formation. "The education of conscience guarantees freedom and engenders peace of heart" (CCC 1784). Pope John Paul II (1993) in his book, *Veritatis Splendor*, wrote about conscience:

> Saint Bonaventure teaches that conscience is like God's herald and messenger; it does not command things on its own authority, but commands them as coming from God's authority.... This is why conscience has binding force. (No. 58)

The virtue seminar offers some of the major guides to conscience formation and moral development. These include the Gifts of the Holy Spirit and the Fruits of the Holy Spirit, which are first received in baptism and strengthened in confirmation. In addition, the Ten Commandments given to Moses by God, complemented by the beatitudes of Jesus Christ, serve as guides for right action. The corporal and spiritual works of mercy further suggest ways to live a life of virtue that places God first and then motivates love of neighbor. Throughout the seminar, various handouts and diagrams show the participants how all of these relate to virtue.

> The Word of God, Gifts of the Holy Spirit, the Sacraments, the teachings of the Church, the Commandments, the virtues, the Beatitudes, the Spiritual and Corporal Works of Mercy, the witness and advice of others, and examination of conscience are like parts of a fan connected to one another, building on each other, and opening to serve as a foundation to guide us first in our own personal formation and then in our responsibility as Catholic educators to help our young people in their own conscience formation. (Earl, 2006, p. 46)

The last major section on content appropriate for faith formation in virtue focuses on leadership. It shows that leadership is not just reserved for the administrator. Each parent is a leader in his/her own home and each teacher is a leader in his/her own classroom. While professional preparation is essential for effective teaching, Pope Benedict XVI (2005) reminds us in his recent Encyclical Letter, *God Is Love,* that

> these charity workers needs a "formation of the heart"; they need to be led to that encounter with God in Christ which awakens their love and opens their spirits to others. As a result, love of neighbor will no longer be for them a commandment imposed, so to speak, from without, but a consequence deriving from their faith, a faith which becomes active through love. (No. 31a)

After each of these major elements for knowing, loving, and acquiring virtue is presented, the virtue seminar then introduces the attendees to ways to promote virtue in school and home, especially by setting up some type of a virtue program. Whether this is a virtue of the month, the quarter, the semester or even the year, participants learn how to start a virtue program either in their classroom or preferably throughout the whole school. This means that principal and faculty need to recognize the true value of virtue and begin to identify the key virtues that they believe need to be reinforced in their students. Drawing from a variety of commercial resources, as well as the experience of the presenters, the participants learn to create several sources that will become ongoing in the school.

These include looking for Scripture passages that speak of the specific virtues, stories from the students' readers or literature series across the grades, and hymns that speak of these virtues. Finally, the faculty needs to think of several practical examples of how the students can demonstrate each virtue. Each of these becomes the source for an ongoing resource. For example, if each teacher starts to keep a list of virtues that can be linked to stories in the children's' readers, then by the end of the first year, there is a comprehensive list of stories. Similarly, this can be done by identifying virtues in hymns as they are used in various services throughout the year. Thus, after 1 year, a school could have a comprehensive list of stories by grade level that highlight specific virtues.

There are many ways that students can be recognized and encouraged for the virtuous actions. Some examples, include a monthly certificate for the best example of the months in each room given out at an assembly or Mass or other service, certificates given to all who exemplify the virtue in each class, or something as simple as creating a chain of virtue and having each student add a link when he/she is caught practicing that virtue.

The important thing is to involve the whole school—all faculty, staff, administrators, and parents too. The weekly or monthly parent letter can highlight the virtue of the month and suggestions offered for its practice at home. This will serve as an aide to parents since they can remind there children that "everybody's doing it!" but this time in reference to positive, sound actions. The more theologically prepared the faculty is, the more they will all see the value of participating enthusiastically in this monthly virtue. Having been renewed in their own appreciation of the spiritual value of virtue, looking for ways to promote the virtue, catch the students practicing it, catch themselves practicing it too will be come more and more integrated into the school day, just as our faith should be integrated into all of life. It will not be yet one more thing "I have to do!"

SPIRITUALITY SEMINAR

For the Christian, the heart of one's faith is the person of Jesus Christ. While it is important to know what we believe and equally important to put out faith into practice, it is absolutely necessary that each person knows Christ personally. Jesus once asked the apostles who do people say that I am? Then he went further and asked but who do you say that I am? This is a major distinction in knowing about something or someone and knowing that someone personally. All of us have seen pictures or in some way know about Blessed Mother Teresa of Calcutta. However, very few of us can say that we know her unless we have been privileged to hear her and watch her speak in person. Similarly, it is easier for us in many ways to say that we know about Jesus Christ. We may have studied his life in Scripture and studied what our faith teaches us about him. Yet, can we say that we personally know Jesus. We come to know Jesus through our prayer, reflection and meditation. Having a personal relationship with Christ brings all of the teachings of the faith alive since they are rooted in Him. Having a personal relationship with Christ means that we know we are never along, we have someone who fully understands and knows us and who invites us to grow daily in knowing Him so that we can imitate his way in all that we do, and say and all that we are.

As teachers, especially in a Catholic school or any faith-based school, we must first know Jesus before we can help our children to know him. He it is who gives life and meaning to all that we teach about him and makes us enthusiastic in how we teach our students about him. How do we come to know Jesus? How do we teach our teachers to know Him? How do we then teach our students to know Jesus Christ, as God and man, as our Savior and our friend? It was in response to this need that the spirituality seminar was created.

This seminar has also been delivered to teachers in the Arlington Diocese since 1997. It includes a series of 2 hour presentations for each of four weeks. Each week, the seminar begins with a different prayer form. Based on the assumption that prayer nourishes the soul as food nourishes the body, prayer is the key to developing one's own spirituality. Thus, by beginning and ending each week with different types of prayer, the participants not only grow to understand more about prayer but they experience different prayer forms or types. Tables 7.1-7.4 provide an overview of the course content.

During the first week of the spirituality seminar, after a short prayer service, the primary focus is on gaining an understanding of the meaning of spirituality and why it is so important for each of us. Much is written today on spirituality even from a secular perspective. However, the seminar looks at spirituality within a Christian context as a way for the individual to come to know God and also develop a deeper understanding of his/her person in relation to God. It is a way to come to know some of the obstacles that stand between the individual and God in living an authentic moral life and growing into the fullness of the image and likeness God intends us to become. If the virtue seminar focuses on how we are to live and act in relation to God and one another in order to fulfill the baptismal call to holiness, the spirituality seminar focuses on coming to know the God who made us and to develop a deep and ongoing relationship with Him so that each person becomes rooted in Christ. The more one realizes the importance of this personal relationship, the more motivated and enthusiastic one becomes in wanting to share this with others, especially one's students. Again drawing from the adage that one cannot give

Table 7.1. PRAYER: KEY TO SPIRITUALITY
By: Sister Patricia Helene Earl, IHM, PhD
Assistant Professor, Director of
the Catholic School Leadership Program
Marymount University

WEEK 1:

I. OPENING PRAYER AND INTRODUCTION

    A. PRAYER

    B. INTRODUCTIONS

II. PURPOSE OF THE PROGRAM

    A. OVERVIEW OF THE TOTAL PRESENTATION

    B. DATES

    C. CERTIFICATE ISSUES

    D. DISTRIBUTION AND LOOK AT THE TEXT

III. WHAT IS SPIRITUALITY

    A. REVIEW OF SPIRITUALITY SEMINAR

    B. KEY IDEAS OF SPIRITUALITY

    C. PRAYER IS THE KEY

        1. CORPORATE SPIRITUALTY

            a. Value as members of the Mystical Body of Christ

            b. Growing in faith, hope, and love with others

            c. Parallel with prayer

        2. INDIVIDUAL SPIRITUALITY

            a. Call to holiness

            b. Personal relationship with Christ

IV. LITURGICAL PRAYER OF THE CHURCH

    A. THE MASS—NEXT WEEK

    B. DIVINE OFFICE—LITURGY OF THE HOURS

        1. VATICAN II—OPEN TO ALL

        2. WHO PRAYS IT?

        3. BASIC STRUCTURE

V. DISCUSSION QUESTION

    A. WHAT STYLE OF PRAYER IS MOST ATTRACTIVE TO YOU? Why?

VI. PRAYER EXPERIENCE—VESPERS

VII. HOMEWORK

Table 7.2.   PRAYER: KEY TO SPIRITUALITY
By: Sister Patricia Helene Earl, IHM, PhD
Assistant Professor, Director of
the Catholic School Leadership Program
Marymount University

WEEK 2:

I.   **OPENING PRAYER—VESPERS**

   A.   PRAYER

   B.   INTRODUCTIONS

II.   **FOUNDATIONS OF SPIRITUALITY:** *THE CATECHISM OF THE CATHOLIC CHURCH* **ON PRAYER**

   A.   WHAT IS PRAYER?

   B.   THE CALL TO PRAYER

   C.   THE TRADITION OF PRAYER

   D.   THE LIFE OF PRAYER

III.   **DISCUSSION QUESTIONS**

IV.   **LITURGICAL PRAYER OF THE CHURCH**

   A.   THE MASS

      1.   LITURGY OF THE WORD

      2.   LITURGY OF THE EUCHARIST

   B.   DIVINE OFFICE—LITURGY OF TE HOURS

V.   **MASS VIDEO**

   A.   WHAT STYLE OF PRAYER IS MOST ATTRACTIVE TO YOU? Why?

VI.   **HOMEWORK**

   A.   READ CHAPTERS 8, 9, 10, 11

Table 7.3.   PRAYER: KEY TO SPIRITUALITY
By: Sister Patricia Helene Earl, IHM, PhD
Assistant Professor
Director of the Catholic School Leadership Program
Marymount University

WEEK 3:

I.   **OPENING PRAYER—LITANY**

II.   **PRAYER FORMS**

   A.   KINDS OF PRAYER

   B.   TRADITIONAL DEVOTIONS

      1.   ROSARY

      2.   STATIONS OF THE CROSS

      3.   NOVENA PRAYERS

      4.   LITANIES

Table continues on next page.

Table 7.3.   Continued
5.   BENEDICTION
C.   LITURGICAL PRAYER—REVIEW
D.   LECTIO DIVINA
III.   DISCUSSION QUESTIONS
IV.   PRAYER EXPERIENCE—MEDITATION
VI.   HOMEWORK

Table 7.4.   PRAYER: KEY TO SPIRITUALITY By: Sister Patricia Helene Earl, IHM, PhD Assistant Professor Director of the Catholic School Leadership Program Marymount University
WEEK 4:
I.   OPENING PRAYER—JOURNALING
II.   *CATECHISM OF THE CATHOLIC CHURCH* ON PRAYER
A.   THE LORD'S PRAYER
B.   GUIDES TO PRAYER
III.   VALUE OF PRAYER OF THE CHURCH AND PRIVATE PRAYER
IV.   DISCUSSION QUESTIONS
V.   PRAYER—CENTERING PRAYER
VI.   EXPERIENCE—CENTERING PRAYER
VII.   HOMEWORK

Knowledge of Christ?

what one does not have, the person who is drawn to this close relationship with Christ is enabled by God's grace to help others to want to know Christ and to make time and space to develop this relationship. Wanting to grow more deeply in this relationship with Christ then motivates the individual to choose to imitate Him more closely through a life of virtue.

During the spirituality seminar, time is spent on exploring two important aspects of spirituality; namely, one's personal relationship with Christ and one's relationship to Christ through a shared membership in His mystical Body, the Church. As human beings, people are by nature social and are meant to live in relationship, just as the Father, Son, and Holy Spirit live in relationship in the Trinity, three Persons in one God. Thus, the individual needs to cultivate a relationship with Christ through community and communal worship and praise and also a personal relationship with Christ through private prayer. To cultivate only a personal relationship with Christ runs the risk of being overly "me" centered rather than God-centered and can lead to introspection without some guidelines and even just personal reflection without God at all. To cultivate only a communal relationship with Christ runs the risk of failing to make time to develop one's individual gifts and talents and to recognize God as their author and inspiration. We need both God and others to be whole. Prayer is the key to spirituality, an action of the will, a choice made to surrender in child-like trust to God which leads to the discovery of a loving and caring God. We join our personal prayer to that of the worshipping community to acknowledge God's love and providential care.

There are two general types of spirituality; corporate and individual. In the corporate form, Christian spirituality comes from and creates the Christian community. This opens up a discussion of the liturgy or public worship of the Church, including the Roman Catholic Mass and the Liturgy of the Hours. Jesus prayer with others and reminded us in Matthew 18:19-20 that where two or more are gathered together in His name, He is there. One's individual prayer helps one to come to know Christ and to grow in holiness. A brief look at some of the saints in the Catholic Church helps us to see how spirituality and prayer were integral to their way of life. They serve as models for us on our spiritual journey through life. Once again, as in the virtue seminar, a look at this call to holiness as found in Scripture and various Church documents broadens one's understanding of the meaning of this call and how we should respond to it. The first week ends with the group studying more intently the Liturgy of the Hours with its use of the Psalms and other Scripture readings that have been prayed at various hours of the day for centuries by priests and nuns and which the laity are also invited to prayer. The closing prayer of the session is evening prayer or Vespers of that day which all pray together to experience this prayer form.

The second week of the spirituality seminar opens with the day's Vesper service. The focus of this session is to examine some foundations for spirituality, looking at Scripture and a variety of Church documents. This segment could certainly be adapted by any faith according to its own religious documents. By examining these valued sources, the participants recognize the value of spirituality based on the Bible, as well as the various Church teachings. They grow in their knowledge which nurtures their desire for this relationship with God through prayer and helps them to appreciate the value of belonging to this community of believers. The Church becomes a source and support for one's relationship with Christ and the influence this has on one's relationship with others. Continuing to focus on the communal dimension of spirituality, a close look at the history of the Mass and the symbolism and ritual it contains helps the individual not only to know and appreciate it meaning and value, but also enlivens one's participation in the Mass. Any religious faith could adapt this to exploring its own religious services, their symbols and meaning. This ultimately motivates the individual in searching for ways to teach this to students.

Some basic principles of spirituality are presented. Essentially these center on the meaning and value of prayer and begin to address the question of how do you pray individually. Pope John Paul II is attributed with saying, "Pray anyway you like so long as you pray."

The third week of the seminar moves from a focus on communal prayer to looking more deeply into personal prayer. The opening prayer is a litany form of prayer, where there are statements of praise of Christ followed by a repetitive response from the group, such as "pray for us" or "have mercy on us." A review of some traditional prayers of the Church begins with a look at the Rosary, the Stations of the Cross, novena prayers, and litany prayers such as the Litany of the Sacred Heart of Jesus or a Litany of Mary. Just as the foundation for communal prayer was traced to Scripture and Church documents and teachings, similarly the call to personal prayer is situated in Scripture and Church documents and teachings. Using the CCC (#2558 ff), prayer is described as gift, covenant, and communion.

There are various kinds of prayer including formal and informal, verbal, and nonverbal, meditation, and contemplation. The traditional general acronym ACTS is explained in terms of the main types of prayer; namely, adoration or praise, contrition or sorrow, thanksgiving, and supplication or petition. *Lectio Divina*, a form of prayer, traditionally practiced by monks and nuns, is presented with its four main parts. These are *lectio* or the sacred reading or careful repetition of a sacred text, *meditatio*, or careful reflection on this sacred text, *oratio*, or a personal prayer response to the text, and *contemplatio*, or a state of seeing or experiencing the sacred text as mystery and reality in God's presence. This session concludes with a guided meditation to introduce the participants to another prayer form.

The final session begins with a Scripture and some journal writing based on the text. This is yet another prayer form and participants are given more of an overview of its purpose. Major emphasis is placed on the Lord's Prayer, given to us by Christ Himself, and the focus of the final section or fourth pillar of the CCC. In addition, a broad overview of the development of various styles or models of spirituality is given. Examples include traditions modeled on such saints as Augustine, Benedict, Gregory the Great, Dominic, Thomas Aquinas, Francis of Assisi, Catherine of Siena, Ignatius of Loyola, Teresa of Avila, John of the Cross, Alphonsus Ligouri, Therese of Lisieux, and Mother Teresa of Calcutta.

Finally, time is spent on ways to get started and to make time and space for personal prayer in the everyday busyness of life. St. Alphonsus says:

> We can meditate in every place, at home or elsewhere, even in walking and at work. How many are there, who not having a better opportunity, raise their hearts to God and apply their minds to mental prayer, without leaving their occupations, their work, or who meditate while traveling. He who seeks God will find Him everywhere and at all times.

This session concludes with another meditative prayer experience for the participants and a closing reminder from Mother Teresa of Calcutta: "Yesterday is gone. Tomorrow has not yet come. We have only today—Let us begin."

Having considered the Catholic dimension, the creation of the seminars which frame the study, and some of its research design, the next chapter looks at the case-focused analysis of the study and provides the reader with some of the teacher commentary on the value of the seminars in their faith formation. The teachers tell their stories and give the reader a glimpse of the actual experience of the seminars.

CHAPTER 8

TEACHER'S RESPONSE TO FAITH FORMATION STRATEGIES

The interviews for this qualitative study explored the influence that a series of virtue and spirituality seminars had on a group of 15 lay teachers' perceptions of the Catholic school. As a retrospective study, it allowed the teachers, who had attended both of these seminars within the past 5 years, to reflect on these studies and their influence immediately and over time. Data analysis for this study incorporated two main approaches to provide a more thorough narrative analysis. Case-focused analysis dealt with the individual respondent's experiences related to the seminars and how they perceived they had been influenced by them. Issue-focused analysis dealt with the collective issues revealed by the respondents (Weiss, 1994).

CASE-FOCUSED ANALYSIS: THE STORIES

Case-focused analysis "make[s] the reader aware of the respondents' experience within the context of their lives: this is what it is like to be this person in this situation" (Weiss, 1994, p. 168). The purpose of the case-focused analysis was to develop an understanding of each respondent's experience

Faith Formation of the Laity in Catholic Schools: The Influence of Virtues and Spirituality Seminars, pp. 97–121

of the virtue and/or spirituality seminar, and of their perceptions of the
influences that these seminars had on them, on their teaching, and on their
understanding of Catholic schools. Understanding the meaning, not only
of events, but also of the participants' perspectives, as well as the influence
of the context within which the participants act, are some of the strengths
of a qualitative study (Maxwell, 1996, p. 17).

Each teacher had a story about her experience in Catholic schools and
the influence of the virtues/spirituality seminars. While some teachers discussed issues, which will be reviewed in later chapters, others presented a
more narrative experience in three major categories. First are the narratives that showed more personal changes, such as, Natalie's. Second are
the narratives that showed more changes in teaching, such as Angel's, and
those that revealed new programs, such as Laura's and Dolores'. Finally,
are those that provided insight into both personal and teaching changes,
especially related to character education, such as, Katherine's, Donna's,
and Cecilia's. All of the stories touched on the seminars' influence on
understanding the mission and purpose of Catholic schools.

Natalie

Natalie, a 53-year-old Baptist, was an aide for the primary grades. She
spent 17 years teaching and taught all of the primary grades. After her
first child went to college, she wanted to return to teaching. A friend and
teacher in one of the Catholic schools told her of an aide position. She had
been an aide and a substitute for 4 years at the time of the interview. Her
story revealed a portrait of the personal changes that she experienced.

Having been raised a Methodist, and currently attending the Baptist
church, Natalie wanted to learn more about Catholicism. Even though she
did not teach the religion in the Catholic school, she felt that since she
had never been close to any Catholics: "I just felt that if I was going to be
working in this environment, I needed to know more about Catholicism
and understand it." Natalie actually attended the spirituality seminar
three times and the virtue seminar once. She came because she found the
seminars to be a source of inspiration.

Given her own motivation for coming, Natalie felt the seminars
affected her each time that she attended, and they continued to influence
her. She wanted to know more about the Catholic faith so that she could
give good example to the children:

> The things I was learning, I wanted to make sure that I could convey that to
> the classroom. Even though I wasn't actually teaching religion, I knew I had

to be living it. So, I wanted that to be real to the children and if they asked questions, I wanted to be able to answer them.

Natalie also felt the seminars increased her interest in reading Scripture. She was looking for information about the Catholic faith, for answers to questions, and for understanding more about Mary, the Mother of Jesus Christ:

> And the other thing it really did for me was it made me want to go more into the Scriptures and find my answers there too. So, it made me, as a Christian, want to know more and make sure that I understand what's in there.

Though Natalie did not teach the formal religion class, she wanted God's love to come through her interaction with the children. This was not a new idea. However, from the seminars, she was impressed with the idea that "anything we do, we need to express God's love through it." She felt that the seminars inspired her "to work on it more." In addition, the materials from the seminars provided her with resources for research, including the manual on the virtues, an explanation of the Rosary as a prayer, and sources to search for answers to her questions.

Natalie and Laura taught at the same school. Natalie was on the original committee that created a virtues program centered on respect. She attributed her involvement with this committee to the seminars:

> Part of that came from going to your seminar because we decided that we really needed to incorporate something in the school because there had been evidence of increasing behavior problems and lack of Christian love and concern for one another, not only in the children but in the staff too, I think. So, I was on the initial committee and worked with several other people and we put together the program and followed it. It was productive and helpful especially with the younger children.

Natalie was enthusiastic about the school-wide program that they created from material that I had presented. She explained that the faculty wanted the students to entertain these virtuous acts, "not for the reward, but because it was the right thing or the Christian thing to do."

Along with the influence that Natalie had on parents and children, whom she attributed to her increased appreciation of spirituality, Scripture, and virtue, Natalie felt that the seminars helped her to understand the mission of a Catholic school and bring it to reality. She did not know much about the Rosary, "before it was just beads." The Mass was a new experience and she acquired an understanding of it. She learned about another liturgical prayer of the Catholic Church, Vespers. While working in second grade, she learned about the children's First Holy Communion, which they receive in second grade: "Knowing all that was involved there and working in second grade that was really important."

Natalie could find nothing negative about the seminars. Instead, as one of several teachers, who attended the seminars several times, even though the content was basically the same, Natalie concluded enthusiastically in her gentle manner:

> I need to keep going back to them because it refreshes me. I just think that they're a wonderful way to prepare teachers to teach children. One of the statements that you kept making that I'll never forget is "You can talk the talk but you have to walk the walk." And those were your exact words but that's all through there. You can teach it, you can preach it, but if you're not living it and the children aren't seeing it in you, it's not the same.

Angel

Angel, a 61-year-old Catholic, taught first grade. Sixteen of her 17 years of teaching were in Catholic schools and 11 of those years were in her current Catholic school. She was proud that she had taught "first grade all the way through." Angel herself was a product of Catholic schools with 16 years of Catholic education. Having graduated from a local Catholic college, and enjoying her Catholic school teaching, Angel needed to change careers when her husband left her and she faced the responsibility of raising and educating her children. After becoming an insurance agent, obtaining a stockbrokers' license and becoming a certified financial planner, Angel decided to get out of the business and return to teaching. She was still very happy teaching first grade for 11 years in the same Catholic school. Angel's story revealed a chronology of events from her background to taking the seminars primarily to the impact that these had on her teaching.

She first attended the spirituality seminar having heard good reports from other teachers who had attended it: "I heard it was very uplifting … and I was also looking ahead towards my Religion certification and choosing classes that I felt would help me not only get certified, re-certified but to help the children that I teach." Her experience with the spirituality seminar influenced her decision to attend the virtue seminar:

> Because I liked the whole presentation, I liked the whole idea. But I want to say that I felt very moved by the spirituality seminar to the point that it helped me improve my own spirituality which then in turn, the way I look at it, helped me teach spirituality to the children. The virtue seminar, I enjoyed that. I learned a lot, reviewed a lot, the virtues, basically what we're

looking at here. So that was more a learning experience for me, or shall we say, a review.

Angel felt that the virtue seminar gave her a good review of the theology related to virtue that she had studied in Catholic schools. The spirituality seminar helped her to improve herself:

> The spirituality just kind of brought me alive again. And then that prompted me to think that this is my role as a Catholic school teacher to continue to foster in these young children. Because I look upon myself as giving them the foundation, giving them the basics as far as the great love that Jesus has for them. That's why, as I mentioned, I call them my angels. We all are here to help each other. The theme throughout my classroom is WWJD, "What Would Jesus Do?" It is on their desks and should there ever be a question, look on your desk, WWJD, well, what would Jesus do? Would Jesus push someone? No, well then you don't.

Angel described some of the concrete effects that she felt she derived as a result of the seminars. Referring back to her own difficult life experiences, she tearfully recalled saying "Why me, Lord?" She acknowledged:

> I was putting Christ aside a little bit. It was through this class that—because I've had some sufferings, some crosses, it does not mean that God doesn't love me, that I'm not going to be as close to Him as anyone else. It just means that I had to work a little bit harder and it just gave me that feeling. It was a renewal that God loves you. You're doing everything you're supposed to be doing, you know. Your spirituality is okay now and I just walked away with a very good feeling.

Angel explained that because of her formal education in the Catholic faith, she believed that the material from the seminars was somewhat of a review as far as the content was concerned. However, she described a sense of newness:

> The newness to it all was the feeling of comfort, the feeling of joy, the feeling of renewal. I think one of the issues in the virtue seminar—the way children are today as opposed to 10 years ago—that is something as teachers, we need to know that so that we can deal with that, because that's what we confront. So I think it gave me a very broad review, the Virtue Seminar. It was a refresher, but the spirituality, it just kind of really drove home, and I was very, very comfortable after I left.

Angel strongly maintained that the seminars, especially the spirituality seminar, still affected her:

I really want to emphasize what I got from it. It has not faded away. It has gotten better. I think about it. My role here as a teacher for these children— it's very significant. And I've been complimented, thank God, that's what keeps me going. You know that this is why we're here. We're in a Catholic school because the parents give us these gifts. I call them gifts for six hours a day. So that we can teach them why they should be here, what God wants them to do, what role is there for them. Times have changed, but that has nothing to do with the doctrine of the Church, what we believe, who we are, or how we act. We don't give into the times, we understand the times and then we work around them with the same philosophy that was given to us 25 years ago or 50 or whatever.

Angel explained that the seminars had influenced how she helped her first graders to learn about virtue and character. Since her students were so young, she obviously did not use some of the more technical or theological terms to talk about virtue to her children. "I felt confident that I'm not putting it above their heads so that they would get bored, not listen, when there were issues that perhaps they hadn't heard about."

Above all, Angel felt that the seminars had renewed her enthusiasm in how she conveyed everything, especially in Religion:

Probably, yes, because you know, this is what we look forward to. I would not teach in a public school because I would be denied the feeling—I'll say boys and girls clear your desks. This is the best time of the day. This is Jesus time. There will always be Jesus time—and I enjoy it. You know, the desks will be cleared, they'd be sitting up, and they'd be listening to me, and responding.

In describing her understanding of the mission or purpose of a Catholic school, Angel believed that parents entrust their children, "the gift they have received from God," to the Catholic school so that:

They will not just learn academics, they will learn all about God, all about the Commandments so that we can all continue in the faith that we have been given, they have chosen, and they are entrusting us with these children. That's our job and to me that's extremely special.

Recognizing the responsibility to carry on the faith was a part of her "teaching job" in a Catholic school. Angel affirmed the value of the seminars themselves and also knowing that so many other teachers are motivated to want to attend them, not only from her own school but also from the other Diocesan Catholic schools:

The more we sit down with each other, we have our team instructor, the more we talk about who we are, the more broadened our scope becomes and then we feel, as we said, that we're doing a good job. We're doing what God wants us to do, it's that sharing. And yes, you do feel this has helped you in your teaching because everybody else is doing it as well you know, and that's why you're here and it's, it's very gratifying.

Angel could not recall anything that she found difficult or negative about the seminars. Instead, she reiterated what she liked best; namely, "the renewal of my spirituality." She was so enthused about the value of the seminars, that she suggested that the Diocese should require attendance by all teachers:

> Well, I just feel that because I derived so much from it that, that it should be like a prerequisite for Catholic teachers coming into the Diocese to experience this feeling. This is who we are, this is what God wants, and just to get that, that uplift before you even walk into a classroom. The parents see us. Yes, we're practicing Catholics. We care about each other. It comes across. And I think absolutely, the more we can foster that, and I think maybe have an in-service at the beginning of the year, just like we have a retreat, that's wonderful. But that could also be a part of it, just to give us that feeling that, yes, you're doing God's work and He's very thankful to you for doing it—keep up the good work.

Laura

Laura, a 52-year-old Catholic, taught art from kindergarten through eighth grade for 4 years. She had been a realtor "for years and years and years" and had volunteered in her children's Catholic school, having studied art history in graduate school: "I found that I could help in the Catholic schools with art programs for my children." When an opening occurred for an art teacher in her children's Catholic elementary school, Laura applied. She "was ready for a change and this was the path to try and I've never regretted it." This was her first and only teaching experience since her "career change." Laura's story revealed a chronology of events from her background to the impact these seminars had, not only on her teaching, but also on creating and introducing a new program into her school.

Laura first attended the virtue seminar. She explained that her school faculty had been looking for "a dimension that was lacking and needed to be developed." They were looking for some way to strengthen the interaction among the students, between the faculty and the students, among the teachers, and between the teachers and the parents. However, they lacked a goal and direction. She and several other teachers from her school thought the virtue seminar might provide the direction for which they were searching. The following school year, Laura attended the spirituality seminar because

> Once you become aware of the need that you have, either personally or in our case at school, and you attend the seminar—the virtue seminar—it's just that you want more, you want more of that spiritual direction and, I will go again, I will go again.

Laura felt that both seminars had a positive influence on her. However, she noted:

> The spirituality seminar seemed to have a greater impact for me personally. But there again, I was probably more focused on myself and I wasn't looking for materials to apply on a school basis. So I think just that my initial outlook was more of a personal focus so maybe that may have colored why that affected me more personally. But they certainly both have personal applications.

Laura clarified how each seminar had affected her. For her, just witnessing the large number of 53 teachers who attended her session of the virtue seminar made her aware of the sense of need that people have for developing this spiritual dimension. She described how she was "impacted by the large number of people lighting up as the material was presented and the time taken and given for prayer, for meditation, for reflecting on these virtues." The virtue seminar made her more aware of how much the virtues were either a part of her life, or how much she really needed them. In the spirituality seminar, Laura recalled the concentration on "the importance of taking time, spending time daily, and then I guess for me, the idea of the centering prayer and that whole experience was probably most powerful."

From the seminars, Laura indicated that the experience of prayer and meditation, as well as the need to set aside time and space had a strong impact on her. Therefore, she remembered:

> Making notes that somehow we need to find time for the children to have time because I think our children are as overbooked as we are and I think, thank heaven we are in a Catholic school and there are these opportunities. I'd like to see those opportunities expanded where there could be time to sit a part. Maybe a class at a time they could sit in the quiet and reflect, you know. Oh something that I took away, definitely.

She explained that it's something that you want to establish as a routine, "guard it with your life, and then you get such a benefit from it, that you want to share it with everyone."

Laura appreciated the resources that were provided to guide the teachers, not only personally, but also in their work with the children. In trying to provide students with time and space for prayer and meditation, she modeled a prayer table similar to the weekly ones created each week in the seminars and brought this into her classroom: "that's always going to be our prayer corner and you have pictures there for reflection." She also copied the idea of having quiet, reflective music as a preparation for this prayer time, similar to the use of music throughout both seminars.

Though Laura only met the students once a week for art class, and felt challenged in how to integrate prayer and meditation, she believed that art enhanced religion. She planned to display and present some religious artwork and have the children reflect on it:

> Certainly not every week, but maybe once a month to get out one or more images for the children to spend even if it's three minutes just looking and meditating on the image.

Laura acknowledged that the religious art program was one that she had before attending the seminars. However, using the pictures and illustrations in this new dimension as a source for meditative reflection by the students was a new idea.

When Laura and her colleagues returned to school after attending the virtue seminar, they were "just on fire" and suggested creating a schoolwide Virtue-of-the-Month Program. The principal caught their "fervor" and supported a committee to design and implement a program for the following school year. They drafted a vision statement for the program and set up some of the procedures to incorporate respect into the "fabric of the school." The school modeled its virtue program after a variety of programs and activities from the virtue seminar.

In addition to designing the program, the teachers created resource and reference pages for each grade level, using materials from the seminar, as well as gathering information from other sources, including the Internet. They wanted the other faculty members to have enough material so that they would be prepared to implement the program and its activities. Laura described the November activities for respect for country, which also included a patriotic sing-a-long that the music teacher had orchestrated. In addition, Laura described a "rewards in discipline program" that the faculty integrated into the virtue activities. Ultimately, as students were caught showing respectful behaviors, each class created a tissue paper stained glass rose window with the various rays representing students' respectful behavior. The teachers also created a skit for a school assembly. Dressed as students in school uniforms, the teachers exaggerated disrespectful behaviors and through the humor, the message of respect "really hit home to them." At the end of the school year, the children were rewarded with a field trip to the Pope John Paul II Cultural Center in Washington, DC.

In reflecting on the seminars and the mission of a Catholic school, Laura stressed her ability to be able to tie these virtues first, to the Religion program in a Catholic school, and then, incorporate it into all subject areas and activities. She hoped that it would be "pervasive throughout the school day." She explained:

> That to me is the greatest benefit, we're so lucky, I mean, that we're a Catholic school and we can focus on God in all of our content areas and in all of our activities. So that idea of respect, I mean, it was respect from your playing during your physical education in the lunchroom, it was everywhere. I thought that was the way the program was implemented. Every time you turned around, it was there. It was kind of like this bubble encompassing the school and it just tied everything together. The students' themselves were genuinely excited about it—all of those intrinsic rewards, somehow they were directly manifested in the school. I really observed the students in their work in the art room, being able to say, "We're not writing on our new tables, because they're new, but also because it's disrespectful."

Laura explained that she also perceived "a heightened level of consciousness" or awareness of this school goal, "to be more respectful of all these different entities." This pervaded throughout the school, not only with the students, but also among the faculty. For example, at a faculty meeting, in response to another's idea, "maybe it would cause you to bite your tongue rather than blurt out a response to something you didn't care for."

Laura reflected that the "whole process" struck her. In addition to attending the seminars, there was a vast amount of material that her faculty reviewed and put together to create their virtue program. She likened it to a gift to be part of a group that was interested in focusing on the students' character. She felt that she grew in her appreciation of her spirituality and of the importance and meaning of virtue. She developed a greater appreciation of the children themselves. She concluded: "it personally affected me as a teacher and I think that school-wide, it had an effect." She noted that it was interesting that the Spirituality Seminar was a small group and the Virtue Seminar was a large group. However, "that didn't seem in any way to affect that you were just given this gift to take with you.... It's just that you want more, you want more of that spiritual direction and, I will go again, I will go again."

Dolores

Dolores, a 50-year-old Catholic, taught in the same Catholic school for the past 20 years of her 21 years of teaching. After teaching physical education for her first 3 years, she started teaching literature, social studies, and religion to seventh and eighth grades, in addition to being a wife, mother, coach, and catechist. Similar to Natalie, Dolores' story revealed a chronology of events from background to the creation and introduction of a new program in her school.

Even though she attended Catholic elementary school for 6 years and Catholic college, Dolores came to the first spirituality seminar to further her knowledge as a teacher, to help her spiritually, and to become more acquainted with Scripture. Dolores was the Religion Curriculum Coordinator for her school. Because the teachers were a little nervous about attending spirituality classes, Dolores wanted to attend in order to motivate her teachers to come, to help them with the religion certification, and "to get them in touch a little more with teaching religion." Her positive response to the spirituality seminar and the materials she gathered for herself, her students, and for the teachers, prompted Dolores to attend the Virtue Seminar:

> I just said, hey this is more, more valuable material that I can send to kids. So I went to the first Virtue Seminar to really gain information for the students—handouts for the students—information that I could incorporate with my teaching.

Dolores was enthused with the Virtue Seminar. She gained information and hands-on materials for the students. She herself gained strength and spirituality as she became more in touch with the virtues and the spirit:

> It just kind of pumped me up, got me excited and so, I went the second time with the virtues. So each time I was energized by what was being presented, what I was taking from the presentation and being able to bring it back and tune the kids into it. It was fantastic—it was a real high.

Dolores admitted that she wanted to come a third time because it was spiritually uplifting, informative and fun: "I gain something every time I go. It's not old information at all."

In reflecting on the personal influence of these seminars, Dolores felt she gained a deeper understanding of Scripture "and how it relates to me as a Catholic educator, how it's sustained me and strengthened me." Dolores believed that being a Catholic school teacher is more than a profession; it is a ministry "that lets me represent the Church and God's Word to these young children." She believed that in order to teach God's Word effectively, a teacher needs to live it. In order to live it, a teacher needs to understand it:

> So by going to the spirituality workshop and the virtues workshop, I gained knowledge. But I also gained strength in my faith, which then helped me to be more effective as a religion teacher. And it's becoming more and more difficult, as the years go by, to be an effective Catholic educator because we're contending with so many other things out there, that we need these workshops. I need these workshops to strengthen and fortify me so that I can get this message out as strong as some of these other media the children are experiencing.

The seminars have continued to affect Dolores. They are a source for renewal and strengthening. Knowing that the seminars are available, Dolores does not feel alone. The resources are there when she feels the "need to be reenergized, to be refortified." She sees herself as having greater access and enthusiasm:

> I also feel that I love this stuff and I can retrieve it—it was so well taught and so meaningful to the educator. We have it stored within us and I can pull out little pieces when I need it. And at the weirdest times, things will pop in ... I don't think it is something that you leave there and it's good for a week or two then it disappears. No. No. I think it's going to restrengthen us but it never leaves, it never leaves, it's always there.

Dolores made a link between the amount of teacher preparation, through the spirituality and virtue seminars, and the ability and spirit with which the teacher can share God's Word and the virtues with students. After a group of teachers from her school attended the virtue seminar, they were so excited that at a faculty meeting, they decided to put a school-wide virtue program into the school. They modeled several methods and ideas from the seminar, including a large bulletin board, a small virtue book, and a monthly virtue in the classes. Each month a new virtue was presented and both teachers and students learned about that virtue and tried to practice it. Students were recognized at school Masses and received certificates for exemplary actions that demonstrated the particular monthly virtue.

Dolores affirmed that teaching virtues and the Holy Spirit were not new ideas for a Catholic school. However, she noted that this was the first time in her 20 years in this Catholic school that there had ever been a program with the whole school "going about different virtues in a month." She described how her eighth grade students were so proud to receive certificates for virtues carried out through the day and into the community, "and to have Father acknowledge it at Mass and to be acknowledged by the parishioners, it really instills a pride in them but it's —about learning the virtues."

As a result of attending the seminars, Dolores observed some changes in her methods and approach to teaching, as well as those of her colleagues who had attended the seminars. Dolores believed that these teachers "were able to teach it even more soundly and with more confidence than before because we felt ourselves that we had a good hands-on." Because the teachers were more familiar with the virtues, what they are, and why we have them or try to practice them, the teachers were able to practice them and interact with the students. As a result, Dolores felt the children could understand what virtue is, see it, and start to emulate it. As a junior high teacher, Dolores was aware of the importance of not only lecturing and giving students notes, but also of demonstration. Especially for the virtues as guides to good character, she explained the importance of showing them that:

> You are first knowledgeable and second, you feel it and are enthusiastic about it and then they catch on. And it makes you an effective teacher. And so I think the seminars and the spirituality class, they just tune you in to your faith—they energize you. I think energize is the word I would use because it gets you excited, because it reenergizes your spirituality so that you, teaching the children, see it and they feel it and then you carry it on among the faculty. And the children see that it's just not what she does in the classroom but what she does in the hallway and what she's doing with other teachers and with other children who aren't in her classroom. I think the children learn a lot by our example, by seeing the teachers that have gone to the virtues program, gone to the spirituality program. Yes, they've gotten their religious education points. I mean that's always there. They're always working towards that. But they've come away with a real sense of who they are as Catholic educators and the importance of being a Catholic educator and that you're a lot more than just being a teacher of a period or subject. You have to be a witness to your faith always. I think the children see that. I think the teachers involved in the seminar classes come away with a sense of a stronger identity of who they are as Catholic educators and what their role is with students.

Since so many teachers in her school attended the seminars over time, Dolores observed that teachers frequently discussed topics and methods and referred one another to the materials. The teachers were able to help each other adapt resources to different grade levels since they were so familiar with the content and enthused about the importance of spirituality and virtues in action. The materials were of value to Dolores because she felt they were "put together by educators who understand what it's like to teach in a Catholic school—it isn't a lot of filler—there's a lot of usable materials." She believed that teachers who attended the seminars could use the materials more effectively than those who had not attended them because:

> They knew how to present it and why it's so important to present it. I think that's another thing too, you need to know why are you doing this, why is it important and that's, that's the root of it all,—why is it important, why are you doing this?

Dolores continued to explain the importance and purpose of a Catholic school and her mission as a teacher in the school. She believed that the Catholic school educator should:

> Try to teach as Christ teaches, as Christ would, make it simple, make it honest, and make it true. Don't make it fake and as a Catholic educator you have to remember you are in a Catholic school and you are representing the Church but you also have to be representing Christ to the children. And as I said so many times, you may be the only link to the Church, to the faith that these children have. Maybe you are a defender of the faith because often virtues seem outdated but you are an advocate for the faith, you have to be representative of Jesus in the classroom and outside the classroom.

In light of her understanding of the mission of Catholic schools, Dolores felt that she had always recognized the responsibility and importance of her role. However, she noted the pressures and struggles that students have today. Sometimes, the teacher may be the major source of information about faith and virtues. In a world of so many mixed messages, where parents are busy, the Catholic school teacher has a more demanding responsibility and "needs to take advantage of everything that's out there to help you." The Catholic school educator has an important job:

> We need to be able to get the right message to them, and as I said with the grade that I teach, we need to teach by example. And to be effective in teaching, you need to be knowledgeable about what you are teaching and you need to feel it, especially religion. If you do not feel it, they're not going to learn it. Forget trying to feel it. They'll just turn you off. But if they see you take the virtue that you're teaching, take it out of the classroom to other teachers, to other students that they do not teach, that's what's important. And that's what you mean by feeling—you have to feel it—it has to be inside of you—it has to be a part of who you are.

Though she taught for 20 years in Catholic school, Dolores felt that the seminars helped her to internalize her role. It became a part of her. The seminars were a source of renewed energy:

It gets you excited. It gets you back in touch. It introduces many new things to you, things that should be important. You know, you become stale, you usually become stale but you go to one of these seminars and you get excited. You learn something new, you see something,... and it goes way beyond, it goes way beyond certification. You know we talk so much about certification in Catholic schools and all and that's important but we don't do it for that. I personally don't. I feel that if I can be effective in what I'm asked to do and sure I teach literature plus I teach Social Studies but I live the virtues, I have to live it, I have to live it. The only way I can live it is to understand it—that's what these Virtue Seminars do for you—those workshops.

Dolores offered only one recommendation; namely, that the seminars continue to be offered to help teachers with heir own spiritual formation and their ability to share these values and principles with their students:

I hope they continue ... to be as dynamic and fulfilling as they have been in the past. I hope that the material that's put together will continue to not only be helpful to the teachers but will continue to motivate them and to help them to continue to grow in their faith.... Those seminars are really important to the teachers. As a religion coordinator who works very closely with the students and the teachers, if you want to know from someone who's been here, it's been very helpful to me. I can see, working with them, over a period, how it's helped them too. And so I think they've become better teachers because of this.

Katherine

Katherine, a 56-year-old Catholic, taught fourth grade. With 18 years teaching experience, 12 of those years were in Catholic schools. She had experience with Grades 3 through 8, as well as serving as an elementary school librarian. Teaching, along with being a mother, was a career for her. She herself had attended Catholic schools for 14 years, including 2 years in college. Katherine's story emphasized both personal changes and changes in teaching.

With her recent participation in the virtue seminar, Katherine commented that it "solidified" what she had heard and had been taught while attending Catholic schools. She appreciated the opportunity to go back and look at some of that material again. She found that the seminars reaffirmed and strengthened her faith. She had studied virtues, commandments, and beatitudes and was grateful to go back and reexamine them as an adult:

That's it. Meet those truths again and I mean, even though I had gone through a Catholic school, I mean, the realness of those workshops, the world is still with us. And I found that it was kind of, yes, the rock is still there and to go there and to have the experience.

This reaffirmation of her knowledge and understanding of virtue and the Catholic faith influenced her teaching. Katherine felt that she was more willing to "allow prayer or to have prayer as more of an element in her room." Before the seminars, she had been comfortable praying a decade or portion of the Rosary with her students, for example, during the month of October, a month set aside to honor Mary and the Rosary. However, she liked the idea of centering prayer and other "tips for spirituality." Consequently, she tried the centering prayer with her students and found that it had "a tremendous calming effect" on them.

She also tried to have her students do some journal writing. Before the seminars, she used journal writing to prepare the students for creative writing in English class. After her seminar experience with journal writing as a form of prayer, she started to use the journal for spiritual writing and reflection. It was a time, for example, to talk about guardian angels or simply to unburden themselves.

Modeling good actions as examples of virtue and good character was one way of teaching students how to act appropriately. Katherine admitted that the seminars had broadened her patience and ability to be more positive and proactive in handling potential discipline issues. Thus, instead of reacting to a child's behavior in an incident, she thought first about giving the child "a chance to redeem herself." She explained a particular incident where she had taken this approach: "it was productive, it was a good thing." A student chose to complete some English sentences "in a very tasteless manner." Rather than immediately calling the child's mother, Katherine talked with her about the content of her sentences and how they "just didn't fit with her being a child of God." Katherine discovered the student had done this for "crowd appeal." She asked her to revise the sentences and to write a note of apology, observing that the student seemed contrite and did, in fact, change her behavior. Katherine acknowledged that she probably would have reacted differently before the discussions on virtue and grace, particularly the idea about "falling and rising every day." With this student, Katherine thought, "okay, let's give her a chance to rise here, we've had the fall, and so let's give her a chance to rise." Not only did the student receive a second chance because of Katherine's reflection and caring, but Katherine also "felt better about it, about having handled it that way then."

Katherine also learned to integrate her teaching about virtue and good character into the entire school day. Her school focused on a particular virtue every month and ways to carry it out. She became more aware that religion needs to permeate the day, especially through the practice of virtue. She found herself "bringing religion into social studies and English and things like that." She admitted that she probably never did that before attending the seminars. In reflecting on how she worked with the monthly virtue before and after the seminars, Katherine felt that the seminars "reaffirmed" some of the things she might have done previously. However, in terms of making the virtue a priority and not "just another" activity or directive from the office, she acknowledged that she had changed. Since attending the seminars, she made "more time" for discussion and activities related to the monthly virtue. She was "less likely to just try to squeeze it in." She agreed that her own enthusiasm and motivation were important in modeling and implementing a virtue. She felt if students see that the virtue is "just another" thing that the teacher has to do, they will learn to approach this behavior in the same manner. However, if the teacher sees a need and personal value to the monthly virtue and activities, then the students may capture some of that enthusiasm.

Reflecting on virtue and the mission of Catholic schools, Katherine first described her understanding of their mission or purpose:

> Well, I feel that we witness to bring our children to Christ and to help them to grow as fully as they possibly can as Christians or Catholics. And to see that their gifts or talents, whatever, are gifts from God that they can use both for the betterment of the world and also for their own growth. And from, through the virtues, it brings them closer to Him.

Katherine felt that the spirituality seminars inspired her and strengthened her awareness of this mission. The virtue seminar gave her "the tools to carry it out, to see how I could bring children to God." She concluded that "There is something deep and personal about that one, about the spirituality, I don't know." She believed that the virtue seminar reminded her of her mission to bring the children closer to Christ, and "that serving with joy is what it's all about so that's what we can impart to the children. But this isn't something to do because we have to."

Donna

Donna, a 46-year-old Catholic, taught fourth grade. The chronology of events, revealed in her story, showed the influence of the seminars on her personally and on her teaching. In her 13 years of teaching in Catholic schools, she had taught in Grades 4 through 8. Having received a public school education, her experience as a teacher in a Catholic school was her first encounter with the Catholic Church. After her first 2 years of teaching in Catholic schools, Donna converted to Catholicism.

Her attendance at the spirituality seminar prompted her to attend the virtue seminar. However, since her school already promoted specific virtues throughout the year, and since she was also a member of the school's virtues' committee, she wanted to know how "to implement that more in the school, to get more information and just figure it out myself about the virtues."

In reflecting on the personal influence of the seminars, Donna recalled "great things to do in the classroom." However, one of the most important things she remembered was the emphasis placed on the importance of teachers or others also taking time to develop their own spirituality: "Take care of yourself spiritually as well, take time to meditate." Donna admitted that she was not doing this before coming to the seminars. However, that directive was one that she took with her and shared with her students and other teachers.

Even 5 years later, Donna believed that she continued to develop her spirituality, using ideas from the seminars. She explained: "I do find myself using my time, down time like in the car waiting for a red light, or in the store waiting in line forever so you can meditate on prayer." Meditation became an important type of prayer, especially at home. Donna made time for prayer and found it valuable for her own well-being, especially after a stressful day:

> I find myself taking time to calm myself down and meditate and to bring God back into my life. So that I can't forget that I'm not alone and that this bad day is just part of life and will go away. So I do use that.

In addition to taking time for personal prayer, Donna found value in the material presented. She put into practice my idea that "you cannot give what you do not have." She commented:

> I just try to apply to my own life first, at home you know. I read some of the Scripture readings. So I have found myself in the past three or four or five years thinking more consciously about my own development because I can't get up and preach something and then not do it. So I've really been focusing more on my own development and part of that's been using this prayer. You don't just put it away and say I don't need it anymore.

Because of engaging in her own prayer and meditation, Donna brought this into her classroom. The material that she studied about virtue, conscience formation and character development also helped her. She explained how she has meditated with her students and encouraged them to turn to God, especially when they are upset or frustrated by their own actions.

Donna explained that she felt awkward the first time that she did a meditation with her students. However, her students now enjoy meditation:

> The first time I did it with the students you, I felt a little bit silly with that. But after the first time, they realize this is real cool, they constantly ask: "Can we meditate? Can we meditate?" So I enjoy it.

Donna described a time when her principal came in to observe her and found her doing a meditation. The principal commented on its value in also helping the students to develop a mature behavior:

> We were meditating and I was thinking that I should be teaching. But she came in and she stayed the whole time and we talked about Scriptures. She came back and said: "What a great gift you're giving these kids! That was truly good." They can meditate mentally or you know become more aware of their surroundings and of God.

Donna explained that she copied many of the ideas from the seminars related to creating an atmosphere for prayer and meditation:

> I use music. Yeah, I use the canticles you told us about and I dim the lights. And I tell you, on a cloudy day, it's perfect, truly perfect, but the kids love it. Yeah, I use "The Pachelbel Canon" is my favorite and the kids seem to like that one. So, I play different things and the kids have actually asked me, from time to time: "Can we meditate?"

After they ended a meditation, Donna noted that the students were calm and relaxed. Having asked them at the beginning to concentrate on Jesus, she took time to discuss what they thought, also hoping that they might not think of anything specific but just be "totally free" in the presence of the Lord. At the end, Donna noted "Everyone's so calm."

Donna acknowledged that she had never done meditation with her students before the seminars. However, now she has done it every year "from eighth graders all the way down to fifth graders and they love it." Just as Donna learned to value making time for prayer and meditation, she felt that her students were learning to value this as well:

> Because they don't have to worry about their friends, they just worry about themselves. Everybody's doing it, it's not like they're singled out. It's kind of like a little escape from having the pressures of the day. I don't know, I think they enjoy it.

Donna agreed that the children were not used to having quiet time. While they did not know how to handle it in the beginning, they learned that they appreciated it, after learning to meditate.

In addition to prayer and taking time to help children appreciate meditation, Donna also believed that the seminars had assisted her in the classroom with developing virtue. As a member of the school's virtues' committee, she tried "not to get them just to say the virtues or memorize the virtues." She wanted them to see them in each other and in themselves. Donna believed that "Religion isn't just words in the book. It's part of everyday life. So I'm always looking for advice and look at the virtues they can do. So I try to be constructive." She explained in detail how here school promotes a monthly virtue, beginning with the principal's monthly assembly and ending with class discussions of how it was practiced.

Donna noted, however, that some of the middle school teachers felt that it was "one more thing that's put upon them." However, they usually feel better about it once they get involved in it. Donna believed that none of these teachers had attended the seminars. Yet, she recalled that it was her attendance at the seminars that encouraged her to get more involved in the virtues program and to realize "the importance of it, too. It's not just a task, it's part of what should be their lives." Donna enthusiastically explained her idea to have each class create a puzzle. Each month, the class would have a piece related to the month's virtue. As the children practiced the month's virtue, a piece would be added and a whole picture would be created by the end of the year. This visual aide would remind the children at the end of the month to continue practicing the virtue. This helped the children to see that the virtues need to build on one another as character develops: "Once we stop talking about courage, it doesn't go away, you know. You just build on it. We take courage and then we add on kindness, then we add on friendship, then we add on all these others." Donna explained that the activities were tools. The behavior of the children would show the value of the various activities. Reflecting on the mission of a Catholic school, Donna described it:

> To be Christ centered. Not only with the academics, to be able to apply it, to the very life in a Christian society. How can you make a better place? So going to a Catholic school, learning the virtues and the values and being able to apply it is going to help. And so you're learning that and your English and your History. But to be a full person, you can get Christ involved in this and then be able to live it, not just say it.

In light of her definition of the mission of a Catholic school, Donna felt that the seminars had deepened her understanding of this mission. She believed that they strengthened and deepened her belief in Christ and encouraged her to get into the practice of attending daily Mass. Though she had prayed before the seminars, she felt that since the seminars, she found herself praying like she "never did before." She reflected back to her days before the seminars:

> So I think it helped me. And I think it's overflowing to the kids, at least I hope it is anyway.... But now I lead the prayer at the teacher's meeting and I'm a Eucharistic Minister. So at the time, I am spreading. I can do this comfortably where I couldn't do it before.

The most significant thing that Donna gained was the desire to "put Jesus first and all things do fit in. It has worked for me, it really has." This became even more important for Donna after the religious sisters who taught in her school were withdrawn because of declining numbers. She became even more aware of her role in the mission of the Catholic school:

> I think, since we don't have the religious sisters there, I feel all of us have to do a little bit more to keep this alive and keep things centered. So I feel like I have to do my part, you know. And so I'm willing to do that. I want to do that. I want to keep the mission going and the vision alive, you know ... keep the virtues going, keep the spirituality going so that you can go out and say: "Yes, this is a Catholic school, not just a school!"

Cecilia

Cecilia, a 50-year-old Catholic, served as a resource teacher for all elementary grades, preschool through eighth, in her school. She had 9 years of teaching experience, all within Catholic schools. She herself attended Catholic schools from kindergarten through graduate school. The chronology of events from her background to taking the seminars also showed the progressive impact that the seminars had on her and on her teaching.

Cecilia was motivated to attend the virtue seminar several years later because of her attendance at the spirituality. Reflecting on the personal influence of the seminars, Cecilia immediately recounted that the spirituality seminar affected her prayer and the prayer of the whole school faculty. Essentially, Cecilia realized that she valued the traditional prayers that she had learned as a child. She agreed that she was now more comfortable in finding many ways to come to know Christ, including meditation or simply speaking in her own words.

Cecilia continued to explain how she integrated the faith throughout the day and introduced character education. She used "Christ as a model in their activities and the way they behave with one another." Her concrete examples of "modeling" showed the importance of teaching the children knowledge about Jesus or about virtue and good behavior, as well as the reality of the effect that this should have on their actions with one another.

Cecilia appreciated the virtue seminar because it provided a specific focus to guide the children in the development of their character. Again, even in a kindergarten class, they learned the meaning of the virtue, as well as how to practice it:

> So, modeling it I think. The virtues were wonderful because we could develop a character every month. When we talk about, honesty, and you could spend the month talking about it. And you could go back to it.

Cecilia acknowledged that she had done some of these things before attending the seminars. However, she still believed that she learned something new. She felt especially strengthened in her beliefs, her teaching, and her ability to encourage her children to do the right things. An example from her second grade experience occurred simultaneously with her attendance at the spirituality seminar when she was able to remind parents of their obligation to help their children receive the Sacraments of Reconciliation or Penance and Eucharist frequently:

> I think I was doing second grade when I took your spirituality, First Communion and Reconciliation, such a beautiful age to teach. It really is! And I think that the seminar strengthened my teaching by making the parents understand how important it is to not rely on me but broaden themselves. Because the parents will have their children at Reconciliation in second grade and the next time they come to Reconciliation they're in eighth grade. You know, that's what human nature is like. So it strengthened me to say, "Okay, let's not forget." And I would even start writing little notes in my little weekly memos, "Okay it's been a month. It's about time to go to Reconciliation. It's just a habit, you know, just a habit. We want to get into a good habit." So, I think that's how it helped me there.

As a Resource Teacher, Cecilia did not think she had as much opportunity to apply the seminars in her classes. However, with further reflection, she realized that they had helped her in how she was able to handle her students, especially in being able to accept their limitations and work more patiently with them. Cecilia felt that she was able to cope with the child's struggles and not get discouraged. Therefore, she could help the child to cope with herself, recognize her own gifts, and not become overly discouraged with her own learning ability.

Cecilia's approach to working with this student was a reflection of her understanding of the mission of the Catholic school. Her understanding showed a link between the mission of Catholic education and forming right behavior as in character education. The children not only learned about the morality of Christ but also learned to model it:

> I think that a Catholic school mission should be to first recognize the quality of the child and be able to teach them a quality education with a Christian, a strong Christian overview. And by that, I mean to be able to give them the gift of Christ and be able to have them model it themselves properly. So I think a Catholic school needs to be able to have as its moral view the identity that they are Catholic, not just Christian, so that we recognize other things like the Mass, the Marian prayers. But we show it and have them deal with the students, the faculty and the parents.

Given this understanding of the mission of the Catholic school, Cecilia felt that her explanation was "a true expression of what I came away with from the seminars." She felt that the seminars broadened her experience and confirmed her understanding:

> So taking those seminars, you're not in a vacuum. You were able to see how others interpret things because we did have dialogue. You were able to see how others are coping with 30 or 35 in a classroom and how do you talk Christ when you want to scream. And you know, you're dealing with no air conditioning on a 90° day, you know, that kind of thing. Yes. It did help me and I think it continues to help me and I think it broadened me, and not just as a teacher but personally._

SUMMARY

These case studies offered a glimpse into some of the participant's experiences of the spirituality/virtue Seminars. The teachers acknowledged the personal influence of the seminars, the influence of the seminars on teaching methods, understanding and implementation of virtue development or character education, and understanding and implementation of the mission or purpose of Catholic education.

All of the participants noted how the seminars affected them personally. At least four of the teachers were filled with tears as they tried to express their feelings about the seminars. Natalie attended the spirituality seminar three times, in addition to the virtue seminar. As a Protestant, she wanted to know more about Catholicism. She continued to attend the seminars because she felt "inspired." Dolores was "energized." Angel felt a "sense of renewal."

However, the seminars had the most notable personal influence on the participants' understanding of prayer and its value as a way of keeping them in touch with God. They learned about various forms of prayer and became more confident in their ability to pray and to feel they were praying correctly. Prayer became an integral part of their daily routines and they felt that they were growing in their love of God. This inspired and energized them in the way that they began to pray with their students. They learned to take time for prayer and they understood and recognized the meaning of my words, "You cannot give what you do not have." They recognized the importance of developing their own spirituality, and they acknowledged that for them, it was rooted in Christ.

Other teachers identified the influence that the seminars had on their teaching methods. They focused on being more sensitive to a parent in need, about understanding their concerns, and seeing the importance of being more caring and nurturing. They recognized opportunities to integrate virtue into other disciplines in ways that they had not done before coming to the seminars.

It was very apparent that the materials provided during the seminars were of value to all of the teachers. The resources, the activities, the use of music, and the interest in having a prayer corner were significant in assisting teachers with teaching methods.

The most significant method seemed to be teaching the students how to meditate. Having experienced their own sense of calm and peace in my classes, the teachers tried to teach this to their students. Several teachers noticed how much their students enjoyed meditation and how it brought a sense of calm and peace to their students.

Inspired by prayer, the participants also felt that they gained a deeper understanding of the theology related to grace, morality, and virtue. They personally grew in their appreciation of virtue and good character. Thus, the personal influence of the seminars seemed to affect their teaching methods and their understanding and implementation of virtue development. Teachers willingly made time for stories and activities to help their students grow in virtue. Laura's school actually created its own program, modeled on ideas from my virtue seminar, to develop respect. Dolores continued to send teachers from her school to the virtue seminar so that the whole school faculty would understand the idea of focusing on and practicing a virtue each month. She was able to build that program within her school.

Several teachers commented that the spirituality seminar had affected them personally. It had helped them to pray and to find time for God in their lives. These same teachers felt that the virtue seminar had strongly affected their teaching. They spoke of a connection between the two seminars.

Similarly, teachers found a strong link between the two seminars and their understanding of the mission of the Catholic school. As they tried to provide for the total development of the child, including the intellectual, physical, emotional, social, and spiritual aspects, the seminars helped them to grow spiritually and intellectually. As they were more aware of trying to love God and neighbor because of the seminars, they felt better prepared to help their children grow in love of God and neighbor. While each teacher's experience was uniquely her own, the similarities among the cases were highlighted through the issue-focused analysis that follows.

CHAPTER 9

TEACHER GROWTH
IN FAITH FORMATION

Issue-focused analysis focuses on what can be learned about specific issues, events or processes from any and all of the respondents (Weiss, 1994). It "is likely to move from discussion of issues within one area of discussion to discussion of issues within another, with each area logically connected to the others" (Weiss, 1994, p. 154). Many themes emerged from listening to the participants throughout the interviews.

Each theme in some way reflects a change that occurred within the individuals, their thinking, or their strategies of teaching. Seven major themes emerged during the interviews; namely, certification, knowledge, prayer, time, modeling, strengthening, and integration. Some of these themes have subsections. The themes are reviewed in relation to personal influence, teaching influence, and character. I will address the seminars' influence on understanding Catholic education in a separate section since this was a culminating topic in my interviews and involved a variety of themes.

CHANGE

The seminars seemed to inspire some type of change within every participant. Some learned more about prayer and incorporated this into their

Faith Formation of the Laity in Catholic Schools: The Influence of Virtues and Spirituality Seminars, pp. 123–133
Copyright © 2008 by Information Age Publishing
123

lives. Others reflected on how they felt they had grown in knowledge, in faith, or in developing their own spirituality. The group shifted and learned to value not only the quiet, but also the opportunity to take time for their own spiritual enrichment and development. This desire for spiritual growth, the recognition of the need for it, and the willingness to change actually prompted many teachers to attend the seminars.

CERTIFICATION

The spirituality seminar and the virtue seminar provided learning opportunities for the participants. Many teachers initially attended the seminars to earn credit toward their religion certification. Eight participants did not make any specific reference to religion certification. This raised the possibility of recognizing that some teachers were looking to do more than fulfill a policy requiring religion certification. Thus, it became important to look for other themes to discover not only personal motives for attending the seminars, but also any personal influence that the seminars could have on the participants.

KNOWLEDGE

Though many teachers initially attended the seminars to earn credit toward their religion certification, knowledge about the theology of the Catholic religion, especially related to spirituality and to virtues, was also important.

Of the various themes related to personal influences of the seminars, acquiring knowledge was the most concrete. Ten participants expressed a lack of theological knowledge about the Catholic religion, either because they had never attended Catholic schools or felt insecure about the validity or correctness of their knowledge. Learning more about the Ten Commandments, the beatitudes and virtues, understanding more about the Catholic Mass and the Liturgy of the Hours, and learning more about prayer were some of the chief academic themes that teachers cited.

Teachers also learned various ways to teach their students about spirituality, prayer, good character, and virtue. The participants gained knowledge about the remaining themes of prayer, time, modeling, and integration. This growth in knowledge helped to explain the theme of strengthening that also emerged.

Of the various themes showing a relationship between the seminars and character education, acquiring knowledge was again the most concrete. All participants were eager to learn more about the Ten Commandments, the beatitudes and virtues. Seven teachers acknowledged acquiring more understanding about grace and the sacraments, and understanding more about conscience formation and moral development. Teachers also learned various ways to teach their students about good character and virtue.

PRAYER

Prayer was an integral part of both seminars. Each session of the virtue seminar opened and closed with a prayer service. The spirituality seminar explored the meaning of prayer and provided a variety of prayer experiences during each session. In addition, it focused on the idea that prayer was the key to developing a Christ-centered spirituality, describing prayer as the oxygen of the soul, and creating an analogy between food and hunger and prayer and spirituality. It explored the liturgical prayer of the Catholic Church, specifically, the Mass, and the Liturgy of the Hours and examined several prayer forms that invited the participants to reflect on Scripture, including meditation, centering prayer, and journal writing. Because prayer was so central to the seminars, all participants spoke at length about their prayer experiences and the effect that these experiences had on their teaching and classroom interaction with students.

Meditation

Theologically, meditation is a form of prayer, but not all prayer is meditative. However, throughout the interviews, the participants used prayer, reflection, and meditation interchangeably. Since this study was not designed to test specific definitions, or to distinguish the influence of specific prayer forms, and since most participants spoke of reflective prayer, meditation, or centering prayer, all of these forms were considered as a type of meditation.

All of the participants included understanding meditation, learning how to meditate, and appreciating the value of reflection as significant ways in which the seminars influenced them personally. Throughout the interviews, all of the participants also used prayer, reflection, and meditation interchangeably as they spoke of the prayer forms in relation to their students. They explained that what they had learned about reflective prayer, meditation, or centering prayer influenced what they, in turn, did with their students. Five of the participants also described how they believed meditation influenced the behavior of students and made them more tolerant and respectful toward one another.

Listening

Listening was also related to prayer and finding time for prayer. All participants acknowledged that the seminars had provided time and taught them to listen to God's Word in Scripture and through prayer. Many associated listening with feeling closer to God. Because they experienced the value of listening, they also saw this as something they wanted to teach their students.

Quiet and Calm

Time for prayer and listening to God's Word about faith and virtue seemed to create an atmosphere of quiet and calm. Music provided a transition from the day's events in school to the time for prayer or instruction on spirituality or topics related to character formation and virtue. Participants not only valued the feeling of calm and quiet for themselves, but also found that this was of benefit to their students.

Atmosphere

The seminars talked about the importance of finding a particular place that would be conducive to personal prayer. They used a prayer table with a Bible and other religious articles, as a way of creating prayer space within the classroom. This also served to show the importance of having a special prayer space, even in the home. Music created a reflective atmosphere for prayer or helped to express the theme of a particular prayer service. Six teachers commented on the contribution of music to their prayer experiences.

TIME

Time for prayer and meditation related closely to prayer and meditation. Almost all participants who attended the seminars felt that the seminars provided them time to grow and time to pray. They became aware of the importance of making time for prayer, as well as focusing on explaining, developing and noticing virtue with their students. Valuing time and space for prayer and listening to God's Word about faith and virtue, teachers tried to share this with students.

Making time for prayer was an important message that influenced the participants. However, making time for virtue also emerged in several of the interviews. They began to recognize the importance of providing time for discussion and activities related to virtue.

Several schools already had some type of school program where they dedicated each month to the practice of a particular virtue. However, several teachers admitted that before the seminars, they either made the announcement, put up a poster, or passed out the information that came from the office. However, they did not make time in their plans to explain, discuss or monitor the practice of the virtue.

MODELING

While the primary focus of the seminars was to provide teachers with theological content, prayer experiences, and activities to do with their students, they also tried to demonstrate teaching methods to the attendees. For example, the classroom space was already set up and materials distributed before the participants arrived. In addition, the format of the presentations varied, providing time for teacher initiated instruction, student experiences, and dialogue and interaction. Many of the participants copied some of the ideas and strategies from the seminars when they introduced the same content to their own students. They mentioned some themes, previously highlighted, including prayer, meditation, listening, and quiet. The teachers provided other examples of modeling, such as, using the ideas from the resources provided during the seminars. Telling or reading stories to portray virtues, creating new programs, and providing examples of virtue, care, and spirituality, were additional ways the participants modeled in their own classrooms what they had seen and heard.

Participants mentioned some themes, previously highlighted, as things to model. These included prayer, meditation, listening, and quiet. However, the concept of modeling in relation to character development expanded to include using stories to teach the virtues, establishing programs that paralleled mine, teaching the virtues, and modeling of the virtues by the teachers to their students. Specifically, they spoke about the content of the manual and resources, the use of stories, and various teaching aides, such as posters, videos, music, and Power Point presentations.

During the virtue seminar, each participant received a binder filled with material related to the theology of topics, such as, virtue, grace, sacraments, conscience formation, and moral development. The materials also included numerous activities for teachers to do with their students. Similarly, during each of the four weeks of the spirituality seminar, they received a folder with theological materials related to spirituality and prayer, as well as numerous activities for the classroom. All participants referred in a positive manner to the manual or resources that they received.

During the spirituality seminar, a prayer table was created each week. The symbols and objects changed each week to reflect the theme of each week's presentation. At the first session, in addition to more theological symbols, a small jar filled with a walnut and rice appeared. Because of its symbolism, it became a regular visual aide. If one filled the jar with rice and then tried to put the walnut inside, it would not fit. However, if one put the walnut into the jar first, it was easy to pour all of the rice into the jar. Symbolically, the walnut represented God, and the rice represented all of the countless activities and events of the day. Thus, if one was busy with all the activities and concerns of the day, there never seemed to be any time left for God or for prayer. Conversely, if one made time first for God, then the events, activities and concerns would still fit into the day. Almost every participant commented about the symbolism and meaning of this jar.

Throughout the seminars, the participants heard many stories in order to show teachers how a story could address a virtue and foster discussion with students, not only about the literary quality of the literature, but also about the actions of the characters. Teachers saw many helpful books and videos as well, including William Bennett's (1993) *Book of Virtues*. Many schools had several teachers who attended the seminars. As a response to the virtue seminar, several schools started a "Virtue of the Month Program" patterned after activities and suggestions given at the seminars. Some schools actually created their own programs, gathering resources, creating a binder, and having faculty in-services to help all teachers to implement the new idea.

As an outgrowth of the seminars, teachers understood more about the meaning of virtue and its importance in the character development of their students. Bennett (1993) maintains that moral education not only involves rules and precepts, but also explicit instruction, exhortation, and training. Moral education must provide training in good habits and affirm the importance of moral example. There is the need for moral literacy, where teachers explain and model good moral practices or virtues (Bennett, Finn, & Cribb, 1999). Based on Aristotle's definition of character as right conduct in relation to others and to oneself, Lickona (1991) offers a way of thinking about character that is appropriate for values education:

> Character consists of *operative values*, values in action. We progress in our character, as a value becomes a virtue, a reliable inner disposition to respond to situations in a morally good way. (pp. 50-51)

The seminars attempted to provide teachers with a better understanding of the theology of virtue in the Catholic tradition, as well as to give them suggestions for ways to instruct their students in the meaning and practice of virtue.

In his review of competencies of caring, Sergiovanni (2000) develops his theory about caring as the cornerstone of the commitment needed for teaching. This commitment includes a sense of being there for the other person and a sense of compassion. Caring and serving for him are the foundation anchors for the profession of teaching. He believes that every pedagogical action shows how one is oriented to children, either living up or failing to live up to teaching responsibilities. Ten participants spoke about the seminars' influence on how they viewed, approached, or handled their students and to look more closely at how they could practice those virtues with their students and, therefore, model them.

The religious belief that God made us in His image and likeness became a foundation for teaching students about respect. The Catholic Church teaches that God calls all people to be holy and this helps to guide one's spiritual growth. Several teachers tried to describe how the seminars influenced how they looked at their students, viewed their concerns, and treated them with greater care.

The spirituality seminar focused on teaching the participants the meaning of spirituality and helping them to develop their own spirituality in the Catholic tradition. Many of the themes, such as, prayer, meditation, listening, calm, strengthening, and modeling relate to spirituality. However, ten of the participants specifically noted spirituality as a major theme that influenced them personally.

STRENGTHENING

The concept of feeling personally strengthened was an unexpected theme that emerged in every single interview. The actual word, "strengthen" occurred in all interviews. In addition, participants conveyed the same concept in the words, "renewed," "confirmed," "affirmed," "deepened," and "broadened." Several of the participants found that the seminars gave them a feeling that they were praying correctly and understanding the faith. The concept of being pedagogically strengthened emerged as an unexpected theme in every single interview.

The concept of being strengthened in efforts to contribute to the character education of students was also an unexpected theme that emerged in every single interview. Teachers expressed more confidence in teaching their students about good character, moral development, and virtue.

INTEGRATION

Catholic schools usually try to integrate some aspects of faith, virtue, and religious content into all dimensions of the Catholic school experience. Integration is a term used here to describe curriculum in which the various academic disciplines are intertwined or integrated. This helps the student to see how the various disciplines relate to each other. Catholic schools usually try to integrate some aspects of faith, virtue, and religious content into all dimensions of the Catholic school experience. The discussion with teachers in these interviews revealed the influence that the seminars had on this integration. Though some teachers included integration among the personal effects of the seminars, the seminars' influence on integration was more prominent in the area of teaching methods.

The discussion with teachers in these interviews revealed the influence that the seminars had on this integration. While the seminars' influence on integration was most prominent in teaching methods, some teachers included integration among the personal effects of the seminars. They appreciated the idea that: "You can't give what you don't have" and that nurturing the spiritual life allowed one to be able to recognize the teachable moments for integrating the faith into the classroom.

While the seminars' influence on integration was most prominent in teaching methods, nine teachers included integration within the effects of the seminars on character education. This grew from the idea that: "You can't give what you don't have" and that nurturing the spiritual life allowed one to be able to recognize the teachable moments for integrating the faith and moral development into the classroom.

INFLUENCE OF THE SEMINARS ON
UNDERSTANDING CATHOLIC SCHOOLS' PURPOSE: THEMES

The spirituality seminar and the virtue seminar provided learning opportunities for the participants. Though many teachers initially attended the seminars to earn credit toward their religion certification, the interviews showed several other areas that personally affected them. The teachers revealed their understanding of the mission and purpose of Catholic schools. The spiritual and character dimensions of the seminars seemed to lead into several themes related to the influence of the seminars on the teachers' understanding of the mission and purpose of Catholic schools. While many of the themes are the same, they are mentioned again to show their influence on understanding the mission of Catholic education, as well as to show that they could also be adapted on this level of mission to serve the needs of any religiously affiliated school.

Modeling and Integration

The seminars primarily planned to provide teachers with theological content, prayer experiences, and activities to do with their students as well as to demonstrate teaching methods to the attendees. Many of the participants copied some of the ideas and strategies from the seminars when they introduced the same content to their own students. Some themes, previously highlighted, were things to model. These included prayer, meditation, listening, and quiet. However, the concept of modeling in relation to understanding the mission and purpose of Catholic schools focused primarily on virtue and prayer, which formed an integral part of the Catholic school experience.

Strengthening

The concept of feeling strengthened in efforts to contribute to the mission or purpose of a Catholic school was an unexpected theme that emerged in every single interview. The actual word, 'strengthen" occurred in all interviews. In addition, participants conveyed the same concept in the words, "renewed," "confirmed," "affirmed," "deepened," and "broadened." They felt better able to see the purpose of the Catholic school and practice it with more motivation.

Care

Many teachers also related the importance of caring to their understanding of the mission of a Catholic school, a place where caring, compassion, and loved rooted in the love of God should have great importance. The notion of being made in the image of God and called to holiness helped teachers to want to show more compassion, sensitivity, and care for their students, their concerns, and their interaction with each other. The seminars helped to increase their impetus, drive, and desire to want to be better at living the virtues and teaching the virtues.

SUMMARY

The themes presented offered a glimpse at the similarities that emerged across the experiences of the teachers who attended the seminars and interviewed for this study. While each teacher's experience was uniquely her own, the participants expressed similar themes. These were in relation to the influence of the seminars on them personally, the influence of the seminars on their teaching methods, the relationship between the seminars and character education, and the influence of the seminars on the participants' understanding of the purpose or mission of the Catholic school. Similar themes emerged across the four areas under review that related to my research questions. Thus, information was gathered about specific issues from all of the respondents that also allowed me "to move from discussion of issues within one area of discussion to discussion of issues within another, with each area logically connected to the others" (Weiss, 1994, p. 154).

As expected, the first themes that emerged related the influence of the seminars on each of the teachers personally. Though many of the participants initially chose to attend one seminar to gain hours toward their required religion certification, it became clear that they ended the seminar with more knowledge and a better understanding and desire for prayer. In addition, appreciation for time, listening, and quiet, associated with prayer, influenced most participants. The notion of personal strengthening was an unexpected theme that every participant cited. They often used similar words, such as, "renewed," "confirmed," or "affirmed." Some even addressed the theme of spirituality itself as something that they felt had grown or developed.

This personal influence seemed to lead naturally to themes related to the influence of the seminars on the teachers' pedagogy. Though the themes were in relation to teaching methods, it was interesting to see that a set of themes similar to the ones associated with the seminars' personal influence emerged. Care and modeling were also associated with teachers' pedagogy.

Because the content of the seminars focused on spirituality and on virtue, both the personal and pedagogical influences helped to establish a link between the seminars and character education and a variety of themes related to it. Knowledge about character education and the theology of virtue was important. Meditation, listening, and quiet were all associated with prayer. Time to explain good behavior and virtue was important. Modeling, including care, feeling strengthened, and integrating character education into all aspects of daily subjects and events continued to be major themes.

Finally, the teachers revealed their understanding of the mission and purpose of Catholic schools. Both the spiritual and character dimensions of the seminars seemed to lead into several themes related to the influence of the seminars on the teachers' understanding of the mission and purpose of Catholic schools. Modeling and integration were associated with each other and included virtue and prayer. Feeling strengthened or affirmed in understanding and living the Catholic school mission was significant.

Finally, the notion of care was almost synonymous with the mission of the Catholic school. In various ways, all participants identified the mission with love of God and love of neighbor.

Having looked at the basic themes that emerged throughout all of the teachers' interviews or stories, the next chapters will focus on the four major outcomes of these programs as discovered through this research. The first is that from attending these seminars that were faith based, the teachers themselves were personally changed. Using an old adage that "you cannot give what you do not have," the next chapter will allow teachers who attended the seminars to describe how they were personally enriched in their own faith lives and thus more motivated to want to share this with students both by example and in the religion class.

CHAPTER 10

CHANGING TEACHERS THROUGH FAITH FORMATION

The first research question asked the following: What significant experiences do the virtue/spirituality seminars produce and how do they affect the participants? Feiman-Nemser (1990) states: "The teacher's own personal development is a central part of teacher preparation" (p. 225).

The spirituality of the teacher is a vital teaching force, especially when matched by the parents' spirituality (Keating, 1990). The task of the catechist is to explain the truths of faith and Christian morality and to encourage the practice of virtue (Pius X, 1905). Formation, therefore, must be a part of and complement to the professional formation of the Catholic school teacher (Sacred Congregation for Catholic Education, 1982). To achieve the goals of religious formation requires a human and well-rounded formation, as well as a formation in spirituality and doctrine (Congregation for the Clergy, 1997).

From this perspective, it seemed valuable first to look for specific ways in which the seminars personally affected the participants. Throughout the interviews, the teachers identified the following themes as specific ways that the seminars affected them personally: certification, knowledge, prayer, time, listening, quiet/calm, change, modeling, including activities such as the walnut and rice, strengthening, integration, and spirituality. At this point, the participants own descriptions will show how these themes came to life.

Faith Formation of the Laity in Catholic Schools: The Influence of Virtues and Spirituality Seminars, pp. 135–147

CERTIFICATION

Seven of the participants initially chose to come to one of the seminars in order to add hours toward their religion certification. Though gaining the certification was a personal goal in coming to the first seminar, attendance at the first seminar prompted all participants to attend the second seminar. This was true, whether they attended the spirituality seminar first or the virtue seminar. Angel chose to attend the spirituality seminar because other teachers had recommended it. She explained: "I was looking ahead towards my religion certification and choosing classes that I felt would help me not only get certified, but to help the children I teach." Dolores, who taught eighth grade, also served as the religion coordinator in her school. She wanted to encourage her teachers to seek their religion certification. She hoped to set the example. She explained her decision to attend the spirituality seminar: "not only to help me spiritually, to become more acquainted with the Scriptures selected for the classroom, but also to help them with certification and to get them in touch a little more with teaching religion."

Elizabeth was new to the diocese. She originally attended the spirituality seminar because she "needed to start certification, religion certification." She explained that she did not feel "really strong" about teaching religion and "wanted to take as much as I could." Jeannice also felt that it would help her with her religion certification. Katherine and Monica also initially attended the seminars because they needed to acquire religion certification.

In contrast, Rebecca specifically noted that she already possessed advanced religion certification. Thus, she noted her decision to attend the virtue seminar: "I don't think it was for religious certification... but I did it for myself." The remaining eight participants did not make any specific reference to religion certification. This raised the possibility of recognizing that some teachers were looking to do more than fulfill a policy requiring Religion certification. Thus, it became important to look for other themes to discover not only personal motives for attending the seminars, but also any personal influence that the seminars could have on the participants.

KNOWLEDGE

Of the various themes related to personal influences of the seminars, acquiring knowledge was the most concrete. All participants expressed a lack of theological knowledge about the Catholic religion, either because they had never attended Catholic schools or felt insecure about the validity or correctness of their knowledge. Learning more about the Ten

Commandments, the beatitudes and virtues, understanding more about the Catholic Mass and the Liturgy of the Hours, and learning more about prayer were some of the chief academic themes that teachers cited. Natalie described why knowledge was important: "just the things I was learning. I wanted to make sure that I could convey that to the classroom and to the children." Dolores wanted to further her knowledge as a Religion teacher. She noted: "I think I've gained a deeper understanding of the Scripture and how it relates to me as a Catholic educator.… I gained knowledge." Lucy, who attended both seminars several times, explained: "Because every time you go, you learn more. You get something different out of it each time."

PRAYER

Prayer was an integral part of both seminars. Each session of the virtue seminar opened and closed with a prayer service. The spirituality seminar explored an understanding of the meaning of prayer and provided a variety of prayer experiences during each session. Because prayer was so central to the seminars, all participants spoke at length about their prayer experiences and the effect that these experiences had on them. Prayer seemed to have the most significant effect on the participants. Some rediscovered the meaning of traditional prayers, such as, the Rosary or the Mass. Some discovered prayer forms that were new to them, such as, centering prayer or journal writing. Others felt they experienced a deeper and more meaningful prayer life, not only at the time of the seminars but continuing to the present time.

Alice recalled the prayers and "the renewal of the prayers that we had learned as little people and what do they mean to us now." She appreciated the Scripture passages. However, a reference to a prayer of St. Theresa touched her: "Christ has no body but yours, no hands, no feet on earth but yours." Alice described this as "a transforming prayer." She had always thought of herself "as trying to follow Christ." She never thought that she "might bring another person closer to Christ."

Five of the teachers admitted that they were never sure if "they prayed right." Lucy came to the spirituality seminar three times. She felt that the seminars had "deepened" her understanding of prayer. She explained:

> Prayer is very important to me and every time I have come to the seminar, I have received more. I have learned more. It has deepened my perspective on prayer. Even though it's the same material, I remember hearing, you know, you can never hear it too often. It touches you differently each time.… It does cause you to look at prayer differently and where prayer involves you, where you are at that stage.

Jeannice expressed uncertainty about prayer. She was not sure whether she "actually prayed right." She explained:

> Sometimes you feel like you're not doing it right, praying right, ... and that helped me.... I realized maybe I'd been praying all along.... I used to stop and say thank you God, you know, just privately, but I never thought much of that as a prayer.

Katherine found that prayer was more important to her after the seminars. She spoke of the importance of prayer in her daily schedule:

> I feel like I try to make prayer more a part of my day.... I find that even if I make more of an effort to say my evening prayers, I even say that I sleep better.... So, it definitely had an effect on me.

Cecilia learned that there were different types of prayer. The spirituality seminar affected her prayer: "It affected me by increasing my daily prayer and by enlarging my prayer group." She and her friends returned to school and encouraged the entire faculty to have more prayer at the beginning of the day, including praying morning prayer from the Liturgy of the Hours that we had examined during the seminars. In addition to appreciating some of the traditional prayers, Cecilia felt a freedom: "It encouraged me to be more free form with my prayers." She acknowledged that she "talked to God all the time." She believed God listened but did not think that she "was really utilizing prayer." She thanked God and asked Him for help. She loved prayers such as the Mass, the Rosary, and structured prayers such as, the Memorare and the prayer to St. Michael. However, after the seminars, she realized that "there's a lot of different ways to get prayer" and "don't be afraid of it."

All participants felt affirmed in their various prayer practices. Others felt that prayer was more important to them after the seminars.

Meditation

Theologically, meditation is a form of prayer, but not all prayer is meditative. However, throughout the interviews, the participants used prayer, reflection, and meditation interchangeably. Participants included understanding meditation, learning how to meditate, and appreciating the value of reflection as significant ways in which the seminars influenced them personally. Teachers learned to recognize little moments for prayer and to value those opportunities.

All of the participants included understanding meditation, learning how to meditate, and appreciating the value of reflection as significant ways in which the seminars influenced them personally. Rose already enjoyed doing some type of "self-reflection" in the morning when she walked her dog. She explained that after the seminars she also tried to do an evening meditation:

> Doing a self-reflection at the end of the day also…. It relaxes me. It gives me a better perspective on what I did, what I've accomplished during the day, what I did, what I can do to make things a little better for myself the next day or anything I need to improve on.

Before the seminars, Mary never felt that she was "meditating properly and that was one of the big things." However, after experiencing a guided meditation that I did with her group, she commented: "It made a big impression on me." She began to reflect on the prayers at Mass. She also started attending Mass "three or four times a week."

Donna explained that she learned to recognize little moments during the day to pray and reflect: "In the car waiting for a red light or in the store waiting in line forever, you can meditate on prayer." She valued moments of prayer: "I find myself taking time to calm myself down and meditate and to bring God back into my life so that I can't forget that I'm not alone." Cecilia realized that she could read someone's prayer or meditation with her faculty. However, she and her colleagues "really tried to do that" after the seminars. Rebecca learned that "there was more time for self-reflection." She explained: "I know you led us through—we did the meditative prayer, and for me, that was very beneficial for me and for developing my own relationship with God."

Atmosphere

The seminars stressed the importance of finding a particular place that would be conducive to personal prayer. In each session, there was a prayer table with a Bible and other religious articles, as a way of creating prayer space within the classroom and an example of the importance of having a special prayer space even in the home. Laura recalled "the importance of having a space that you find that's always going to be like your prayer corner."

Music and pictures helped to create a prayerful atmosphere. Six teachers commented on the contribution of music and art to the prayer experiences. It also helped to set a tone or provide for a prayerful atmosphere and transition from other activities.

Listening

Listening was also related to prayer and finding time for prayer. Nine participants acknowledged that the seminars had provided time and taught them to listen to God's word in Scripture and through prayer. Many associated listening with feeling closer to God. Elizabeth enjoyed listening about "faith and virtues and how to teach the kids." She liked to listen to words on some of the tapes and to the interpretation of Scripture and spirituality because it reminded her to see "Christ as our center."

Quiet/Calm

Time for prayer and listening to God's word about faith and virtue seemed to create an atmosphere of quiet and calm. Teachers found this to be comforting, especially after an active day in the classroom. After a meditation, Rose felt "closer to God" and more at peace; Mary felt that she was on "a path to closeness with God." She usually rushed into things but felt that she was able now "to sit quietly and slow down and let God take over and that quietness and that time … helped."

Several teachers felt the seminars were like a retreat. They felt refreshed and renewed by the peace, calm, and quiet. Elizabeth felt that the classes provided:

> A chance to relax and slow down and take in all this stuff that we use every day, spiritually. And it's an opportunity to get that back because with being so busy every day, I don't think of it until the very last.

Alice shared an observation throughout the seminars. Each week as the group assembled, they developed a sense of calm, having been somewhat frenzied the first week they arrived. By the last week, no one watched a clock, and people were almost reluctant to leave and go back to their busy routines. By the third session, Alice recalled her observations:

> The chatter became, boy, it's really important to do something for yourself. We need it and I feel other people were saying it.… With such running, busy lives, we never take time to sit down quietly.… Everything is on the rush, including our praying.

Lucy also observed the quiet and calm and its value. She agreed that she was more aware of the importance of listening "in order to go beyond the words and to come to know Christ." She continued:

> It just really showed the importance of quiet. Everything, every day is so noisy. The TV is on and the noise of the cars and the music. Your car is quiet and there's something going boom, boom, going next to you.... There has to be time when you're awake that you're quiet because your soul needs to think and needs to grow just like your body needs to grow.

Following the seminars, Donna appreciated meditation and the quiet and calm that accompanied it. This was especially true after a stressful day: "I also do it at home ... when I'm really stressed out, ... I find myself taking time to calm myself down and meditate and to bring God back into my life so that I can't forget that I'm not alone." Rebecca shared this insight. She valued prayer, the time for it, and the quiet: "I think that the class, that seminar helped me with that, and just that quiet prayer, that meditation. Do you remember when you would read to us?"

Most participants learned to appreciate the quiet of the prayer experiences and looked for ways to continue to make time and space for the quiet of reflection.

Time

Time for prayer and meditation was closely related to prayer and meditation. Most participants who attended the seminars felt that the seminars provided them time to grow and time to pray. They became aware of the importance of making time for prayer, as well as focusing on explaining, developing and noticing virtue with their students. They appreciated the time that the seminars provided for prayer and felt that, as Rebecca said, it "was very beneficial" in developing a relationship with God.

Laura acknowledged that because of "the time taken and given for prayer, for meditation" she realized: "how much they were a part of my daily existence and how much I really needed those things." She recognized how much she wanted to develop her spirituality and "all the importance of taking time, spending time daily. And then I guess for me the idea of the centering prayer and that whole importance was probably most powerful."

Elizabeth felt that both seminars gave her the opportunity to find time. She commented: "Oh yes time, time to slow down and listen about my faith and the virtues, and how to teach it to the kids, how to include it in our every day well." Mary echoed the same idea:

Temperamentally, I'm the type of person who rushes into things—bump, bump, bump. When I was remembering just a year ago, you made a point to me to sit quietly and slow down and let God take over. And that that quietness and that time to come in that helped me quite a bit.

Donna also noted that after the seminars she was able to find time for prayer that previously she missed:

I do find myself using my time, down time like in the car waiting for a red light, or in the store waiting in line forever…. I find myself taking time to calm myself down and meditate and to bring God back into my life.

Jeannice also noted that prayer affected all aspects of her life. The seminars reminded her to find time for prayer: "Yes, it helped me…. I need to make the time for prayer and also I liked it…. It just reminded me of, like, you know, to take time to say thank you, appreciate, I notice things much more." Because she learned to be more attuned to making personal prayer time, Monica made this observation about herself: "Just loving, letting God love through me, I feel that my family is becoming close to God too." Cecilia commented about "another message" that she "took away" from the seminars; namely, making prayer time a priority: "You need to begin your day with prayer. You need to find a time and give that time because if you don't, you won't find it later."

The seminars reminded Rebecca of the need and perhaps "obligation" to know Scripture "and to spend more time better understanding the teachings of the Catholic Church." Laura described the influence of the seminars in relation to time and listening:

It did influence me, especially because it's something that you want to establish a pattern, a routine of it, guard that with your life and then you get such a benefit from it that you want to share that with everyone.

CHANGE

In one way, all of the themes associated with personal influence of the seminars could be considered changes within the participants. However, five of the participants specifically spoke of feeling changed because of the seminars. The seminars seemed to inspire change within many of the participants. Some learned more about prayer and incorporated this into their lives. Others reflected on how they felt they had grown in knowledge, in faith, or in developing their own spirituality. For example, Donna felt that she could take a more active role in her school in their virtue program because she did not feel as "naïve" about the meaning of virtue.

Similarly, because she understood more about the virtues, Monica described an inner "transformation" that inspired her personally to practice the virtues more deliberately and consciously. Jeannice understood that the virtues were not just "something expected." She recognized the spiritual dimension of virtue and felt that she started "looking at things in a different light." As the seminars were repeated, participants admitted that they came because they were looking to change, and to seek some spiritual direction.

Alice had observed a change in the participants as they moved from the first to the subsequent sessions of the spirituality seminar. As noted in the section on "Quiet and Calm," the group shifted and learned to value not only the quiet, but also the opportunity to take time for their own spiritual enrichment and development. This desire for spiritual growth, the recognition of the need for it, and the willingness to change actually prompted many teachers to attend the seminars. Laura commented that she and other teachers came to the virtue seminar because they "were kind of seeking something, some changes, looking to make some changes, but we really didn't have a direction on that." From others who had attended the seminars, Laura thought the virtue seminar "might be what we're looking for." After she arrived, she was more convinced: "I mean the minute we got there, we were soaking everything up because it just seemed to be exactly what we needed…. We were just on fire after that." Similarly, Laura then attended the spirituality seminar because she wanted "more of that spiritual direction."

STRENGTHENING

The concept of being personally strengthened was an unexpected theme that emerged in every single interview. The actual word, "strengthen" occurred in all interviews. In addition, the same concept was conveyed in the words, "renewed," "confirmed," "affirmed," "deepened," and "broadened."

Rose had acknowledged that she engaged in some type of self-reflection in the morning before attending the seminars. However, after the seminars, she wanted to do this again at the end of the day: "But after the Spirituality Seminar, I found myself doing more meditation…. It's, I think, actually probably deepened my own spirituality and has encouraged me to do a little bit more."

Mary commented on the seminars' influence on her and her colleagues:
They had a great influence on me … and any of those teachers there when I

took them were all very much impressed and it sounds like they were enlivened too by both of the virtues and spirituality seminars.

Similarly, Natalie, who attended the seminars several times, concluded: "I need to keep going back to them because it refreshes me…. I just think that they're a wonderful way to prepare teachers to teach children"

Alice expressed these same sentiments: "You know, I think everybody who came out of the seminars felt enriched and passed that on. When people were debating back at school about whether they should go or not, your seminars were champions of the place to go to be renewed." Though she also attended Catholic school, Alice explained the reason for the need or desire for renewal:

> I, somebody once said to me how sometimes when we have gone through Catholic school with 2 years of college, that our religion kind of, our religious experience, our learning of religion stops at the level that you stopped your formal education. And that if you don't continue to grow as a person in your spirituality, well, that sinks into your body, and that's where you are, back where you were at your last class…. I still felt that I was rusty, so I hadn't gone deep enough or thought enough about what I was doing. So, I needed to have a mature, I needed to have a dose of what I call mature religion, mature theology to kind of, to grow up from a sophomore in college to becoming that adult that I was supposed to be in the classroom…. We all needed to be renewed…. This is not just a course but a spiritual awakening, renewal to connect with the God we all love. It becomes habit forming!

Katherine agreed that the seminars "reaffirmed" her Catholic school experience and reminded her that "the rock is still there." Dolores also explained that she appreciated having the seminars available to her so that she could continue to attend them when she felt "the need to be reenergized, to be refortified."

Participants referred to the seminars as a source of refreshment. They motivated some participants to pray more or read Scripture more often. Some felt renewed in their role as teachers in a Catholic school and better able to bring the love of Christ to their students. Some referred to the seminars as "a place to go to be renewed" or to be enriched. For some, it recalled and confirmed their own Catholic school experiences; for others, it helped them to feel that they were "praying right." Dolores captured the idea of being strengthened and the idea of growth or renewal in her personal life: "I realized that I was gaining far more than hands-on material for the students. That I myself was gaining strength, spirituality, and that I was becoming more in touch with the virtues." Others, like Rebecca, felt that they gained strength "from within" and that the seminars "nourished their inner self."

Several of the participants found that the seminars gave them a feeling that they were praying correctly and understanding the faith. Jeannice acknowledged that she could think more about faith. She felt that it helped with her prayer and affirmed that she "actually prayed right." Rebecca already spent time in prayer before the seminars. However, after attending them, she felt that she had "more information on our faith." In addition, the seminars took her prayer "to a higher level." Rebecca felt that she gathered her "strength from within." She felt that the seminars "nourished" her "inner self."

INTEGRATION

Catholic schools usually try to integrate some aspects of faith, virtue, and religious content into all dimensions of the Catholic school experience. The discussion with teachers in these interviews revealed the influence that the seminars had on this integration. While the seminars' influence on integration was most prominent in teaching methods, some teachers included integration among the personal effects of the seminars. Participants spoke of a link they recognized between developing their own spirituality and relationship with Christ and the positive influence this had in their teaching and in aspects of their personal lives.

Donna recalled this idea. She had learned "great things to do in the classroom." However, she noted one thing I had said: "Take care of yourself spiritually as well." She admitted that at the beginning of the seminars, she found herself "not doing that." However, after the seminars, she saw a link between her own spirituality and "spreading it with students."

Dolores also recognized a link between what she personally gained and how it influenced other aspects of her life: "They go because they want to get something spiritually uplifting from the Scriptures…. That's why they continue to go because they're doing it for themselves and by doing it for themselves, the kids are going to benefit." Angel also described the seminars as becoming an integral part of herself. They influenced her: "It helped me to improve my own spirituality, which then in turn, the way I looked at it, helped me teach spirituality to the children.

SPIRITUALITY

The spirituality seminar focused on teaching the participants the meaning of spirituality and helping them to develop their own spirituality in the Catholic tradition. All of the themes developed within this section were themes that the participants expressed as ways in which the seminars influenced them personally. All of these themes are related to spirituality. However, some of the participants specifically noted spirituality as a key theme that influenced them personally.

Three of the participants recognized a connection between the virtue and spirituality seminars. Growing in the spiritual life seemed to help with practicing virtues. Elizabeth expressed this idea that the spirituality seminar offered her the opportunity for personal reflection and growth in her relationship with Christ. However, after the virtue seminar, she then felt "enriched with that spiritual animation." Most participants felt better able to talk about and share their faith as a result of attending the seminars.

SUMMARY OF THEMES RELATED TO
THE PERSONAL INFLUENCE OF THE SEMINARS

All of these themes seem to be connected as ways in which the seminars personally influenced the participants. Perhaps this is because all forms of spirituality have a common thread, "the quest of the human spirit for something that is above, that is bigger, deeper, 'more than' the ordinary surface reality of life (Guinan, 1998, p. 1). Christian spirituality could be broadly defined as "our life in the Spirit of God" or "the art of letting God's spirit fill us, work in us, guide us" (p. 2). It deals with the whole person, body and soul, calling the individual to live life to the fullest. Each of these themes in some way seemed to touch the participants and help them in their personal quest for meaning.

In addition, since all participants were teachers, this desire for the spiritual seems even more likely in light of Groome's (1998) approach to education. For Groome, every teacher and parent has a call or vocation to be a "humanizing educator, to teach with a spiritual vision" (p. 37). This calling (vocatus) is heard within one's being and comes from beyond oneself. As a result, philosophers, including Plato and Aristotle, "have understood educator as a spiritual vocation, implying that its surest foundation is the educator's own spirituality" (p. 37).

Finally, if teachers felt personally enriched because of these seminars, it seems incumbent on principals and diocesan superintendents, in their roles as spiritual leaders, to look for and sponsor this type of program, especially for their teachers. Sergiovanni's (1984) distinction between the competent and the excellent school principal makes this clear. Muccigrosso (1994) affirms that to be excellent the Catholic school principal must accept the challenge of articulating a Christian vision and the development of spiritually self-aware and motivated Christian individuals.

Having looked at the basic themes that emerged throughout all of the teachers' interviews or stories, the next chapter will focus on the second of four major outcomes of these programs; namely, that those who attended not only were personally enriched but also gained insight into how to improve their teaching pedagogy, especially in the area of sharing the faith or teaching religion, so that it was not just a subject but a way of life that they wanted to suggest to their students. You may find repetition in themes and in some of the stories. However, this is a deliberate attempt to show the similarity of themes in each of the four areas of research as well as to ask the reader to reflect on teacher stories and how they can overlap and suggest multiple ways in which the seminars have influenced their faith formation.

CHAPTER 11

IMPROVING
TEACHER PEDAGOGY

The second research question asked: In what specific ways have the seminars been reflected in participants' teaching or influenced their thinking about their teaching pedagogy? Doyle (1990) describes teacher education research as "a loosely coordinated set of experiences designed to establish and maintain a talented teaching force" (p. 39). He states that the study of teaching practices "shifts ... to an explanation of how a practice works and what meaning it has to teachers and students in a particular context" (p. 20). If teachers' personal development is essential to their preparation for teaching (Feiman-Nemser, 1990), and if the seminars personally influenced the participants in this study, then it is important to examine the influence of the seminars on teachers' teaching and thinking about teaching pedagogy. Many of the themes related to the personal influence of the seminars were also relevant for the influence of the seminars on teaching methods and how they approached their students. The following themes related to teaching methods emerged in the interviews: prayer, listening, quiet/calm, time and space, the manual of resources, modeling, care, strengthening, and integration.

Faith Formation of the Laity in Catholic Schools: The Influence of Virtues and Spirituality Seminars, pp. 149–167
Copyright © 2008 by Information Age Publishing

PRAYER

Because prayer was so central to the seminars, all participants spoke at length about their prayer experiences and the effect that these experiences had on their teaching and classroom interaction with students. Since the Mass is the most central prayer in the Catholic Church, seven teachers not only recalled the video on the Mass, but also explained how they spoke more to their children about the meaning and importance of the Mass.

Rebecca singled this out as a significant area that had an impact her teaching methods:

> You gave us ideas to try this and show your children. I remember you showed us a video on the Mass that talked about the Liturgy of the Word and the Liturgy of the Eucharist. And I remember how important that was to show that to the children, and make sure that the children understood the different parts of the Mass. And I know there were also some methods in there. And I thought they were very helpful.

Some teachers felt they were better able to remind their children that all are wonderful creations by God. With this added respect for differences, they also felt that they could introduce the children to a variety of prayer forms, according to their age and ability. Rebecca also believed that the seminars strengthened her ability to bring an important message to her children: "that they are a wonderful creation of God." Respecting the differences of all people, Rebecca explained how the seminars strengthened her ability to discuss various types of prayer with her students and show them that all forms of prayer were important:

> The message that I take to the children is that God created all of us. We all have differences. We are all very unique, but we are all very special to Him. And again, there are many ways to pray. I always pray with the children. We can always do a prayer that we've memorized. Sometimes we do more of that just talking to God.... I have always had a love for the Rosary. And perhaps even that was strengthened for me.

Scripture played a central part in the seminars and some teachers felt that they understood more and felt more comfortable in teaching about Scripture. As a result, they used it more frequently and included it more easily in their lessons. Monica appreciated the time spent in the seminars looking at parts of Scripture. She learned to value and use Scripture more with her students:

> I refer them more to Scripture, ... And I would point out to them the parts in Scripture, different passages that meant a lot to me, and where it would

say this is what God thinks of you and this is what God expects of you....
And so I used a lot more of that in the classroom than I did before.

A few of the participants felt that what they learned about prayer not only influenced their own prayer, but also allowed them to have a better relationship with their students, either feeling more connected with the students or more willing and comfortable praying with them. Lucy explained: "I'm sure it has had an impact on that because every time that I have attended the seminars... it just brings such a heightened awareness to my personal prayer and my personal connection with the children and with myself."

The seminars also affected Katherine's interaction with her students, especially in the area of prayer:

> I feel that I'm more willing, maybe willing is not the right word but more, you know, to allow, to allow prayer or to have prayer as more of an element in the room. Yes, it is important that we get our decade of the Rosary in every day during October and I like the idea of centering prayer that you talked about, and the tips for spirituality. And I've used that and that has a tremendous calming effect with the children.

Meditation

Throughout the interviews, the participants used prayer, reflection, and meditation interchangeably, even as they spoke of the prayer forms in relation to their students. Most participants believed that they had learned personally about reflective prayer, meditation, or centering prayer influenced what they, in turn, did with their students. Teachers experienced meditation and centering prayer and learned how to do it in the seminars. They enjoyed it. Taking time to teach students to mediate and finding out that they enjoyed it was one of the strongest themes that emerged. Rose was in the practice of doing some type of daily self-reflection. However, after the seminars, she made time for an evening meditation. In addition, since meditation had become so meaningful to her, she decided to try this with her students. She remarked:

> Personally, it has had an effect, like I said before, we did the meditations. I did incorporate that last year into my class quite a bit off and on. I had a very challenging group last year for my first year and I found that the meditation and getting them to do self-reflection, it calmed the children quite a bit and it got them to actually be a little bit nicer to one another.

In two cases, the principal visited the class and commented to the teacher about the positive effect this had on the students. Rose affirmed that what she had started with herself was so positive that she decided to do it with her students. She recounted an experience of doing a meditation with her students when her principal visited her class:

> I did and actually one of my principal's evaluation of me—it just so happened that that's what I had planned for that day as a closing. And I received quite a few comments that made me feel very pleased with myself and pleased that I went ahead and took the seminar before I started. She thought it was a wonderful idea with this group of kids. And actually she encouraged me to use more of the meditation and self-reflection with them.

Donna started to meditate with her students, and regardless of the grade she has taught, she noted: "It's been wonderful. I've done it every year from eighth graders all the way down to fifth graders and they love it." Donna recounted a similar experience, showing the positive effect of doing meditation with her students:

> I talk with my kids. You get very upset and you get frustrated. You find yourself doing things that you shouldn't do or wouldn't want to do or wouldn't want to react to. So, I find myself stopping and thinking, you know, it's more thinking and being aware you can turn to God and say, "time out, I need to refocus." The first time I did it with the students, you know, you get to breathing slowly and I feel a little bit silly with that. But after the first time, after they realize this is real cool, they constantly ask, "Can we meditate? Can we meditate?" So, I enjoy it. And actually, Mrs. Schwenk came in and we were meditating. And I was thinking that I should be teaching. But she came in and she stayed the whole time. And we talked about Scriptures. She came back and said, "What a great gift you're giving these kids! That was truly good." That's true, because they had actually gotten in trouble in the art room. She came in and said: "What are you doing?" I said, "We're just meditating." And then we talked about when they get themselves stirred up and they're talking too much or whatever, that they can stop, and even if they can't put on a CD at that particular time, they can meditate. They can meditate mentally or you know, become more aware of their surroundings and of God.

Lucy recalled that she had never meditated with her children before the seminars. However, in thinking about something we had done in the seminars that helped her do something different with her children, she responded:

> Oh yes, the quiet centering prayer. You know, I had done that but you can only do it for a short time with this level because they really, some of them do it really well. The others just want to look around and see who has their

eyes closed and you know, and who is really quiet and thinking. And it does cause everyone to be still. And I just, I have talked to them about listening to God, that God speaks to them all the time, but you can't hear Him if you are surrounded all the time by noise. You have to be still and you have to listen.... I know I do it now. And I remember coming back from one of those—the last one and I started doing that—the one with the ocean, the meditation, calming of the sea.

Lucy added that personal prayer and prayer with her children affected the way she looked at her students. She hoped that it influenced the way she handled her children:

I'm sure, I'm sure it has had an impact on that because every time that I have attended the seminars you know, for the weeks, the ongoing weeks, it just brings such a heightened awareness to my personal prayer and my personal connection with the children and with myself.

Listening

Listening was also related to prayer and finding time for prayer. Many participants acknowledged that the seminars had provided time and taught them to listen to God's word in Scripture and through prayer. Because they experienced the value of listening, they saw this as something they wanted to teach their students. Elizabeth appreciated "time to slow down and listen about my faith and the virtues and how to teach it to the kids, how to include it in our day."

Alice explained that she felt that the seminars helped her to be more open and attentive to God's will, not only in prayer but also throughout the day. She was better able to listen and respond to the needs of her students:

I think I looked at my children completely differently when I walked back into my classroom.... It also did other things for me. You get stressed in your classes you know, but you have to be listening to God, open to God and in touch with God.... And that's what you would say, that our spirituality wasn't just on a time zone. When you started your classes but you blessed yourself and you said your morning prayers. You had to be more in tune and open, I mean, open to the message of God. You are listening for His call throughout the day. And I had not been doing that prior to that. I would pray and then I would kind of, you know, turn the dial down and go on with the next chore or the next job or the next activity. But you were saying you keep the dial on and listen throughout the day. For there were many circumstances in my class when children would come to me or situations would arise where the dial was on, and I directed it differently.

Lucy valued the centering prayer. After attending the seminars, she taught her children how to do a short meditation:

> It does cause everyone to be still. And I have talked to them about listening to God, that God speaks to them all the time, but you can't hear Him if you are surrounded all the time by noise. You have to be still and you have to listen.

Lucy felt that the seminars, therefore, helped her with her "personal connection with the children."

Donna also valued prayer and meditation. She began to talk to her students about the value of silence as a way to develop a relationship with Christ:

> I keep stressing to them not to just keep thinking and talking to God, but stop and listen. You know you don't have to keep thinking and talking in your mind. You can just listen. And I said, "He's not going to come out and just talk to you verbally, He's going to talk to your mind, talk through your thoughts." And that's what you need to do is just—actually, I actually had my major concern with this if it bothers you, put it on a piece of paper on your desk and just offer it up and listen. And they seem to know how to do that well.

Quiet/Calm

Time for prayer and listening to God's word about faith and virtue seemed to create an atmosphere of quiet and calm. Music provided a transition from the day's events in school to the time for prayer or instruction on spirituality or topics related to character formation and virtue. Participants not only valued the feeling of calm and quiet for themselves, but also found that this was of benefit to their students. Prayer brought a sense of calm and quiet to the children. Many participants commented that their children initially were not accustomed to quiet, given all the activities, games and electronic devices that occupy them. After learning how to be quiet for prayer, students found that they really liked it. They noticed that it affected how they viewed their students and they were happy to see the positive effect it had on them.

Katherine was more comfortable praying with her students after the seminars. She appreciated the centering prayer and the tips for spirituality and found "that has a tremendous calming effect" on the students. Lucy also observed that the "quiet centering prayer... does cause everyone to be still."

Donna recounted that her class loved meditation and even asked when they could do it. She agreed that many of our children today are not accustomed to "having quiet." However, once they experience it, "they love it." Mary admitted that because of teaching her students more about prayer and meditation, she felt "closer" to her homeroom. She "explained to them about sitting quietly and letting God speak to them."

Alice explained that the peace and calm of the seminars influenced how she looked at her students and interacted with them:

> I think I looked at my children completely differently when I walked back into my classroom—I saw them the way you were presenting the people of God as people who long to be in union with Christ.... Therefore, I looked at those children as more God-centered people and I was horrified. It really scared me to think that I hadn't been thinking enough that way all those years before. But I was thinking more in terms of children, children who need to become acquainted with Christ.... And it was through your messages, your Scriptures, your review of those sacraments, I mean, you did that too sister. You talked a great length about the sacraments and the sacramental grace that flow from those sacraments that gave us the courage to do what we needed to do. We needed to rely on those sacraments and to frequent them. And therefore, I was now, I was looking at my children in a much more spiritual sense than I had before. And therefore, I responded to them differently.
>
> You were so tranquil and peaceful in the class. You never got angry. You never lost your sense of peace. It was there from the first class to the end and that sense of love of God. And that, I really, I felt that that, that love was kind of massaging everyone that was there because it was sinking into our hearts as well. And you were simply showing us the grace that pours forth from the heart of Christ. You were showing us how and giving it to us in a very special, very dynamic but peaceful way. And I think that the first thing I know I did at home and in the classroom was to remember that sense of peace, to remember that sense of Christ-ness, to look at things, situations with amazing a little more mercy and a little more forgiveness in the people that I was dealing with, especially the little children with whom you sometimes tend to loose your patience. You know you can't, but you're holding on. And now I recall I was keeping my patience through a much better channel, the channel of God, not just because I was supposed to be a good teacher.

Time and Space

Time for prayer and listening to God's word about faith and virtue seemed to create an atmosphere of quiet and calm. In general, teachers learned to take more time with prayer and tried to create a prayer corner or table. Following the seminars, Katherine felt that she had a better understanding of virtue and prayer. She was more enthusiastic about the idea of having a specific virtue each month. Instead of just mentioning it or giving out a paper on it, she acknowledged: "I think I feel more, probably I would tend to make more time for it. I would tend, I would be less likely to just try to squeeze it in … in that sense, it's probably made a difference."

Donna had learned to appreciate taking time for herself in meditation. She taught prayer and meditation to her students, and was enthusiastic in recounting how much "they loved it." She agreed that her students learned to appreciate the quiet time for prayer once she gave them the opportunity to experience it.

Laura expressed these same sentiments. She valued meditation for herself. However, she recognized the importance of teaching her students to appreciate quiet time:

> But the need for taking time for setting aside time—I remember making notes that somehow we need to find time for the children to have time because I think our children are as overbooked, as we are. And I think, thank heaven we are in a Catholic school and there are these opportunities. I'd like to see those opportunities expanded, where there could be, you know, just an occasional visit to church that wasn't going for Rosary or Mass or Benediction or just to go or confession. Just to go and sit apart, maybe a class at a time. They could sit in the quiet and reflect, you know. Oh, something that I took away, definitely.

Laura taught art and acknowledged that she had pictures and illustrations that she normally used with her students. However, after the seminars, she felt that she had new ideas to help the children not only to appreciate art, but also to deepen their experience of God. Time and space became more important for her:

> It's not a short-term experience for me. It is continuing, definitely continuing. You know, personally having, and this I think you put out this idea, if I'm not mistaken both in the spirituality and the virtues, the importance of having like a space that you find that's always going to be like your prayer corner. And you have pictures there for reflection or whatever, music, whatever, things you're going to use so, the idea continues with me. But my difficulty in translating that to the students is with my limited contact with the students, seeing them only, basically for one hour or a little bit less a week to plug that into the art room, that's a little bit of a challenge. But we do have a program. Art enhances religion. And we do have a lot of religious artwork that I can present, that I can put up for the children. Because the spirituality. At the end of the year I didn't implement that but I am hoping this year to do that, too. Certainly not every week, but maybe once a month to get out

one or more images for the children to spend, even if it's 3 minutes, just looking and meditating on the image.

Lucy also focused on the idea of taking time to listen. She agreed that the seminars provided her with the opportunity for time "to focus on listening and quiet, because you forget. You really forget that it's so loud and that there's so much going on." She explained how this influenced her thinking about her own students: "I think that there's so many demands on kids and adults. The only quiet time they have is when they fall into bed. That's just not right." She valued finding this time for quiet for children: "I think the little exercise with be still and listen and be very quiet, helps them to realize how noisy the world is and how nice quiet is sometimes. What a gift to have quiet sometimes!"

In addition, in schools that had already started to focus each month on the practice of a virtue, participants found that they gave more time to teaching the virtue, discussing it with their students, and noticing it when children practiced the virtue. Time for the virtue became a priority because the teachers understood more and valued the activity. Jeannice related a similar practice before the seminars. Her school had a virtue each month but she "didn't do a lot of teaching." She explained: "I didn't know how to approach it so much, but I would always read it" She might put up a poster, or teach a short lesson when she received the paper. However, after the seminars, she tried to find books and stories. She spent time thinking how to focus on the virtue. She took time to plan and make it more important for her students: "I needed to, you know, try to make it a part of them, make it more for them. And it was a daily thing, instead of one class or a definition."

RESOURCES

During the virtue seminar, each participant received a binder filled with material related to the theology of topics, such as, virtue, grace, sacraments, conscience formation, and moral development. It included numerous activities for teachers to do with their students. Similarly, during each of the 4 weeks of the spirituality seminar, they received a folder with theological materials related to spirituality and prayer, as well as numerous activities for the classroom. All participants referred in a positive manner to the manual or resources that they received. Specifically, they spoke about the content of the manual and resources, the use of stories, and the jar filled with a walnut and rice.

Manual and Activities

All of the participants valued the manual and resources. They provided them with knowledge on the theological topics from Scripture, and various Catholic Church documents, as well as understanding more about how to teach children of various ages. Many participants used the activities as a springboard to create other activities.

Donna was a member of a school committee that helped to plan activities to emphasize monthly virtues. She found the manual useful. She observed: "I use your book a lot. They have great ideas in there." She explained how each class had made a banner for the virtue of courage. She noted that the manual was a practical resource of ideas: "The handouts, the Scripture readings, the others that applied to each virtue, they were all in the book there. They were practical."

Lucy expressed a similar opinion. She had attended the seminars several times. She expressed that this was partly because of the materials: "They're usable. I could bring them into my classroom, and the worksheets that came with my virtues' book, I have used." She explained that she had gathered several ideas for the school program on respect from these resources.

Rebecca noted that the seminars included methods. She expressed gratitude for some of these ideas:

> You gave us ideas to try this and go back and show your children. I remember you showed us a video on the Mass that talked about the Liturgy of the Word and the Liturgy of the Eucharist. And I remember how important that was to show that to the children and make sure that the children understood the different parts of the Mass. And I know that there were also some methods in there. And I thought they were very helpful.

Rebecca also found the resources helpful in teaching virtue to her students:

> In terms of the virtues, I think it gave me a great resource because there is a lot of information in that virtues' binder. To go back and to share with the children, talk about what they mean, and how at the different grade levels you can put that in place.

Rebecca also used the manual as a resource for her own knowledge. She felt that if she had a better understanding of the theology, then she would be able to use the various activities and methods:

> I remember learning when you taught about the theological virtues of faith, hope and love. That part was really interesting when you were teaching

about the Catholic Church in terms of the virtues.... I found that to be very enlightening. And I know that I have that binder at home in my little library on a shelf and I will go back. I used it as a resource to go back so that I could have a better education and understanding of the virtues in accordance with the teaching of the Catholic Church.

Because the manual was available as a faculty resource, Cecilia was motivated to attend the seminars so that she could have a better grasp of the underlying meaning of the various activities. Natalie found the manual valuable: "Yes, it gave me places to go for research. This book was a big help." Natalie explained: "There's a lot in there about explaining the Rosary, where to look for answers to questions. I found that very helpful." Alice commented about "that beautiful loose leaf binder." She found it useful because it contained many things:

> Many things that you had covered: a Catholic theology, the virtues, the cause of virtues, the prayers, the renewal of prayers that we had learned as little people and what do they mean to us now, and the Scripture packages.

Dolores noted: "It was a ready resource created by Catholic educators for Catholic educators." She explained what she felt made this manual and these resources different from another Religion text:

> That book's put together with thought—that book is put together—that book is put together by educators who understand what it's like to teach in a Catholic school. It isn't a lot of filler. There's a lot of usable materials— materials that's used, used effectively. It's different than a regular teaching manual. It's usable, hands on things that you can use now. It's not—I call filler. It's not called filler, to fill up a book. It's material so usable that's put together—a book that's usable—it's a resource that's usable. It's usable with kids. It's usable for teachers and it really addresses some of the areas as quickly as we need to address them.

Dolores also suggested that the manual is valuable for anyone. However, she strongly believed that teachers needed to attend the seminars in order to derive the greatest benefit from its use:

> I think some of the materials you could pull out and have them do it. They are good. But most of the material just substantiates, just enhances what's taught in the seminar classes, the spirituality classes. You gain the knowledge, the insight at the seminar classes but then you have this manual to take a step further. But I don't think you can separate them. I do not think you can give that manual out to a teacher and they just use it. They probably could. But I don't think they could use it effectively or as effectively as if they had gone to the seminar and to the virtues' workshops and they knew how to present it and why it's so important to present it. I think that's

another thing too. You need to know why are you doing this, why is it important and that's, that's the root of it all. Why is it important? Why are you doing this?

Dolores also noted that because a number of teachers from her school had attended the seminars, they were familiar with the manual and resources. They can share the resources and "help each other" by recommending different ideas or activities contained in these materials.

Walnut and Rice

Just as with the personal influence, the participants singled out the walnut and the rice as a valuable visual aide that was meaningful to all age groups. Several teachers created prayer tables similar to mine and included the walnut and the rice. Others used this idea as a student project so that every student had a symbolic jar. The visual aide of the jar with a walnut and rice became a useful classroom symbol. Donna explained:

> Exactly right, I, the thing with the jar and the rice and the walnut. I love that one because you get so busy in our lives, the kids have sports, and all kinds of stuff like that, so if you don't put God in there first, you never really do get Him in. It all fits if you put God in there first. But if you try to put Him in last it's never going to work.... So I did love that one because it's a visual thing.... As a matter of fact, you know, every now and then I say to the kids, you know, "What in Religion did you particularly like" and they mention that. And they said if you're going to put something like the rice and the walnut, it's visual and you can see it. They actually mention that.

Rose was attracted to the prayer table that I arranged for each session. She commented on the "different artifacts, books or articles." The jar with the walnut and rice reminded her of the importance of developing her spirituality. Her class looked at it and enjoyed talking about it. It made them aware of the prayer table so that Rose eventually began to create other visual objects to encourage them to explore and discuss.

The symbolism of the walnut and the rice inspired Cecilia. She explained how valuable its message was to her prayer life. However, she also felt that her kindergarten class could understand this visual aide: "But I thought, my kids will get this and they did, and, you know, I still remember."

Modeling

The seminars provided teachers with theological content, prayer experiences, and activities to do with their students as well as demonstrations of teaching methods. For example, the classroom space was already set up and materials distributed before the participants arrived. In addition, the presentations provided time for teacher initiated instruction, student experiences, and dialogue and interaction. Participants copied ideas and strategies, including meditation, creating a prayer table, and activities specifically related to teaching commandments and beatitudes. In addition to modeling methods related to prayer, meditation, listening, and quiet, a few of the participants noted that they were impressed with my own peaceful and calm manner of presentation. They tried to copy this and discovered that with patience, they were able to be more tranquil with their students, and their students, in turn, were often calmer. This also caused those teachers to handle some class and home situations with a greater sense of forgiveness and mercy. I had emphasized the importance of listening attentively to God and people. Several teachers commented on the value they found in copying this action. I had often used the expression: "You can't give what you don't have." Several participants quoted this back to me. They indicated that they had applied this motto to developing a spirituality and relationship with God. They were able to share this with their students. They tried to seek a better understanding of the knowledge and methods needed to plan and more effectively teach their students.

Jeannice had been nervous about talking about God or faith in God. She admitted that when she started teaching, "it was okay in religion class" to mention God. However, outside of the formal religion class, she "didn't do a whole lot with it, with the philosophy." She concluded that the seminars were helpful: "helped me to get things together personally, I guess, and then once you've done that, you're better able to pass it on."

In another example, Alice described my emphasis on listening to God and to people. She recalled a meeting with a parent. She tried to model this behavior:

> I remembered your approach. And your approach was one of listening, of sitting back and letting people get settled, of opening yourself to what that person had to say. And I could feel myself doing that. I just sat down. I welcomed her. I greeted her and I listened.

Natalie commented that the seminars were "a wonderful way to prepare children." She took these words seriously, especially in relation to prayer and authentically teaching the content of the Catholic faith: "You can teach it. You can preach it. But if you're not living it and the children aren't seeing it in you, it's not the same."

Rose also used materials related to the beatitudes and the commandments that she found to be helpful. Her students especially liked "a word scramble on the Ten Commandments." She also used these same materials to create her own PowerPoint presentation. She incorporated music, not just in meditation, but art projects. I would put on a religious tape that had some tale, which talked about God. And they really got into it. They enjoyed it so much that it got to a point that they would start asking if they could listen to it during art.

Though Rose had a prayer table in her classroom before attending the seminars, she noticed that each week of the seminar, the objects on the table changed to coincide with the specific topic or theme for study and discussion. She admitted that after the seminars, she copied this idea: "To be honest with you, I don't think I would have changed my or had as many items on the prayer table as I did." She noted that "changing it keeps up their interest in it, draws their attention to it, and draws them away from the computer and more to the prayer table."

Mary also tried to teach her students about meditation and sitting quietly. In addition, she noted that each week the participants received a copy of the plan for that session, Mary "tried doing even better planning." She felt "a little bit more aware of the duty and responsibility" to help the children learn about God. Mary cited modeling as one of the benefits of the seminars, especially for schools that lack the presence of religious sisters:

> I think it's very, very important, even vital that they have the Catholic school teachers, especially those without any religious sisters at their school. It is vital that they have training, not just in philosophy and theology, but in the basics of spirituality like what you did, since they do not have any role models in terms of the religious sisters there. So I think it's very, very important.

Katherine noted that she was willing to pray with her students, and especially liked "the idea of centering prayer, … and the tips for spirituality" because of their "tremendous calming effect." She also modeled the idea of having the children not only write in a journal "to get them ready for a creative writing," but also have "more of a spiritual journal" as she had learned in the seminars.

CARE

Our Catholic belief that we are made in the image and likeness of God and called to holiness served as a foundation for teaching students about respect and a guide for their spiritual growth. As already evidenced in their own dialogue, several teachers tried to describe how the seminars influenced how they looked at their students, viewed their concerns, and treated them with greater care.

Dolores also addressed the importance of being sensitive to her students and teaching them by example to care for and respect each other. She explained that the seminars helped her to know how to present virtues or topics related to character education. In addition, she emphasized, "You need to know why you are doing this, why is it important. And that's the root of it all." The seminars helped her "to get the right message" to her students and "to teach by example."

Monica explained that the seminars had helped her to have a more compassionate view of her students. She noted that she felt she was able "to recognize them more as individuals and to try to meet their individual needs." She believed that:

> We're at the point in education where we are teaching multi-intelligences, that appealing to their positive, good sides, their assets rather than their negative sides. And I think in doing that, in trying to have each one of them be successful in their own way or in their own right. You know, I'm teaching the same lesson to all the kids. I think the benefits have come to me.

Participants related how they tried to make more effort to see each child as a special creation by God, how they were more understanding toward parents, especially during conferences, and how they were more focused on sharing God's love with their students.

STRENGTHENING

The concept of being pedagogically strengthened was an unexpected theme that emerged in every single interview. The actual word, 'strengthen" occurred in all interviews. In addition, the same concept was conveyed in the words, "renewed," "confirmed," "affirmed," "deepened," and "broadened." Just as they felt a spiritual sense of renewal as a personal effect of the seminars, participants also felt strengthened in their teaching. Part of this was because they felt more knowledgeable about religious topics related to prayer and spirituality, as well as to virtue. They had greater confidence that what they were teaching and doing, especially in religion, was right. They felt affirmed and saw the seminars as a confirmation of what they were doing. In addition, if teaching religion topics was new to them, they felt strengthened because they had some accessible resources from which to draw. Other participants were more confident in talking and sharing the faith with students, as well as entering into discussion with parents. Dolores recounted that teachers were able to "teach more soundly and with greater confidence." The seminars helped her as a Catholic educator:

> I think I've gained a deeper understanding of the Scripture, how it related to me as a Catholic educator, how it's sustained me and strengthened me as a Catholic educator. Most importantly, I really feel that as a teacher in the Catholic school, it's more than just a profession. It's a ministry that lets me represent the Church and God's Word to these young children. To teach God's Word, to teach it effectively, we have to live it. And to live it, we have to understand it. So, by going to the spirituality workshop, I gained knowledge, but I also gained strength in my faith, which then helped me to be more effective as a religion teacher

The concept of being pedagogically strengthened emerged as an unexpected theme in every single interview. After the seminars, Mary described how she planned her religion lessons:

> Some days were after I'd get back from church, I went about five in the morning and I spent that time going through the whole week's religion and thinking about it and so forth. It made me a little bit more aware of the duty and responsibility that I had to help the children about God.

Cecilia explained that the seminars helped her with her teaching as well as her ability to involve the parents. From all of the seminars, she felt that she had "come away with something from each one where I could really reinterpret things." Preparing children to receive the Sacraments of Reconciliation and Eucharist in second grade, she said: "The seminars strengthened my teaching by making the parents understand how important it is not to rely on me but to broaden themselves." She further explained that she felt prepared to encourage and remind the parents to take their children to the sacraments more frequently.

Dolores explained that those who attended the seminars were able to teach "more soundly and with more confidence." She noted the importance of demonstration, especially in working with middle school students. She expressed a link between the seminars and a renewed ability to teach:

> You have to demonstrate your teaching. So getting up in front of the class and teaching about a virtue or about the Scriptures or whatever you're teaching, you have to show them that you are first, knowledgeable and second, that you feel it and are enthusiastic about it. And then they catch on, it makes you an effective teacher. And so I think the seminars and the spirituality class, they just tune you in to your faith. They energize you. I think energize is the word

I would use because it gets you excited because it reenergizes your spirituality so that you—teaching, the children see it and they feel it.

INTEGRATION

Integration is a term that may be used to describe curriculum in which the various academic disciplines are intertwined or integrated so that the student learns to see how the various disciplines may be related to each other. Catholic schools usually try to integrate some aspects of faith, virtue, and religious content into all dimensions of the Catholic school experience. The discussion with teachers in these interviews revealed the influence that the seminars had on this integration. Though some teachers included integration among the personal effects of the seminars, the seminars' influence on integration was more prominent in the area of teaching methods. Teachers were also able to recognize more ways of integrating ideas related to good character and virtue, and other religious themes into other subjects and daily events. All participants reported being more sensitive to recognize opportunities to integrate virtues or prayer or other religious themes into any subject. Others felt a sense of confirmation and were less hesitant. A few commented that it was good to hear other teachers talking about doing this and to know it was an acceptable thing to do. Monica, who attended the seminars several years ago, was so accustomed to integrating the religion that she initially found it difficult to give specific examples. Several participants provided examples, with stories in literature being one of the first opportunities to integrate good character and virtue into subjects other than religion.

SUMMARY OF THEMES RELATED TO
THE PEDAGOGICAL INFLUENCE OF THE SEMINARS

All of these themes seem to be connected as ways in which the seminars influenced the participants' teaching or thoughts about teaching pedagogy. In coding for common themes, almost every theme discovered in relation to the personal influence of the seminars was also a significant theme in the seminars' influence on teaching pedagogy. Thus, many of the teachers' descriptions are included in more than one chapter, not to be redundant but to emphasize a parallel between the personal influence and the pedagogical influence. Many things taught, as well as the manner in which there were taught, influenced participants to teach the content and to use many of the teaching methods they had witnessed during the seminars.

From this perspective, I would suggest that the participants and I formed a relationship similar to that found between a parent and child where emergent literacy (Strickland & Morrow, 1989; Sulzby, 1994; Sulzby & Teale, 1991; Teale & Sulzby, 1986; Teale & Sulzby, 1996; and Yaden, Rowe, & MacGillivray, 2000) occurs. Sulzby and Teale (1991) offer a definition of this area as behaviors in reading and writing that precede and develop into conventional literacy. Teale and Sulzby (1996) note that the functions of literacy are an integral part of the learning process that takes place. Children learn through active engagement, constructing understanding of how the written language works.

In their study, the Santa Barbara Classroom Discourse Group (1994) proposed a broader understanding of literacy:

> As members of a group accomplish the events of everyday life, they construct a model or models of literate action that define the boundaries of what counts as literacy in their particular group. In turn, this model serves as a frame for future interactions, which in turn modify the model. (p. 146)

The Santa Barbara Classroom Discourse Group (1994) definition of literacy shows how literacy was defined, redefined, constructed, and reconstructed with a group. Thus, "the outcome of this process is not a single definition of literacy, but an understanding of the multiplicity of literacies individuals face as they become members of ever-expanding groups and communities" (p. 147). They conclude: "like their students, the teachers were influenced by the opportunities they have to learn new ways of being teachers and engaging students in learning" (p. 148). In addition, they conclude that issues of literacy and professional development are intertwined.

In addition to finding a similarity between the influence of the seminars on teaching pedagogy and Emergent Literacy, the concept of "scaffolding" (Sulzby & Teale, 1991) also seems to describe a link between what and how I taught these teachers and what and how they, in turn, chose to teach these religious truth, elements of prayer and spirituality, and virtue and right conduct to their students. Sulzby and Teale explain "scaffolding" in relation to storybook reading. The language of the adult and the child surrounds the author's words. The participants cooperate and seek to negotiate meaning by using verbal and nonverbal means. The adult supports the child's performance through successive engagements. Gradually, the adult transfers more and more autonomy to the child (Sulzby & Teale, 1991). Based on this "scaffolding" concept, reading aloud is an act of construction. Language and the accompanying social interaction are an integral part of the influence of storybook reading on literacy development. Thus, through cooperation, interaction and routine, the scaffold is built so that gradually, the adult reader does less and the child begins to do more and more of the reading, gradually becoming independent.

This model of learning and acquisition of literacy was used in the design of the seminars. hoping that by teaching, guiding, and providing experience, and repeating that each week or in each seminar session, the participants would become more assured and confident and able to teach their students what they had been taught, but in an age appropriate manner. Many participants commented about copying or modeling teaching methods, as well as perceptions of listening, and attitudes of patience and calm. In addition, they repeated these same things with their students. Thus, the "emergent literacy" and "scaffolding" seem to be good models of learning both in my incorporating them into my plans, and listening to how participants followed this same model in their plans.

Having looked at the basic themes that emerged throughout all of the teachers' interviews or stories, the next chapter will focus on the third of four major outcomes of these programs. This chapter takes us into some of the specifics of the importance of character education; namely, making time for it, modeling it through stories, programs, virtue education, and care, and integrating the virtues into the daily activities of the classroom and even the home.

CHAPTER 12

FAITH FORMATION AND CHARACTER EDUCATION

The third research question asked: How do participants, upon completion of the seminars, define character education and articulate whether or not a relationship exists between the seminars and character education? Coles (1986) examines moral thinking and how influences, outside the home, shape it. He also examines the issue of moral conduct (Coles, 1997) as it develops in response to the way a child is treated at home or in school, a response to moral experiences as they take place in a family or a classroom. Moral intelligence (1997) is acquired and grows not only by memorization of rules and regulations but also "as a consequence of learning how to be with others, how to behave in this world, a learning prompted by taking to heart what we have seen and heard" (p. 5). The child witnesses adult morality or lack thereof, looks for cues about how to behave, and finds them in parents and teachers. Life's experiences, as well as stories (Coles, 1989) provide nourishment for the moral imagination.

Many of the themes related to the personal influence and the pedagogical influence of the spirituality seminar and the virtue seminar provided learning opportunities for the participants. Though the interview questions always referred to character education, all of the participants consistently spoke about virtues or virtue programs. They attended a virtue seminar, and knew that virtue and moral development are more commonly used terms in the religion curriculum of the Catholic schools. Therefore,

Faith Formation of the Laity in Catholic Schools: The Influence of Virtues and Spirituality Seminars, pp. 169–185

they automatically identified the virtue and moral concepts with character education, suggesting that character is the fruit of virtue. Though many teachers initially attended the seminars to earn credit toward their religion certification, the interviews showed that the seminars were also relevant in showing the relationship between the seminars and character education or moral development. Knowledge was important since the seminars attempted to expand the participants' theological knowledge as related to virtue development or character education. Some earlier themes were combined, such as, prayer, meditation, listening, and quiet. Other significant themes related to character education included time, modeling, strengthening, and integration.

KNOWLEDGE

Of the various themes showing a relationship between the seminars and character education, acquiring knowledge was the most concrete. Several participants expressed a lack of theological knowledge about the Catholic Religion, either because they had never attended Catholic schools or felt insecure about the validity or correctness of their knowledge. Learning more about the Ten Commandments, the Beatitudes and virtues, understanding more about grace and the sacraments, and understanding more about conscience formation and moral development were some of the chief academic themes that teachers cited. Teachers also learned various ways to teach their students about good character and virtue. Gaining a better understanding, for example of the Beatitudes, made some of the participants focus on helping their students understand the importance of not only knowing the beliefs of their faith but also the importance of putting them into practice. Deeper knowledge also made it easier for some teachers to assist students in having a better understanding of themselves.

Donna acknowledged that the seminars helped her to realize the importance of virtue for herself and her students: "It's not just a task. It's part of what should be their lives." Thus, greater understanding and knowledge of virtue, grace, conscience formation and moral development provided a stronger foundation for the participants so that they could make a better effort to guide their students. In essence, all of the remaining themes related to character education could be considered topics that provided the participants with some type of knowledge.

Mary agreed that she had gained a better understanding of the beatitudes. She felt that she then tried to help her students understand the importance of not only knowing the beliefs of their faith but also the importance of putting it into practice. She commented about the beatitudes and virtues: "I think the beatitudes or virtues are a great way to put into practice what you believe. That's what I tried to get over to the children."

Rose felt that she had gained "a better understanding of the virtues." She explained that "it has been quite a while since I actually sat down and learned from them." She felt the seminars helped her with her "teaching" and "in a personal way for a better understanding." She regretted not having attended the virtue seminar earlier. She described a challenging class of students that she had during the previous year. She felt that the knowledge she gained could have helped her to assist her students in having "a better understanding of themselves."

Lucy found information about the meaning of the virtues "enlightening" and "helpful." She admitted that "it was material I would never have bought or looked for that was important." Donna acknowledged that the seminars helped her to realize the importance of virtue for herself and her students: "It's not just a task. It's part of what should be their lives."

PRAYER, MEDITATION, LISTENING, AND QUIET/CALM

We have already seen that prayer and its various related themes were an integral part of both seminars. While prayer, meditation, listening, and quiet were separate themes in relation to the personal and pedagogical influence of the seminars, in relation to character development, the participants included them as part of one activity. Listening was also related to prayer and finding time for prayer. Many participants acknowledged that the seminars had provided time and taught them to listen to God's word in Scripture and through prayer. Time for prayer and listening to God's word about faith and virtue seemed to create an atmosphere of quiet and calm. Several of the participants noted that prayer and meditation, along with listening and quiet, also helped students to reflect on their own actions, understanding their appropriate behaviors, and recognizing actions, such as bullying, that needed to be changed. Some of the participants noticed a subtle change for the better in some students' actions. Their principals affirmed this observation. This may have helped students to become more accountable and responsible for their actions. Several participants noted that the meditation experience seemed to help their students, not only grow in understanding themselves and the value of good behavior, but also grow closer to God.

Reflecting on whether she noticed any change in her students' behavior as a result of their reflection, Rose told a story of a girl in her class who was "a bit of a bully." Rose explained that during the year as they continued the meditation and self-reflection, "we told them to ask God to help you in some way today to be nicer on the playground or to help someone who doesn't understand. Ask God to give you a little bit of guidance." Rose explained that this student changed over the year. "She was not a bully anymore, not so much." Rose observed that "she actually went from having a few friends to having many friends." The children wanted to sit with her. Rose believed that taking time for quiet prayer and reflection helped this student to change her behavior.

Donna also related how she used the meditation experience to help her students not only grow closer to God, but also grow in understanding themselves and the value of good behavior. Her experience of meditating with her students while her principal came to visit gave example not only of the influence of meditation on her teaching methods, but also on her conscious effort to help her students grow in virtue and moral character.

TIME

Making time for prayer was an important message that influenced the participants. However, making time for virtue also emerged in several of the interviews. Several schools already had some type of school program where each month was dedicated to the practice of a particular virtue. However, several teachers admitted that prior to the seminars, they either made the announcement, put up a poster, or passed out the information that came from the office. However, they did not make time in their plans to explain, discuss or monitor the students' practice of the virtue. Katherine explained that after the seminars, she was more aware of making the virtue a priority, and not just another activity:

> I think I feel more, probably I would tend to make more time for it. I would tend to be less likely to try to squeeze it in. So, I think in that sense, it probably has made a difference.

They tried to make it a part of their students' lives and a daily activity. Jeannice related a similar practice before the seminars. Her school had a virtue each month but she "didn't do a lot of teaching." She explained: "I didn't know how to approach it so much, but I would always read it" She might put up a poster, or teach a short lesson when she received the paper. However, after the seminars, she tried to find books and stories. She spent time thinking how to focus on the virtue. She took time to plan and make it more important for her students: "I needed to, you know, try to make it a part of them, make it more for them. And it was a daily thing, instead of one class or a definition."

Valuing time and space for prayer and listening to God's Word about faith and virtue, teachers tried to share this with students. Many teachers also commented on time. Following the seminars, Katherine felt that she had a better understanding of virtue and prayer. She was more enthusiastic about the idea of having a specific virtue each month. Instead of just mentioning it or giving out a paper on it, she acknowledged: "I think I feel more, probably I would tend to make more time for it. I would tend, I would be less likely to just try to squeeze it in … in that sense, it's probably made a difference."

MODELING

Modeling was as important in influencing the participants' appreciation of virtue as it had been in the previous two areas of influence. Some themes, previously highlighted, were also mentioned as things to model. These included prayer, meditation, listening, and quiet. However, the concept of modeling in relation to character development expanded to include using stories to teach the virtues, establishing programs that paralleled mine, teaching the virtues, and modeling of the virtues by the teachers to their students.

Stories

During the virtue seminar, many materials relevant to virtues and moral development were displayed. These included a variety of videotapes, as well as William Bennett's (1993) *Book of Virtues*. Several of the participants modeled these suggestions and made an effort to use stories to teach their students about good character. Depending on the age of the students, teachers identified characters that possessed particular virtues in the stories. They discussed morals that were portrayed by certain themes and guided their students in discussions to understand the value of virtuous living, noting again that good character is the fruit or result of virtue.

Rose thought of various stories in the children's readers. She could see "incorporating virtues" and having the children talk about characters and their actions. Jeannice reported doing the same thing with her stories from her literature series. She cited a story her class had just read and explained how she would guide her students to find a virtue in the story similar to William Bennett's (1993) *Book of Virtues*.

Programs

Many schools had several teachers who attended the seminars over a 5-year period. As a response to the virtue seminar, several schools started a "Virtue of the Month Program" patterned after the activities and suggestions provided in the seminars. Dolores was in a school that had not previously had a virtues' program. The regular religion curriculum included virtue. However, a group of teachers had attended the virtue seminar. They came back to school and were "excited about the virtues' program" Dolores explained what happened as a result of their faculty meeting:

> At the faculty meeting, we decided that we were so excited about the virtues' program; let's put it into action in our school. Let's put it into action school wide—Grades K-8. Let's expose them to what we ourselves were exposed to. So we formed a committee on the virtues program within our school. And so we had a bulletin board in the cafeteria for the school where everybody shared. And we had a virtues' book and noted virtues displayed in the classes and the students received acknowledgement at school Masses and they received certificates. And the children, each month a new virtue was presented to them and they worked all that month on the virtue and learned about it. And we've been able to take the material that we as teachers had gained and now the students are able to practice the virtue, know about the virtue, and when they receive a certificate, they are excited about that. They are acknowledged for practicing the virtue. The virtues program started from going to the virtue seminar.

The teachers followed guidelines from the seminars, using ideas for bulletin boards, student and family activities, and even recognition of good character through periodic awards. Some schools actually created their own programs centered on a specific theme, such as respect. They gathered resources, created a binder to organize the materials, and hosted faculty in-services to help all teachers to implement the new idea. Laura explained that her school developed a committee after several teachers attended the virtue seminar. She continued:

> We developed a whole comprehensive program that we put in place last school year. And the idea was that we focused on the one virtue of respect because we felt that that just underpinned all the other virtues. And so by focusing on the one, we could tie it to a number of different things throughout the school year. So, we designated each month to focus on a different aspect of respect and we assigned one grade level—we started in ascending order we started with kindergarten and went to eighth grade. Each month a different grade had the responsibility for presenting that particular respect theme. Now, for instance, September we started from kindergarten and worked our way to eighth grade. September, Kindergarten started with

respect for God. And so the teacher, the home room teacher for kindergarten did some research from the materials that we collected from the Virtue Seminar and picked out some ideas and examples and materials distributed and discussed during the seminars. And then she made the materials available to the rest of the faculty. And then we also, the principal designated a little column in our weekly newsletter that was for respect. And the classroom teacher, the homeroom teacher that was responsible for the month would give information to the principal to insert in that corner of the bulletin every week. And that was an attempt to send the program home to the parents as well and have them hopefully not only become aware of what we are doing but sometimes there would be suggested activities that they could do with their children at home to try and involve them in the project or in the whole theme of respect. So that would go on a monthly basis. It would just be different homeroom teachers.

In the "Ambassadors for Christ Program" that Laura described, the principal actually asked her to create an in-service just on respect. She hoped to motivate her entire faculty to implement this new program in the same way the virtue seminar had motivated two or three teachers in her school to venture to create a program on respect. Not only did the program "incorporate respect into the whole thread, the fabric of the school," but also all the teachers pledged their support of it. In addition, they created a system for rewards, and many artistic displays around the school, including a lighthouse with rays for all acts of respect that they had taken from the seminars.

Natalie was also a member of the committee that created this adaptation of the virtue program. She explained the origin of the project. Several teachers had attended the seminars. They decided that their school "really needed to incorporate something in the school because there had been evidence of increasing behavior problems and lack of Christian love and concern for one another, not only in the children, but in the staff too." She affirmed that their program "was productive and helpful."

Virtue

Bennett (1993) maintains that moral education not only involves rules and precepts, but also explicit instruction, exhortation, and training. Moral education must provide training in good habits and affirm the importance of moral example. There is the need for moral literacy, where teachers explain and model good moral practices or virtues (Bennett, Finn, & Cribb, 1999). Based on Aristotle's definition of character as right conduct in relation to others and to oneself, Lickona (1991) offers a way of thinking about character that is appropriate for values education:

Character consists of *operative values*, values in action. We progress in our character, as a value becomes a virtue, a reliable inner disposition to respond to situations in a morally good way. (pp. 50-51)

Following the seminars, teachers felt that they gained a better understanding of the Catholic theology on virtues and issues of conscience formation and character development. They believed that they could talk to their students and help them to express their feelings about virtue in order to help them understand it. Several participants felt more confident that they were saying and doing the right things when they spoke about good habits, virtues, and moral behavior. Natalie felt that if she had a better understanding of the Theology, then she would be able to use the various activities and methods:

> I remember learning when you taught about the Theological Virtues of faith, hope and love. That part was really interesting when you were teaching about the Catholic Church in terms of the virtues.... I found that to be very enlightening. And I know that I have that binder at home in my little library on a shelf and I will go back. I used it as a resource to go back so that I could have a better education and understanding of the virtues in accordance with the teaching of the Catholic Church.

Others commented that they acquired a new view of virtue and began to understand that it had a spiritual dimension, that it was both a gift from God and a means of growing closer to God. In schools that practiced a monthly virtue, some participants related that it became more than another activity or directive from the principal. They perceived its value and meaning as a way of life, and, therefore, devoted more time to it throughout the month. A few participants also commented on their own conscious, increased practice of virtues, being more open and patient with students, able to respect their unique gifts and differences, and, therefore, being able to give better example of the virtues associated with good character. After attending the seminars, Elizabeth felt that she was better able to talk about virtue with her students and help them to express their feelings:

> You made me feel like that I was on the right track as far as Religion and teaching our morals, values, and virtues to the children. And that what I was saying with love, that I was doing the right thing, not only that I was doing the right thing, but morally and spiritually, I was on the right track. I was teaching.

Teachers focused not only on teaching the concepts of virtue but also on helping students value virtue, moral actions, and good character as a way of life. Jeannice had admitted that the seminars had broadened her understanding of virtue. She realized that there was "something spiritual about it. It was coming from God." Her deeper understanding of virtue influenced her decision to focus on virtues and discuss them with her students. The Virtue of the Month was not "just another" activity. She tried to "make it a part" of her students. She tried to practice the virtues and give example to her students. She described herself as being "more open" to her students and to their thinking. She believed the seminars helped her "to be a little more gentle" in helping them to understand and practice the virtues. She agreed that she began to see herself and her students "more in a relationship with God" and on "a journey." She recognized that:

> Religion's not taught just as a Religion course, but they're seeing it always, you know, in all kinds of subjects, or in all kinds of ways. And hopefully, they'll be mindful of that, maybe when they go home, or maybe they'll learn a lesson or something.

Jeannice explained that virtue had become not "just a topic. It's a life." She spoke about focusing on bullying. She admitted that she had been afraid to say anything to the students about their behavior. However, because she felt more comfortable, she would now take the time to talk to the students. She gave an example:

> Now I say, "Why should you ridicule somebody because they're not good at math or maybe they're not good at athletics? I think, you know, God's given us all talents. God gives us all skills and who's to tell God that He's made us defective, you know. But I do try to integrate it even in everyday conversation.

Donna was a member of her school committee to plan their Virtue of the Month Program. She enjoyed building on ideas from the manual of resources that she had received at the seminars. However, she explained that her goal was now "to get the kids to realize that religion isn't just words in the book. It's part of everyday life." She found herself more open and aware of constructive ways to promote good behavior. She wanted her students not "just to say the virtues or memorize the virtues." She tried to direct them to focus on their actions: "Do you see them in each other? Can you see the virtues in each other and in yourself?" She explained that her goal was "to try to get them to live it and to recognize it in other people." As her students became more aware of their good acts and virtues, Donna was amazed at how their own understanding grew. When the principal would visit and ask them for examples of how they practiced a particular virtue, Donna noted: "The kids were so good about it. They were saying things I didn't even realize. They were saying things that I didn't think were the virtue but were picking up as part of the virtue." Donna valued the importance of promoting virtue with the children. She now believed that: "It's not just a task. It's part of what should be their lives."

CARE

In his review of competencies of caring, Sergiovanni (2000) develops his theory about caring as the cornerstone of the commitment needed for teaching. This commitment includes a sense of being there for the other person and a sense of compassion. Caring and serving for him are the foundation anchors for the profession of teaching. He believes that every pedagogical action shows how one is oriented to children, either living up or failing to live up to teaching responsibilities. Several participants spoke about the seminars' influence on how they viewed, approached, or handled their students. Cecilia acknowledged that the seminars served as a reminder and "a review" to look more closely at how she could practice those virtues with her students and, therefore, model them. She explained that she used "Christ as a model in their activities and the way they behave with one another." She offered several examples of how she tried to remind them that Jesus was their model, recognizing the need to address behavior issues as they happened. She acknowledged that she now introduced virtues by "modeling it." She appreciated the opportunity to have children focus on one virtue each month. Yet, she could refer back to virtues when a child called someone a name or exaggerated a story:

> One example I would use, if a child was having an altercation or if somebody said something. Little kids do this so off hand, you know. "I don't like your shoes, or why are you doing that?" And I would always remind them, "You're talking to Christ, He's right there. He's right there in this little boy's or this little girl's heart." And they just kind of look at you like—"what's she saying?" Even though they hear it, they're too little to understand it. But if you catch them right when they're saying something that is not nice, I don't mean just being impolite, I'm not talking about anything horrible, just being a little kid, punching and kicking in line. I think that's, this is, you know, a child of Christ and Jesus is inside everyone of us. "Why are you talking that way?" Oh, okay, you can bring it back. So, modeling it I think. The virtues were wonderful because we could develop a character every month. Then we talk about honesty. And you could spend the month talking about it. And you could go back to it you know. I don't remember the order now but I think honesty was in September and in December we would talk about honesty again, you know, and make it real for them. For instance, talking about things people did on vacation. And if he starts to embellish it, "and we went on a sleigh ride" (laughing).

Some addressed the importance of becoming more sensitive to students and teaching them by example to care for and respect each other. Dolores explained that the seminars helped her to know how to present virtues or topics related to character education. In addition, she emphasized, "You need to know why you are doing this, why is it important. And that's the root of it all." The seminars helped her "to get the right message" to her students and "to teach by example." However, she added that in addition to knowledge and example, "You need to feel it, especially Religion." She explained:

> Because if you do not feel it, they're not going to learn it…. They'll just turn you off. But if they see you take the virtue that you're teaching, take it out of the classroom to other teachers, to other students that they do not teach, that's what's important. And that's what you mean by feeling—you have to feel it—it has to be inside of you—it has to be a part of who you are.

Monica noted that she felt she was able "to recognize them more as individuals and to try to meet their individual needs." She believed that:

> We're at the point in education where we are teaching multi-intelligences, that appealing to their positive, good sides, their assets rather than their negative sides. And I think in doing that, in trying to have each one of them be successful in their own way or in their own right. You know, I'm teaching the same lesson to all the kids. I think the benefits have come to me.

Understanding the importance of virtue from an adult perspective made teachers more committed to teach about it and model it. Taking this further, a few participants now recognized that it was necessary for the teacher to have it first before she could teach her children about developing a relationship with God or others. Rebecca agreed that if she could recognize that love of God in me as the presenter of the seminar and make it a part of herself, then it was possible that she was witnessing to the love of God with her students. There was a good possibility that her students would then recognize that love of God in her and make it a part of themselves, and share it with others.

Monica explained how her spiritual growth, as a result of the seminars, helped her in her practice of virtue:

> I think that's more or less what the virtue seminar said to me. Part of it is, you're happy, you're joyful you know, virtues helped me with the consistency. Sometimes it's hard when you say good morning to somebody and they don't respond, and to keep trying to be positive. What happened as a result of that, it just comes naturally now, because, as I teach the kids, a virtue is a good habit, one that you have to develop. So, no matter where I am, I greet people, say hello, strike up a conversation, and make new friends.

And it's funny that a lot of times what ends up happening is that we end up talking about something spiritual. And I think that's the unique part of all of it, that somehow or other it brings us back to our place with God. And I have felt my spiritual life grow. I found that I needed more Scripture and I looked for hope and other virtues in the Scriptures. I might open up the Scriptures. I get a good idea of what to do today, or how to practice a good life today or how to bring God into my life and or recognize Him in my life and let Him be recognizable to somebody else through my life. I think that's the biggest part of what happened to me, first of all, conscientiously trying to live those virtues, and then somehow naturally I think they have come through to my students.

STRENGTHENING

The concept of being strengthened in efforts to contribute to the character education of students was an unexpected theme that emerged in every single interview. The actual word, "strengthen" occurred in all interviews. In addition, the same concept was conveyed in the words, "renewed," "confirmed," "affirmed," "deepened," and "broadened." The teachers believed that they gained confidence, first to teach about virtue, moral development, and good character, and then to feel that what they taught was accurate and correct, especially within the Catholic tradition.

Dolores explained that she believed the seminars "reenergized" her and gave her more confidence in teaching her students about good character, moral development, and virtue:

Teach it differently—that's a good question. I think that the students focused on how the faculty—once they became familiarized with the virtues, once the children themselves first learned just what a virtue is and what are virtues and why do we have them. First, I think we were able to teach it even more soundly and with more confidence than before because we felt ourselves that we had a good hands-on. But then as we practiced among the staff and we started to interact, I think the children now understand what is a virtue or what is—they see it and they start to practice, to emulate it. And I think, especially, I was thinking for the junior high school, you have to demonstrate for them to really be taught. You can lecture to them and you can give them notes, but you have to demonstrate. That's the best type of learning in junior high. You have to demonstrate your teaching. So getting up in front of the class and teaching about a virtue or about the Scriptures or whatever you're teaching, you have to show them that you are first, knowledgeable and such and second, that you feel it and are enthusiastic about it. And then they catch on and it makes you an effective teacher. And so I think the seminars and the spirituality class, they just tune you in to your faith. They energize you. I think energize is the word I would use because it gets you excited because it reenergizes your spirituality.

For some participants who had attended Catholic schools, the seminars reawakened their association of virtue and right action with God's love. They felt renewed in recalling that God loves us, and gives us the grace to respond to His love, and to love Him and others through the practice of virtue. They were more resolved to teach and guide their students to practice the virtues and develop good character.

Angel expressed this sense of renewal and strength in working with her first grade. She recalled that "the spirituality just kind of brought me alive again." She was renewed in thinking about her role as a Catholic school teacher and more committed to "giving them the foundation, giving them the basics as far as the great love that Jesus has for them." She continued to reflect on "the newness of it all" with feelings of "comfort," "joy," and "renewal." This was especially important to Angel in trying to teach virtue and help her little children develop a foundation for good character:

> I think one of the issues in the virtue seminar—the way children are today as opposed to ten years ago, which is something as teachers, we need to know that so that we can deal with that, because that's what we confront. So, I think it gave me a very broad, a review, the virtues, the virtue seminar. I knew most of it. It was a refresher. But the spirituality, it just kind of really drove home, and I was very, very comfortable after I left.

Rebecca also felt renewed and strengthened by the seminars. The seminars "strengthened and better helped" her to teach her children "that they are a wonderful creation of God." In addition, she felt strengthened in her resolve to teach her students how to be moral and virtuous people of good character. She reflected on this idea:

> I think it was an awareness to me that other people are doing this. I think that I left with more of a sense that others, my colleagues in other Catholic schools in this Diocese, are doing it also. I think that from that, the 2-day workshop, I think to take back to my school the sense of increasing the individual's value, the worth of the child, no matter at what grade level they are at. That was important. There is something you can do with that virtues' program at all levels. I think the core of it is showing the child their value, increasing self-esteem, and helping them to see that they really are a very special creation of God.

INTEGRATION

Catholic schools usually try to integrate some aspects of faith, virtue, and religious content into all dimensions of the Catholic school experience. While the seminars' influence on integration was most prominent in teaching methods, some teachers included integration within the effects of the seminars on character education. I had taught that: "You can't give what you don't have." I had suggested in my teaching that nurturing the spiritual life allowed one to be able to recognize the teachable moments for integrating the faith and moral development into the classroom. They tried to integrate the recognition of virtue and moral living, not only in literature stories, but also in other subjects, including, history, science, and math. A few participants even gave examples of how they had deliberately integrated virtue into their interaction with students. In their response to students' inappropriate behavior, they tried to show more tolerance and acceptance, while they seized a teachable moment, recalling a theme of the virtue seminar, that if we "fall down," with God's grace we are able to "get up." Katherine expressed that after the seminars, she made more time within her daily schedule for focusing on the particular virtue taught each month in her school. She shared a story that revealed how she integrated virtue into her own interaction with a student. She described a situation in which she could have reacted to a child but instead, thought:" Let's see if giving her a chance to redeem herself would be the way to go." Katherine continued:

> Well, it was, she'd written, she was to have completed some sentences. She completed them in a very tasteless manner and the aide picked up on it and she forgot her mother needed to be contacted on this one. But then I thought my impulse was to agree. I talked with her. And I talked about how this was beneath her and affecting her, about her own personal limits, and how this just didn't fit with her being a child of God. And I said, "Did you have somebody with you when you did this?" And she said, "Yes." And she, I knew, I thought that she had done it for crowd appeal. And so, I just had her do them over. I had her write up a note of apology, and I thought she was quite contrite. And I've seen quite a change in her.

Katherine felt that she had seized a teachable moment and handled the situation in a different manner than she would have done before the seminars. She explained:

> Well I think had I not stopped, yes, and thought about it and thought about and remembered this summer we were talking about falling and rising every day. And I thought, "okay, let's give her a chance to rise here, we've had the fall. And so let's give her a chance to rise."

Jeannice took a greater interest in taking time to integrate virtues into her other plans, especially since she had more understanding about their meaning. After introducing the virtue being practiced for the month, she "started trying to find books for them to read." In addition, she tried to include the virtues and moral choices in her other subjects. She explained:

> Yes, and I would try to focus on that. We would discuss it regularly. If I saw something in History, when I'm teaching history, and if I could relate it to a virtue, I would start trying to make it more—. Whenever I could plan it out because I got ideas. And I realized just how important it was not to just keep everything inside, saying it once, constant repetition, write them on the board and by example and trying to find a student who was practicing it. And you might point it out. I try to find examples. I didn't do so much of that before the seminars.

Jeannice realized that "Religion's not taught just as a religion course, but they're seeing it always." She continued to incorporate examples of moral conduct in all of her subjects:

> Because right after the virtue seminar, I was still self-contained and so I was teaching everything, you know. I looked at it in terms of science, or if we're reading a literature story I try to pick out a virtue. Or I try to relate it to something that they might be reading in religion. You know, we might be like, today we were reading a story called "Wreck of the Zephyr." And the boy gets in trouble. He ends up wrecking his boat because of his arrogance and he won't listen to advice. So I tried to incorporate what they might find in religion or even a virtue.

Participants believed that they recognized the need and were able to teach their students to recognize God's gifts and use them to the best of their ability. Monica tried to integrate the virtues into all of her subjects:

> I think it does come across that way because no matter what subject I'm teaching, I can always stop and bring in a spiritual point. I think no matter what, especially when I teach literature. It seems like almost every poem or story we read, it all goes to some virtue. And I reference the kids to something we had in religion class. "See how this fits in here and what would you do with regard to being respectful or loyal here?" So, in Literature, yes. In History, I've noticed it too. And I think the kids, it's funny, I'll get off track and seems like we're having a religion lesson instead of a history lesson. But we can look at different persons in history and how did they contribute to the common good, how did they help to build our nation to be this nation under God and caring about other people? It's funny, but sometimes in mathematics also it comes out. I can't think of anything recently but often-times I'll say to the kids, "This is one of the reasons why I teach in Catholic school because I can share my faith with you in all the subject areas. And I can point out the presence of God in this situation where I couldn't do that in a public arena, you know."

Laura played a role in helping her school create a whole program centered on respect. It was inspired and modeled after the ideas presented in the seminars. The school integrated respect, looking for different aspects of respect to be practiced each month. The principal included comments and suggestions for home practices in her weekly bulletin to the parents. The program was also tied in with the school "Rewards in Discipline Program." At the beginning of the year, the teachers pledged to support the program at a school ceremony. The pledge explained how the teachers "were going to incorporate respect into the whole thread of, fabric of the school, throughout the school." The teachers, in turn, modeled respect and tried to teach it to their students. All subject areas and activities incorporated the virtues. Laura added:

> That idea of respect I mean, it was respect from your playing during Physical Education in the lunchroom. It was everywhere. And I thought that was the way the program was implemented. Every time you turned around, it was there. It was kind of like this bubble encompassing the school. And it just tied everything together.

SUMMARY OF THEMES: RELATIONSHIP BETWEEN CHARACTER EDUCATION AND THE SEMINARS

Throughout the interviews, participants seemed to recognize the personal influence of the seminars, which, in turn, seemed to help them in general with their teaching, and in particular with their understanding and ability to teach students to understand and practice virtue in order to develop sound moral character. The positive personal influence of the seminars affected the relationship between the seminars and character education in a manner suggested by the themes related to teaching pedagogy. The patterns of knowledge development, reflected in the theory of emergent literacy (Sulzby & Teale, 1991) and the concept of scaffolding, could apply to the development of character.

In addition, the acquisition of good character, morals or virtue may suggest that they could be considered within the broader understanding of literacy suggested by the Santa Barbara Classroom Discourse Group (1994). The participants seemed to progress in their understanding and practice of virtue, as well as their ability to teach this to their students.

The participants' comments and behavior supported Lickona's (1993) view that "We progress in character as a value becomes a virtue, a reliable inner disposition to respond to situations in a morally good way (pp. 50-51)."

The participants seemed to progress in their value for character and in their ability to care for their students. This suggests that the participants' actions also support Sergiovanni's (2000) about care and character. With care as the cornerstone and character a goal for education, Sergiovanni believes that teachers are concerned about maintaining and nurturing higher levels of competency, while paying attention to caring and community building. Sergiovanni seems convinced that competence alone is not a sufficient goal for education. Competence and care need to join together in the practice of teaching.

Having looked at the basic themes that emerged throughout all of the teachers' interviews or stories, the next chapter will focus on the final major outcome of these programs. Since it is important for those in a Catholic school to understand the mission of Catholic education, this chapter will show how the experience of the seminars helped attendees to understand and participate more in the mission of Catholic education. However, it will continue this discussion by looking at the core of the mission or purpose, to educate and form students to know and live the Catholic faith. Yet, the mission of any religiously based school, while educating the child intellectually for life, is to form that child in that faith and teach him or her to value it as a way of life. The chapter will also show how regardless of doctrinal content which is specific to each faith, Christian as well as non-Christian, understanding virtue and spirituality, living it, and sharing it with students are applicable to any faith, with the appropriate modifications of doctrine. Thus, the results of this study, while gathered from Catholic schools, can apply to any school that promotes a religious formation for its students.

CHAPTER 13

UNDERSTANDING THE MISSION OF CATHOLIC EDUCATION

The final research question asked: Is there an impact on lay teachers' perceptions of Catholic education as a result of participation in the seminars? The spirituality seminar and the virtue seminar provided learning opportunities for the participants. As the teachers revealed their understanding of the mission and purpose of Catholic schools, both the spiritual and character dimensions of the seminars seemed to lead into several themes related to the influence of the seminars on the teachers' understanding of the mission and purpose of Catholic schools. The most notable themes were modeling and integration, strengthening and care.

MODELING AND INTEGRATION

While the seminars primarily planned to provide teachers with theological content, prayer experiences, and activities to do with their students, they also demonstrated teaching methods to the attendees, as discussed in relation to the pedagogical influence of the seminars. Many of the participants copied ideas and strategies, especially when they spoke about

Faith Formation of the Laity in Catholic Schools: The Influence of Virtues and Spirituality Seminars, pp. 187–198
Copyright © 2008 by Information Age Publishing
187

moral development and introduced the meaning and practice of virtue. Some themes, previously highlighted, were also mentioned as things to model. These included prayer, meditation, listening, and quiet. However, the concept of modeling in relation to understanding of the mission and purpose of Catholic schools focused primarily on virtue and prayer, which were integral parts of the Catholic school experience, yet, could equally be a part of any religious school. While this chapter focuses on an increased awareness of the mission of Catholic schools, since this is the group studied, many of its conclusions can be applied to other religious school experiences.

Vatican Council II's *Declaration on Christian Education* (Pope Paul VI, 1965) showed that education is an important concern of the Church, which "is under an obligation, therefore, to provide for its children an education by virtue of which their whole lives may be inspired by the spirit of Christ" (No. 8, p. 730). The U.S. Catholic Bishops in their 1972 document, *To Teach as Jesus Did,* affirmed that the Catholic school is distinguished by the integration of religious truths and values with life. The Congregation for Catholic Education (1988) stressed the importance of the "climate", which, "if it is not present, then there is little left which can make the school Catholic" (No. 26, p. 13). This climate should be noticed as soon as one enters a Catholic school as though one had entered a new environment, permeated by a Gospel spirit of love evident in a Christian way of thought and life and the presence of Christ. The crucifix alone does not create the climate, but the people, who, by word and example, make the spirit of Jesus present and active (Keating, 1990). Instruction in religious truths and values is important, but it is not simply one additional subject. It should be "the underlying reality in which the student's experiences of learning and living achieve their coherence and their deepest meaning" (U.S. Catholic Bishops, No. 103, p. 29).

VIRTUE

As each participant described her understanding of the mission or purpose of a Catholic school, the idea of drawing closer to God or acting with Christ as a model invariably helped to establish a link between moral development or practicing virtue and the mission of the Catholic school. Jeannice described the purpose of a Catholic school. It is a place "to educate." However, she emphasized that in a Catholic school, "we're here not only to do the basic subjects, but try to show them that those subjects are ways to get closer to God." She believed that what we learn and how we use what we learn "are ways to get closer to God and do what God asks us to do for our neighbors." In view of her understanding of the mission of a Catholic school, she admitted that before the seminars, she "didn't think much about the philosophy" of the Catholic school. She qualified this: "I mean I paid attention to it, but I never thought much about how to teach it or how to, you know I think I always figured it would kind of come." After attending the seminars, she realized:

> It's there or it's not there. You have to teach it. You have to be vigilant about commenting to students, you know, and incorporating the virtues in every aspect and bringing it out. And I think after the seminars, I realized that. And I also don't feel so scared to tell others about it, especially after the Spirituality Seminar. I don't feel so nervous about saying, you know, where, you know, why or where it's coming from.

Jeannice had been nervous about talking about God or faith in God. She admitted that when she started teaching, "it was okay in Religion class" to mention God. However, outside of the formal religion class, she "didn't do a whole lot with it, with the philosophy." She concluded that the seminars were helpful: "helped me to get things together personally, I guess, and then once you've done that, you are better able to pass it on."

The seminars helped participants to look more closely at the Catholic school's philosophy and to make it a reality. Several participants believed that the seminars assisted them in two ways. The spirituality seminar provided inspiration and focused them on the mission; while the virtue seminar provided "the tools to carry it out" and bring children to God. Katherine described the purpose or mission of a Catholic school:

> Well, I feel that we witness to bring our children to Christ, and to help them to grow as fully as they possibly can as Christians or Catholics, and see that their gifts or talents, whatever, are gifts from God. That they can use both for the betterment of the world and also for their own growth, and from, through the virtues, it brings them closer to Him.

Katherine believed that the seminars influenced her ability to continue this mission. She explained that "the tips on spirituality" "inspired" and "focused" her on this mission. She felt that "the virtues" provided her with "the tools to carry it out to see how I could bring children to God."

Lucy described how she viewed the mission of the Catholic school. She believed that the purpose related to character education:

> It's to, the purpose is to help these children get to heaven and to realize that their actions, their thoughts, their knowledge of God and their faith and their service is what's going to help them get there. And it's the values that

you teach, your faith values, that I think is so important for children in schools now.

She felt that the seminars helped her to understand and help with this mission because they had increased her "focus in that direction." She explained how she had a better understanding:

Teaching the virtues, you know, when we went through the different virtues in the Virtue Seminar. Just the little ideas to get it across to the kids, the little activities. It really helped because you know, they say, well teach this, teach that. But then, you just kind of flounder—how am I going to do that—and sometimes just a little sheet will drive a little point home.

She specifically referred to the material that she had gathered from the seminars on the beatitudes, the Ten Commandments, and the "O Antiphons" or Advent psalms.

PRAYER

I had described prayer as the "key to spirituality" and a means of developing a relationship with God. When participants spoke about helping the students to have a better understanding of God and helping them to grow in their faith, they often remarked again about what they had learned about various forms of prayer. They recalled their personal need for prayer as well as the importance of teaching their students so that they would see its value in coming to know and act more like Christ. Prayer was a means of learning about Christ and virtue was a means of putting Gospel values into practice.

Natalie, a non-Catholic, viewed the purpose and mission of the Catholic school as "educating the children with Catholicism as the primary thing to be taught." She felt that "everything else falls underneath that and should flow up to that." From this perspective, she believed the seminars had helped her to understand the mission of the Catholic school, especially to know more about prayer. She explained:

I didn't know what the Rosary was all about. Before, it was just beads. And the Mass, understanding the Mass, learning about Vespers, and learning about children's First Communion, all that was involved there and working in second grade, that was really important.

Rose had attended Catholic school and found that she described the mission of a Catholic school based on that experience. She believed that the mission was "to give the children a better understanding of God" and "to help them grow in their faith." She added:

> Being in a Catholic school helped me tremendously to grow in my faith and to bring me closer to God. And I think that would be the mission of the Catholic school—to help children grow in their own spirituality and to give them a better understanding of the Catholic faith.

Rose admitted that as a student, she did not see the purpose, with "the benefit of Religion, of attending Mass." In trying to explain how the seminars influenced her in the classroom, she provided a concrete description of the prayer table that I had set up with various symbols for each week's lesson, including the "walnut and the rice." From this, she created a prayer table that she changed weekly in her classroom to "get the children to develop their own spirituality."

Donna described the mission of the Catholic school, "to be Christ-centered." She explained the need to put this into practice:

> Not only with the academics, to be able to apply it. But again, I'm more of an apply person, but to apply it to the very life in a Christian society. Like you can read the paper and go through the news and it can be very depressing. But how can you make a better place, how can you?... So going to a Catholic school, learning the virtues and the values and being able to apply it is going to help. And so you're learning that, and your English and your History. But to be a full person, you can get Christ involved in this and then be able to live it, not just say it. And so I think that's pretty much it.

Donna believed that the seminars had helped her with her "belief in Christ and the practice going to Mass every day." Before the seminars, she felt:

> I didn't take care of myself. I wasn't really living it in a sense. I mean, I was going through the motions but I wasn't praying. Yeah, I was praying but not that kind of prayer. But today, I find myself praying like I never had before. So, I think it helped myself and I think it's overflowing to the kids. At least I hope it is anyway.

Because of the seminars, Donna gained confidence and became more involved in the school and church community. She explained:

> But now I lead the prayer at the teacher's meeting and I'm a Eucharistic minister. So at the time, I am spreading. I can do this comfortably where I couldn't do it before.

STRENGTHENING

The concept of being strengthened in efforts to contribute to the mission or purpose of a Catholic school was an unexpected theme that emerged in every single interview. As previously noted, the actual word, 'strengthen" occurred in all interviews. In addition, the same concept was conveyed in the words, "renewed," "confirmed," "affirmed," "deepened," and "broadened." Participants felt that they could understand the mission of the Catholic school more clearly and help to contribute to it. Some were more motivated to make their students more aware of the purpose of the Catholic school mission and show them how to live as caring, compassionate, honest, and respectful Christ-centered people. Those with less experience in Catholic schools felt that they knew more about the schools and were more confident in speaking to students about their faith and its meaning in daily life. Some participants felt a renewed sense of commitment to their role as a Catholic school teacher.

Elizabeth believed that the seminars had "reaffirmed" and "confirmed" her awareness of God's importance in her life. She felt better able to see the purpose of the Catholic school and practice it with more motivation. She believed that the Catholic school was "the only place where you could teach that on a daily basis." She explained the importance of the seminars:

> So I feel that the seminars helped me to realize that, how important these things are to everybody, everyday. From living the virtues and being spiritual are necessary in our society. So because we have a chance to teach in the Catholic school, then that helps explain why it is so important to bring this to the kids and to show them how to live and how to care for others and be compassionate and be honest. And so the seminars I think helped me realize the importance of Catholic schools and having the kids and what to teach and what's important for them to know as far as our faith and as far as the social, when they go out in society.

Dolores described the mission of the Catholic school and the Catholic school educator:

> I think the purpose of the Catholic school, of the Catholic educator is to try to teach as Christ teaches, as Christ would. Make it simple, make it honest, make it true. Don't make it fake. And as a Catholic educator, you have to remember you are in a Catholic school and you are representing the Church. But you also have to be representing Christ to the children. And as I said so many times, you may be the only link to the Church, to the faith that these children have. And maybe you are a defender of the faith because often virtues seem outdated. But you are an advocate for the faith. You have to be representative of Jesus in the classroom and outside the classroom.

Dolores noted that in her 20 years of teaching in Catholic schools, it has changed. "It becomes more difficult" to "get the right message to them." Aware of her "awesome responsibility," she recognized "the need to take advantage of everything that's out there to help you." She believed that the seminars, which she had attended several times, "reenergized" her. "You know," she said,

> It gets you excited. It gets you back in touch. It introduces many new things to you, things that should be important. You know, you become stale. You usually become stale. But you go to one of these seminars and you get excited. You learn something new. You see something, going. So these seminars are so important.... Sure I teach Literature plus I teach social studies. But I live the virtues, I have to live it. I have to live it. The only way I can live it is to understand it. That's what these virtue seminars do for you, those workshops.

Mary felt that charity should be evident in a Catholic school, where all are aware of the importance of God in their lives. With this perspective, she believed that the seminars "gave great inspiration." She felt that they made her "feel more emotional in a sense" about her religion. She felt that she "wanted to do more and continue teaching in a Catholic school."

Angel described the Catholic school mission to help parents with "the gift they have received from God, which is their child." Specifically, she believed parents sent their children to Catholic schools, not only to learn "academics," but also to "learn all about God, all about the Commandments, so that we can all continue in the faith that we have been given." She felt that parents entrusted their children to her care as a Catholic school teacher to carry out an "extremely special" job. She strongly believed that the seminars had been a source of renewal:

> Definitely, you're learning more, you're more enthused. Therefore, that's going to prompt you to go forward. You know, it's just like it's a camaraderie. If we're all doing the right things, everybody's happy and we know we're doing the right thing because we're within God's plan. So it's just a wonderful opportunity to feel that we're where we should be.

Laura explained that in a Catholic school she feels that teachers "can focus on God in all our content areas and in all of our activities." The seminars not only prompted her school to create its own program on respect, but also produced "a heightened level of consciousness." She explained that not everyone was knowledgeable of all the details of their program. However, she was sure that for everyone on staff "there was an awareness of 'Oh, this is our goal. Our goal is to be more respectful of all the different entities.'" She continued, "I just think that there was this heightened level of consciousness that was pervading the school."

Cecilia felt that the seminars had broadened her, "not just as a teacher, but personally." She felt she would have "stayed kind of stagnant" without the seminars. She had learned to share with others, to see how "others interpret things" while "coping" with their students, and how to "talk Christ when you want to scream." She explained that her description of the mission of the Catholic school "was a true expression of what I came away with." She described her gains within her description of the mission of a Catholic school:

> Well, my understanding. Well, let's see. I'm not sure I can answer in a few sentences. The Catholic School has, by its mission, I'm not talking about the mission statement that we flounder over and we spent years working on, but from my own purpose. I think that a Catholic school mission should be to first, recognize the quality of the child and be able to teach them a quality education with a Christian, a strong Christian overview. And by that I mean to be able to give them the gift of Christ and be able to have them model it themselves properly. So I think a Catholic school needs to be able to have as its moral view the identity that they are Catholic, not just Christian. So that we recognize other things like the Mass, the Marian prayers, and to show it…. So, that's how I see.

CARE

Throughout the seminars, I had explained our Catholic belief that we are made in the image and likeness of God. I had used this as a foundation for teaching students about respect. I had also explained that the Catholic Church teaches that we are all called to be holy. This helps to guide our spiritual growth. Several teachers tried to describe how the seminars influenced how they looked at their students, viewed their concerns, and treated them with greater care.

This was similar to Noddings (1984) concepts of distinguishing between "the one caring" and "the one cared-for." Several researchers (Arlin, 1999; Elbaz, 1992; Noddings, 1984, 1988, 1991, 1993, 1999) have emphasized that schools should be centers of care that promote human development and respond to human needs. Sergiovanni (2000) summarizes the importance of caring: "To teach is to profess something, and professing requires standing for certain virtues that include making a public commitment to serve ideas and people. Caring is the cornerstone of this commitment" (p. 35).

If this is true for all teachers, then how much more important it must be for a Catholic school or any school that claims to be rooted in Christ.

To teach students that Christ first loves us and enables us to love others suggests the importance for any teacher, especially in a Christ-centered Catholic school, to demonstrate Christ's care for students so that they will learn how to care for others. Every participant included the concept of care in the mission of a Catholic school, recalling either learning more about Christ's love through prayer and spiritual growth or the importance of modeling that love of God by trying to live the virtues. Teachers recalled not only the mission of the Catholic school, but also their mission as Catholic school educators, to spread the Gospel and bring Christ's love to others through their vocation as a Catholic school educator.

Monica's description of the mission of a Catholic school showed the importance of the concepts of caring, compassion, and love rooted in the love of God. She described the mission in these words:

> I think the continuing of the study of the Good News. I feel that God uses me and other teachers as His instruments to spread the Gospel and bring His love. That's what it is, His love to these children. I feel it is very important that the Catholic school is a place that nurtures God's children that He has brought us here to be His hands in taking care of His children. And that's what I think it is, to have us live our faith. That's why I'm here. I need the support of the community. That in religion class we talk about the Church is not a building. It's the people. So we are a Church here. When you talk about mission, I guess, I see this as a vocation not a job. And I don't know if I equate vocation with mission as much as I guess, I have a hard time putting things into words, it's doing God's will. I feel strongly that God has a job for me to do here, a job and job is kind of an ambiguous word I guess. But through me, His presence will be known and through my faults, his presence won't be known.... I guess probably without getting too wordy is to spread the Good News and to bring an awareness about the presence of God in our lives and to help others to become closer to Him.

Monica believed that the seminars "renewed" her sense of dedication to this mission. It reminded her: "I need to get going again. So it increased the impetus and the drive and the desire to want to be better at living the virtues and teaching the virtues."

Rebecca's understanding of the Catholic school mission was also associated with care and the love of God. She described the mission:

> I think it is to educate the entire child, and I think it would go spiritually emotionally and academically. I always tell the children if you get the spiritual in order first, the academics will come. I think that the purpose of a Catholic education, what should come first, would be your love and obedience to God. And if you have that in place, then you can take on the academics and the physical education of the child. We tell the children, if we don't have the first

in place, the other, even though we might think it very significant, it really is not.

Her understanding of mission was rooted in her belief that "we are able to love because of God's love for us." Rebecca believed that the message of the seminars strengthened this belief. She explained:

> I think it was definitely a strengthening of what I had always felt in my heart. It was a verification so to speak that this is what we are about, this is what we need to be doing with our children. And then again through you, that tremendous love that you have for God is always so evident to me. And that strengthens me to take that back to the students.

Rebecca emphatically affirmed "that gift of loving comes from God. So, absolutely, because God is love, and it is because of that, we are able to love others."

Alice also identified the Catholic school mission with a spirit of caring and of love. She described the mission of the school:

> To guide a child and my mission as a Catholic school teacher was to guide a child spiritually, intellectually, emotionally, physically throughout the year that that child was with me. Probably the most important thing that I could do as a Catholic educator was to instill a love of Christ in the heart of that child. To show Christ to that child as a friend who is something, something really special, more than just your next door neighbor, because that's what a child understands. But also to develop a dialogue with Jesus' Mother, the Blessed Mother, because we, in my life, how I was brought up, I think the Blessed Mother was so utterly important.... So, I think that a very small part of the mission, the mission of the Catholic school, I think is to reach the parents. You are reaching those parents as well as instructing those children, because many times, it is very surprising to me that many of those children attend the Catholic school.

Alice felt that the seminars had "reminded her" of why she was there, and of the importance of understanding and practicing the virtues in relating to students, their parents, or coworkers. Very simply, the seminars "reinstated" this understanding for Alice.

SUMMARY

In order to evaluate the influence of the spirituality and virtue seminars on the understanding of the mission or purpose of the Catholic school, each participant was asked first to describe her understanding of the mission. Then within that context, each teacher could explain the influence of the seminars. Though each one was unique in describing the Catholic school mission, it was interesting to see that they all captured the idea of a school that could be recognized as guiding its students to know and love God and to bring this love to others. With this guiding principle, the Catholic school could educate the whole child, intellectually, physically, emotionally, socially, and spiritually.

The Congregation for Catholic Education (1988) stressed the importance of the "climate", which, "if it is not present, then there is little left which can make the school Catholic" (No. 26, p. 13). This climate should be noticed as soon as one enters a Catholic school as though one had entered a new environment, permeated by a Gospel spirit of love evident in a Christian way of thought and life and the presence of Christ. The Catholic school must motivate the student to come to the faith, to integrate it into life, and to accept and appreciate its values (Keating, 1990).

Hellwig (1998) believes that spirituality must try to be in harmony with the source and meaning of our being in contemplation and in action. Christian spirituality seeks this harmony in a continuing discipleship with Jesus of Nazareth. With discipleship or apprenticeship, "Christian life is a continual learning from and empowerment by the person of Jesus of Nazareth" (p. 7). Many participants felt spiritually enlivened and renewed to model this spirit to the students and to make a deliberate effort to integrate this Christ-centered modeling, incorporating moral and virtuous acts, as well as prayer in its varied forms throughout the school day.

The U.S. Catholic Bishops in their 1972 document, *To Teach as Jesus Did*, affirmed that the Catholic school is distinguished by the integration of religious truths and values with life. The Bishops note the importance of this in light of the current "trends and pressures to compartmentalize life and learning and to isolate the religious dimension of existence from other areas of human life" (No. 105, p. 29). The participants, who felt enlivened spiritually from the seminars, also felt that they could see the importance of integrating religion, especially living the virtues, into all subjects. They believed that they made more of an effort toward this integration because of their deeper understanding.

The concept of caring was not only integral to the Catholic school but also synonymous with any effort to model Christ. This vision of Catholic education resembled the spiritual experience noted by Groome (1998). He believes that the ultimate goal of this education enables people to become fully alive human beings and to fulfill their ultimate human vocation with a horizon that stretches to the Transcendent. Reflective of the value of caring in education as developed earlier, Groome believes that a humanizing education seems more likely for educators who have an abiding faith in the worth of their vocation, the potential of their learners, and in gracious mystery.

Modeling virtue and prayer, integration of religion and concepts of moral development, and nurturing and caring for students as a sign of God's love were major themes that participants identified as signs of the influence of the seminars on their own growth in understanding the mission of Catholic education. If the teacher in the Catholic school is called to assist with the formation of students, helping them to grow and develop in faith (Keating, 1990), then teachers must also be well formed in this faith. Skilled in the art of education, they should also "bear testimony by their lives and by the teaching to the one Teacher, who is Christ" (Pope Paul VI, 1965, No. 8, p. 733). Formation must be a part of and complement to the professional formation of the Catholic school teacher (Sacred Congregation for Catholic Education, 1982). The seminars seemed, in the spirit of these Church documents, not only to provide teachers with the information, but also with the necessary personal formation needed to guide students to a deeper love of God and neighbor, to fully develop and learn to use their gifts and talents, and to become caring and responsible individuals. Modeling and strengthening, integration and care were the major themes that described the influence of the seminars on teachers' understanding of the mission of the Catholic school.

The final chapter offers some suggestions where we need to do more research, not only in Catholic education, but also in any faith-based education primarily in the areas of the formation of lay teachers and the development of some type of character education for students. It suggests how this type of program needs to be developed in more areas so that further study of its effects can take place. It will also suggest how the models that are provided and developed for Catholic schools could be adapted for any faith-based school. This would suggest an even greater avenue for future research.

CHAPTER 14

FAITH FORMATION AND THE FUTURE OF CATHOLIC SCHOOLING

Findings from this study may be helpful in creating additional programs to assist teachers in Catholic schools with their formation. The findings, however, should be considered with an awareness of the limitations of the study. After the initial survey of several hundred participants, the sample size, 15 female Catholic school elementary teachers from one diocesan school system, was very small. Additionally, the selection criteria, teachers who attended both seminars, were broad. No effort was made to look at the individual seminars. Instead, the choice was made to include only those who attended both seminars in order to capture the collective impact of the seminars. The group included teachers from all elementary grades with a diverse number of years of teaching experience. Though a random sample provided the initial survey, the smaller purposeful sample created the group to be interviewed. Out of the 300 teachers who had attended both seminars at the time of the study, less than 1% was male and less than 1% taught on the high school level. Thus, the sample for interview was representative of all of the teachers who attended both seminars within the selected diocese. Discussion and feedback were encouraged relevant to the findings of this study. To preserve the accuracy of the participants' responses, the interviews were audio taped. A third party transcribed the

Faith Formation of the Laity in Catholic Schools: The Influence of Virtues and Spirituality Seminars, pp. 199–208
Copyright © 2008 by Information Age Publishing

tapes and each participant received a copy of her transcription along with her case analysis with a request for feedback before including the material in the study. As a result, common themes across the interviews emerged. Thus, the summary conclusions could show internal generalizability across the group.

However, the issue of external generalizability raises the question of whether the findings from this study can be applied to other people, Catholic schools or dioceses, or other religion courses. The size of the study and the limitation of the content taught make this questionable. However, while the findings may not apply to the general population, it is hoped that this study will produce implications that, with further study, may have significance in the area of teacher formation and character education, not only for Catholic schools throughout the country, but also for other schools as well.

This interview study has implications in the areas of educational leadership, literacy, teacher formation, and character education.

EDUCATIONAL LEADERSHIP

Sergiovanni (1984) distinguishes between school competence and school excellence. Included in the "relational force" of school competence, the principal is able to build a human environment of cordiality, respect, and cooperation. School excellence is created when two additional forces are evident: symbolic and cultural. The symbolic force refers to the ability of the principal to assume the role of "chief" and model goals and behaviors that signal a vision to others of what has meaning and value. The cultural force refers to the ability of the principal to articulate the purposes and values of the school in order to create a meaning-filled experience for staff and students. The Catholic faith provides principles, norms, customs, traditions, and common meanings that enliven Sergiovanni's terms:

> From the first moment a student sets forth in a Catholic school…. Everyone should be aware of the living presence of Jesus … [His] inspiration must be translated from the ideal to the real. The Gospel spirit should be evident in a Christian way of thought and life that permeates all facets of the educational program. (Congregation for Catholic Education, 1988, No. 25).

The Catholic school leader applies these forces of leadership to meet the challenges of nurturing spiritual growth and formation. However, to be excellent, the Catholic school leader must accept the challenge of articulating a Christian vision and the development of spiritually self-aware and motivated Christian individuals (Muccigrosso, 1994). The role of the faith leader may be divided into two parts: the spiritual attributes that a person brings to the job through a personal faith experience, and the pastoral competencies to create a prayer environment, develop a sense of community service, witness to the faith, and integrate the Gospel message into the curriculum (Drahmann & Stenger, 1989).

Leadership occurs at various levels, including the superintendent for a diocesan system, the principal for a school, and the teacher for a classroom. Given the various ways that the spirituality and virtue seminars influenced the participants, these programs seem to help one to develop the spiritual attributes that a person brings to the job and the pastoral competencies needed to create the Catholic school environment. With the apparent influence of these seminars on a small sample, the current seminars could help the classroom leader as well as serve as a resource for principals, as they try to provide programs for their faculties. The spirituality and virtue seminars could potentially contribute to continuing to create Catholic schools of excellence within the Arlington Diocese, as well as in any diocese in the United States.

LITERACY AND CARING

In their study, the Santa Barbara Classroom Discourse Group (1994) proposed a broader understanding of literacy:

> As members of a group accomplish the events of everyday life, they construct a model or models of literate action that define the boundaries of what counts as literacy in their particular group. In turn, this model serves as a frame for future interactions, which in turn modify the model. (p. 146)

If this broader view of literacy is combined with the theories related to scaffolding (Sulzby & Teale, 1991) and emergent literacy (Strickland & Morrow, 1989; Sulzby, 1994; Sulzby & Teale, 1991; Teale & Sulzby, 1986; Teale & Sulzby, 1996; and Yaden, Rowe, & MacGillivray, 2000), then William Bennett's (1993) notion of "moral literacy" could gradually emerge through this scaffolding. From the material gathered in these interviews, many teachers explained how they appreciated my guiding them through repeated experiences of meditation. As a result, they not only were able to meditate, but also were able to recreate these same experiences with their students, in much the same manner as that in which storybook reading takes place. They gave similar examples related to modeling virtue by watching me and trying to capture the same peace in their interaction with students. They gained an understanding of virtue, felt better able to teach it and show care for their students. Guided by these literacy theories, the spirituality and virtue seminars could be a scaffold for emerging personal spirituality, and character development, allowing the teacher to respond to the call of the vocation, "to be a humanizing educator, to teach with a spiritual vision" (Groome, 1998, p. 37).

Larrivee (2000) maintains that the foundation of a caring community begins with a teacher who bonds with and nurtures thoughtful interactions among students. Teachers who cultivate respect are concerned with the dignity and worth of the individual, with acceptance and listening. Noddings (1988) develops the idea of caring as a moral orientation to teaching and the aim of education. Her concept of moral education involves modeling, dialoguing, practice, and confirmation. The themes of modeling, and confirmation were integral aspects of the various ways in which the seminars influenced the participants. Care was an integral part of the mission of the Catholic school. Again, these theories lend support for the validity of the seminars as an effective model to prepare lay teachers in the Catholic schools. However, the integration between the spirituality and the virtue seminars could serve as an added reason that the Catholic school, with adaptation, and the combined seminars, with adaptation could help to establish a program of moral education in any school.

TEACHER FORMATION

Doyle (1990) describes teacher education research as "a loosely coordinated set of experiences designed to establish and maintain a talented teaching force" (p. 3). His five stages or paradigms create a set of stages in which teacher education moved from seeking to prepare teachers in practices at one end to fostering reflective capacities of observation, interpretation, and decision making at the other, with knowledge, personal development, and proactive innovation in the middle. Feiman-Nemser's (1990) notion of reflective teacher education emphasizes the teacher's personal development as a central part of teacher preparation. These theories add to the credibility of helping teachers to develop their own spirituality so that they can better guide their students' faith and virtue development in a Catholic school. However, they may also suggest that the Catholic school, with adaptations, and the combined spirituality and virtue seminars, with adaptations, could serve as a model for any school to develop a program of character education.

However, in addition to reflecting the value of caring in education, as suggested earlier, the spirituality and virtue seminars are rooted in Christ, as the source, model, and goal for spiritual and character development. Groome (1998) supports this faith-centered approach and believes that a humanizing education seems more likely for educators who have an abiding faith in the worth of their vocation, the potential of their learners, and in God. In addition, faith in a religiously held conviction makes it more possible for that conviction to become a source of educators' commitment in their educating. United by their spiritual vision, drawing from a variety of "depth structures" and providing the practical guidance to make this vision a reality in the educator's soul, style, and space, Groome develops his total vision of "educating for life for all."

The last two implications related to teacher formation are related to personal observations about the interviews in this research study. That the spirituality and virtue seminars influenced teacher's pedagogy, character education, and understanding the mission of the Catholic school seems to be supported by the interviews with the participants. The majority of the teachers who were interviewed attended Catholic schools at some point in their lives. This variable emerged during the interviews and was not originally factored into the criteria for selecting the participants. However, another implication of this study emerged. If the majority of the interviewees who attended Catholic schools at some point in their lives felt renewed, strengthened, and more confident that they were praying correctly, teaching correctly, and growing in the spiritual lives as a result of the seminars, then the seminars could have even more to offer to those who never attended Catholic schools.

Finally, I observed that the participants did not feel that my position as assistant superintendent or my vocation as a religious sister inhibited their responses or observations. However, this discussion with the interviewees caused several of them to digress from the questions to the topic of the presence of religious sisters in the Catholic schools. Since the current decline in religious vocations was one reason for the focus of this research on the formation of the laity in Catholic schools, the participants' comments on this topic were of interest. It was apparent that several participants trusted that a sister was more qualified to speak about religious topics, such as, spirituality and virtues. Lucy commented:

> Because you are a religious and because you have a calling to be a religious person, that in itself gives you the graces that a professor wouldn't have. And because you are so important in my Church as a religious, it makes me want to come.

Katherine felt that I, as a sister, through my service, joy, and example, reminded her "that serving with joy is what it's all about." Donna had been inspired to convert to Catholicism because she had observed the Religious sisters in her first school "going to Mass" and "listening to them pray." She was currently in a school where the religious sisters had been withdrawn because of declining vocations. She felt coming to the seminars helped her:

to do a little more to keep this alive,..., to keep the mission going and the vision alive, ... keep the virtues going and the spirituality going so that you can go out and say, yes, this is a Catholic school, not just a school.

Angel recalled being taught by "nuns." As a result, she commented:

What you're saying to me, naturally, I'm going to perk up and listen to everything you're saying, as opposed to me being a Catholic lay person saying it ... because you're representing exactly what the Catholic Church teaches.

Monica summarized these sentiments of trust and confidence in the Religious, but also of hope for the future of Catholic education:

Whenever we have the opportunity to have religious sisters with us. You know, people have said, "We're not going to have a Catholic school. The Religious sisters are gone." Well, we may not have as many religious sisters as we had, but I do think that the ones we have are still very important to us because we do look to you for guidance, for leadership, to teach us, and to pray for us. I know I still think it would be great to have religious sisters here with us in school, whether it be principal or co-teacher or whatever. But there's an element there that, even though we don't have to be in Religious Life to develop this spirituality, it is a different vocation. And I hope that it doesn't dwindle so much that we don't have religious life because I think that we do need it. But I think it's, but I think it will take a different direction. And you being a part of that to nurture it. And I do think we need the seminars to help develop these ideas in us rather than just having the knowledge. The knowledge is important but you need to have the experience.

The reflections of the participants on the topic of religious sisters have several implications. They have identified Catholic schools with the presence of religious. Many of the teachers expressed a feeling of inadequacy in teaching about religious topics. Many of them look to the religious for the correct information on matters of their faith. These thoughts imply the need for doing these seminars and others like them so that the laity will feel qualified to continue the spirit of the "mission" and the "vision" of Catholic schools. Their thoughts may also raise the question, would the same seminars, taught by a lay person, be as well received? If future research shows that the seminars are effective with a broader population, should religious teach them in a spirit of handing on the faith? Finally, since several teachers were prompted to attend the seminars because they knew me through my professional work with them, would that imply that a key ingredient for future seminars is that the facilitator should be someone known and respected by the group?

RECOMMENDATIONS FOR FUTURE RESEARCH

This qualitative study of 15 lay teachers who explored the influence that a series of spirituality and virtue seminars had on them, their teaching pedagogy, character education and their perceptions related to the Catholic school resulted in recommendations for future research. The research recommendations that follow may potentially provide greater insight into the formation of lay teachers in Catholic education, as well as the moral formation or character development of students, primarily in Catholic schools, but also in any educational setting.

Formation of Lay Teachers in Catholic Education

In recent years, there has been an emphasis in Catholic education to define and characterize the Catholic identity of Catholic schools. In addition, programs to assist with the formation of Catholic school principals have been developed. However, the lay teacher in the Catholic school in most Catholic dioceses has been required to pursue and maintain the courses necessary for teacher licensure and the religion courses needed to obtain religion certification within the specific diocese. In both cases, the focus has been on teacher development, both professionally and theologically.

The results of this study suggest that, in addition to the necessary educational and theological content, teachers also need guidance to develop their spirituality. Teachers attending the spirituality and virtue seminars felt renewed. They learned to recognize the need to develop their own personal relationship with Christ, which, in turn, motivated them. They not only felt that they did a better job of teaching the content of the religion, but they also discovered the importance of their own underlying relationship with Christ. They no longer taught just a subject called religion, they taught a way of life. They grew in understanding how to live this Christ-centered life and were, therefore, enthusiastic in sharing this with their students.

However, approximately 300 teachers in the selected diocese attended both of these seminars. Additional research needs to be done first within the selected diocese, and then across multiple Catholic dioceses in the United States. In addition, the specific doctrine taught in these seminars could be adapted to other religious denominations and similar seminars created to determine the consistency of the influence of this model in assisting with the faith formation of teachers in other religious schools, the effect on their pedagogy, their understanding and development of character education, and their understanding and integration of their own school mission within their specific roles in their schools.

Within the original diocese, more teachers need to attend the seminars so that more data can be gathered from a larger number of participants. Studies also need to be done with teachers on the secondary level to see if the seminars have the same influence on this level as on the elementary level. Studies also need to be done with more variation in the sample based on gender and number of years teaching. Since the majority of teachers in the sample for this study had attended Catholic schools for some period in their lives, more work needs to be done to see how if there are significant differences in the seminars' influence on teachers who have never attended Catholic schools. If the increased numbers within the original diocese continue to support the positive influence of the seminars, other dioceses would be more likely to want their teachers to attend the seminars. This, in turn, could lead to a national database to try to confirm these initial findings.

Another area for research related to the formation of lay teachers could focus on the influence of each of the seminars on participants. Approximately 500 teachers in the selected diocese attended one or both of the seminars. In the current study, several participants seemed to imply that the spirituality seminar influenced their own spiritual growth, while the virtue seminar provided the content so that they could teach this to their students. However, they were only questioned about the total influence of the two seminars. Thus, studying the separate influence of each seminar could provide more data about the nature and specific influence of each seminar. This could serve as a guide for the creation of additional seminars to build on the foundation provided by the spirituality and virtue seminars.

This current study related to lay teacher formation was broad in the sense that the spirituality seminar offered general tips to help participants with their spiritual growth. The study could be expanded by creating a spirituality seminar that would focus on the charism or spiritual characteristics of a particular religious community or religious denomination. Based on the outcome of this current study and the positive influence it had on the participants, this could be a means for current religious communities to nurture the charisms of their founders and continue their community's influence on Catholic education, despite declining numbers of religious vocations. It could also serve as a model or foundation for other schools, not necessarily Catholic, to nurture their own spirit and charism.

Character Education

In recent years, many materials have been created related to character education. These have included stories, videos, and manuals filled with a wide range of activities to do in the classroom. However, this current study was more focused on the teacher's personal preparation. Teachers' personal spiritual growth and development of their relationship with Christ, along with a plethora of theological and psychological content to give them an understanding of virtue and human development, seemed to take them from simply doing activities to looking to inspire students to act morally and virtuously as a way of life modeled after Christ.

A future topic for study would be the students who are involved in some type of character education. Does a Virtue of the Month Program, implemented by teachers who have attended the spirituality and virtue seminars, produce more positive and lasting character development in students than a set of character or virtue activities, implemented by teachers who have not had this type of preparation?

An additional topic for future research, and specifically teacher education research, could be to adapt the seminars to provide a character education preparation for teachers in any school, including any religious or public sector. While I personally believe that the faith dimension and Christ-centered approach provides an essential foundation for a character education program, I supported my spirituality and virtue seminars with several educational theories that are recognized, regardless of the religious dimension. These included the role of the educational leader to create schools of competence and excellence (Sergiovanni, 1984), the pattern of emergent literacy (Strickland & Morrow, 1989; Sulzby, 1994; Sulzby & Teale, 1991; Teale & Sulzby, 1986; Teale & Sulzby, 1996; and Yaden, Rowe, & MacGillivray, 2000), and scaffolding (Sulzby & Teale, 1991), a broadened view of literacy (Santa Barbara Classroom Discourse Group, 1994), the recognition that the role of the educator, noted by Plato and Aristotle, has been seen as "a spiritual vocation implying its surest foundation is the educator's own spirituality" (Groome, 1998, p. 37), a program of character education built on respect and responsibility (Lickona, 1991), the importance of caring as the cornerstone for the commitment of teaching (Sergiovanni, 2000), the need to recognize the relationship between the one caring and the one cared for (Noddings, 1984), the importance of building a moral literacy for youth (Bennett, 1993), and the notion that "We progress in our character as a value becomes a virtue, a reliable inner disposition to respond to situations in a morally good way" (Lickona, 1991, pp. 50-51). Character is the fruit or outgrowth of virtue. Therefore, a series of seminars to strengthen the teacher's own spirituality and to provide an understanding of the meaning and values associated with virtue could provide the enrichment and motivation to make the character education manuals come alive.

CONCLUSION

Traditionally, Catholic schools in the United States were staffed exclusively by priests, religious brothers, and religious sisters. Today, however, they are predominantly staffed by laypersons. This change in teaching staff has inevitably altered, to one degree or another, the essential religious character and culture of Catholic schools. To provide assistance in the overall mission, spirit, culture, and charism of Catholic schools, a series of spirituality seminars and virtue seminars was created. Based on this qualitative interview study, the seminars had a positive influence on the individual participants, especially in developing their spirituality. The seminars also assisted them with their teaching and thinking about their teaching pedagogy. The participants found a relationship between the seminars and character education. Finally, the participants perceived that they had a deeper understanding of the mission or purpose of a Catholic school and how to implement this in their daily interaction with students, staff and parents. The seminars not only provided the participants with information, but also provided for the formation of the participants.

This qualitative study examined these topics by reviewing each case study, as it was audio taped. In addition, the study identified specific themes that emerged in trying to determine the influence of the seminars. Some of the themes, including prayer, modeling, strengthening, and integration, existed within and across the four areas being studied for the influence of the seminars. The implications of this study reveal that the seminars could be valuable for Catholic education, as well as character education in any school setting and faith formation in any religious school setting and thus, are important for future study.

REFERENCES

Aborn, S. (1998, November). 30 days to a more spiritual life. *Ladies Home Journal, 115*(11), 156-161

Arlin, P. (1999). The wise teacher: A developmental model of teaching. *Theory and Practice, 38*, 12-17.

Augenstein, J. J. (1989). Socializtion differences among principals in Catholic schools. *The Living Light, 25*(3), 226-231.

Augenstein, J. J., & Konnert, W. W. (1991). Implications of informal socialization process of beginning elementary school principals for role preparation and initiation. *Journal of Educational Adminsitration, 29*(1), 39-50.

Aumann, J. (1985). *Christian spirituality in the Catholic tradition.* San Francisco: Ignatius Press.

Benedict XVI, Pope. (2005). *God is love.* Boston: Pualine Books and Media.

Bennett, W. (Ed.). (1993). *The book of virtues: A treasury of great moral stories.* New York: Simon & Schuster.

Bennett, W. J., Finn, C. E., Jr., & Cribb, T. E., Jr. (1999). *The educated child: A parent's guide from preschool through eighth grade.* New York: Simon & Schuster.

Bryk, A. S., Lee, V. E., & Holland, P. B. (1993). *Catholic schools and the common good.* Cambridge, MA: Harvard University Press.

Buetow, H. A. (1985). *A history of Catholic schooling in the United States.* Washington, DC: National Catholic Educational Association.

Burrett, K., & Rusnak, T. (1993). Integrated character education. *PDK Fastback Series 351.* Bloomington, IN: Phi Delta Kappa Educational Foundation.

Catechism of the Catholic Church. (1992). New York: Catholic Book Publishing.

Ciriello, M. J. (Ed.). (1994). *The principal as spiritual leader: Expectations in the areas of faith development, building Christian community, moral and ethical development, history and philosophy.* Washington, DC: United States Catholic Conference.

Coles, R. (1986). *The moral life of children.* Boston: Houghton Mifflin.

Coles, R. (1997). *The moral intelligence of children.* New York: Penquin.

Congregation for Catholic Education. (1988). *The religious dimension of education in a Catholic school: Guidelines for reflection and renewal.* Washington, DC: United States Catholic Conference.

Congregation for the Clergy. (1997). *General directory for catechesis.* Washington, DC: United States Catholic Conference.

Convey, J. J. (1992). *Catholic schools make a difference.* Washington, DC: National Catholic Educational Association.

Cook, T. J. (2001). *Architects of Catholic culture: Designing & building Catholic culture in Catholic schools.* Washington, DC: National Catholic Educational Association.

Doyle, W. (1990). Themes in teacher education research. In W. R. Houston, M. Haberman, & J. Sikula (Eds.), *Handbook of research on teacher education* (pp. 3-29). New York: Macmillan.

Drahmann, T., & Stenger, A. (1989). *The Catholic school principal: An outline for action.* Washington, DC: National Catholic Educational Association.

Earl, P. H. (2006). *Building the builders: Faith formation in virtue.* Washington, DC: National Catholic Education Association.

Edgington, W. D. (2002). To promote character education, use literature for children and adolescents. *The Social Studies 93*(3), 113-117.

Elbaz, F. (1992). Hope, attentiveness, and caring for difference: The moral voice in teaching. *Teaching and Teacher Education, 8*, 421-432.

Feiman-Nemser, S. (1990). Teacher preparation: Structural and conceptual alternatives. In W. R. Houston, M. Haberman, & J. Sikula (Eds.), *Handbook of research on teacher education* (pp. 212-233). New York: Macmillan.

Fortosis, S. (2001). Theological foundations fro a stage model of spiritual formation. *Religious Education, 96*(1), 49-64.

Fowler, J. (1991). *Weaving the new creation.* New York: Collins.

Fowler, J. (2004). Faith development at 30: Naming the challenges of faith in a new millennium. *Religious Education, 99*(4), 405-422. Retrieved March 5, 2007, from http://www.proquest.umi.com /pqdweb?index=146&sid=5&srchmode=1&vinst=PROD&fmt=3&s...

Galda, L. (1984). Narrative competence: Play, storytelling, and story comprehension. In A. D. Pellegrini & T. D. Yawkey (Eds.), *The development of oral and written language in social contexts* (pp. 105-117). Norwood, NJ: Ablex.

Gardner, H. (1999). *The disciplined mind: What all students should understand.* New York: Simon & Schuster.

Gorman, M. (1989). The spirituality of the Catholic school principal. In R. Kealey (Ed.), *Reflections on the role of the Catholic school principal* (pp. 29-33). Washington, DC: National Catholic Educational Association.

Groome, T. (1998). *Educating for life for all: A spiritual vision for every teacher and parent.* Allen, TX: Thomas More.

Guinan, M. D., OFM. (1998). Christian spirituality. *Catholic Update #C0598.* Cincinnati: St. Anthony Messenger Press.

Haitch, R., & Miller, D. (2006). Storytelling as a means of peacemaking: A case study of Christian education in Africa. *Religious Education 101*(3), 390-402.

Halford, J. M. (1999). Longing for the sacred: A conversation with Nel Noddings. *Educational Leadership 56*, 28-32.

Heft, J. (1991). *The Catholic identity of Catholic schools.* Washington, DC: National Catholic Educational Association.

Hellwig, M. (1998). The hallmarks of Christian apprenticeship. *Momentum 29,* 7-8.

Hersey, P. (n.d.). *NASSP assessment handbook.* Reston, VA: National Association of Secondary School Principals.

Horrell, H. D. (2004). Fostering hope: Christian religious education in as postmodern world. *Religious Education 99*(1), 5-23.

Hughes, L. W., & Ubben, G. C. (1984). *The elementary principal's handbook: A guide to effective action,* (2nd ed.). Boston: Allyn & Bacon.

Jacobs, R. M. (1996). *The vocation of the Catholic educator.* Washington, DC: National Catholic Educational Association.

John Paul II, Pope. (1979). *On catechesis in our time.* Boston: Daughters of St. Paul.

John Paul II, Pope. (1993). *Veritatis splendor.* Boston: Daughters of St. Paul.

Keating, J. R. (1990). *A pastoral letter on Catholic schools.* Arlington, VA: Diocese of Arlington.

Keating, T. (1987). *The mystery of Christ: The liturgy as spiritual exercise.* Rockport, MA: Element.

Kelly, E. M. (Ed.). (1996). *Numerous choirs: A chronicle of Elizabeth Bayley Seton and her spiritual daughters* (Vol. II). Saint Meinrad, IN: Abbey Press.

Kimbrough, R. B., & Burkett, C. W. (1990). *The principalship: Concepts and practices.* Englewood Cliffs, NJ: Prentice Hall.

Larrivee, B. (2000). Educational culture and climate: Creating caring learning communities. *Contemporary Education 71,* 18-21.

Leadership Conference of Women Religious. (2007). *Pioneers, poets, & prophets: Catholic Religious sisters in America.* Silver Spring, MD: Author.

Leseman, P. P., & deJong, P. F. (1998). Home literacy: Opportunity, instruction, cooperation and social-emotional quality predicting early reading achievement. *Reading Research Quarterly 33,* 294-318.

Lickona, T. (1976). *Moral development and behavior: Theory, research and social issues.* New York: Holt, Rinehart, & Winston.

Lickona, T. (1991). *Educating for character: How our schools can teach respect and responsibility.* New York: Bantam.

Lickona, T. (1993). The return of character education. *Educational Leadership 51*(3), 6-11.

Lickona, T., & Ryan, K. (Eds.). (1992). *Character development in schools and beyond.* Washington, DC: The Council for Research on Value and Philodophy.

Martin, J. (2000, July 1-8). The business of belief: Living a spiritual life in the corporate world. *America, 183*(1), 16-19.

Matthaei, S. H. (2004). Rethinking faith formation. *Religious Education 99*(1), 56-71.

Maxwell, J. A. (1996). *Qualitative research design: An interactive approach.* Thousand Oaks, CA: SAGE.

McGuffey, W. H. (1836). The eclectic first reader for young children. Cincinnati, OH: Truman and Smith.

McNeil, B. A. (1996). Elizabeth Seton—mission of education: Faith and willingness to risk. *Vincentian Heritage, 3,* 185-200.

Melville, A. M. (1951). *Elizabeth Bayley Seton, 1774-1821.* New York: Charles Scribner's Sons.

Merkel, J. (1998). Sacred circles. *Momentum, 29,* 36-38.

Merriam_Webster collegiate dictionary (11th ed.). (1996.) Springfield, MA: Merriam-Webster.

Miles, M. B., & Huberman, A. M. (1994). *An expanded sourcebook: Qualitative data analysis* (2nd ed.). Thousand Oak, CA: SAGE.

Moore, J. P., Jr. (2005). *One nation under God: The history of prayer in America.* New York: Doubleday.

Morneau, R. F. (1995). *The importance of religious imagination: A talk.* Canfield, OH: Alba House Cassetttes.

Morneau, R. F. (1996). *Spiritual direction: Principles and practices.* New York: Crossroad.

Morris, T. H. (1998). Rooted in the paschal mystery. *Momentum, 29,* 24-26.

Muccigrosso, R. (1994). Nurturing faith: The principal's trust. In M. J. Ciriello (Ed.), *The principal as spiritual leader* (Vol. II, pp. 3-7). Washington, DC: United States Catholic Conference.

Muto, S. A. (1984). *Pathways of spiritual living.* Petersham, MA: St. Bede's.

National Catholic Educational Association. (n.d.). *Shepherding the Shepherds* [Program] Available from National Educational Association Programs Web site http://www.ncea.org/departments/secondary/programs/shepmain.asp

National Catholic Educational Association. (2002). *United States Catholic elementary and secondary schools 2001-2002: The annual statistical report on schools, enrollment and staffing.* Retrieved from National Educational Association News and Information 2001-2002 Web site http://www.ncea.org/newinfo/ nceacommunications/cswhighs2002.asp

National Catholic Educational Association. (2007). *A brief overview of catholic schools in America.* Retrieved June 20, 2007, from http://www.ncea.org/about/ HistoricalOverviewofCatholicSchoolsInAmerica.asp

National Conference of Catholic Bishops. (1979). *Sharing the light of faith.* Washington, DC: United States Catholic Conference.

New England Primer. (1805). Albany, NY: Whiting, Bacjus and Whiting.

Noddings, N. (1984). *Caring: A feminine approach to ethics and moral education.* Berkeley: University of California Press.

Noddings, N. (1988). An ethic of caring and its implications for instructional arrangements. *American Journal of Education, 96,* 215-230.

Noddings, N. (1991). Stories in dialogue: Caring and interpersonal reasoning. In C. Withrell & N. Noddings (Eds.), *Stories lives tell: Narrative and dialogue in education* (pp. 157-170). New York: Teachers College Press.

Noddings, N. (1993). Beyond teacher knowledge in quest of wisdom. *The High School Journal, 76,* 230-239.

Noddings, N. (1993). Conversation as moral education. *Journal of Moral Education, 23,* 107-118.

Noddings, N. (1999). Caring and competence. In G. A. Griffin, M. Early, & National Society for the Study of Education (Eds.), *The education of teachers* (pp. 205-220). Chicago: NSSE, Distributed by the University of Chicago Press.

Palmer, P. J. (1999). Evoking the spirit. *Educational Leadership, 56*, 6-11.

Patel, E. (2003). On nurturing a modern Muslim identity: The institutions of the Aga Khan development network. *Cross Currents, 53*(2), 209-211.

Pius X, Pope. (1905). *On the teaching of Christian doctrine.* Boston: Daughters of St. Paul.

Paul VI, Pope. (1965). *Declaration on Christian education.* Boston: Daughters of St. Paul.

Peck, M. S. (1993). *Further along the road less traveled.* New York: Simon & Schuster.

Powers, B. (1982). *Growing faith.* Nashville, TN: Broadman Press.

Purcell-Gates, V. (2000). Family literacy. In M. L. Kamil, P. B. Mosenthal, P. D. Pearson, & R. Barr, (Eds.), *Handbook of reading research* (Vol. III, pp. 853-870). Mahwah, NJ: Erlbaum.

Riessman, C. K. (1993). Narrative analysis. In J. van Maanen (Ed.), (Vol. 30). Thousand Oaks, CA: SAGE.

Rite of Christian Initiation of Adults. (1986). Washington, DC: United States Catholic Conference.

Ryan, K. (1993, November). Mining the values in the curriculum. *Educational Leadership, 51*(3), 16-18.

Sacred Congregation for Catholic Education. (1982). *Lay Catholics in schools: Witnesses to faith.* Boston: Daughters of St. Paul.

Santa Barbara Classroom Discourse Group. (1994). Constructg literacy in classrooms: Literate action as social accomplishment. In R. B. Ruddell, M. R. Ruddell, & H. Singer (Eds.), *Theoretical models and processes in reading* (4th ed., pp. 124-154). Newark, DE: International Reading Association.

Schaps, E., Battistich, V., & Solomon, D. (1997). School as a caring community: A key to character. In A. Molnar (Ed.), *The construction of children's character* (pp. 127-139). Chicago: NSSE, Distributed by the University of Chicago Press.

Schwartz, E. (2001). Three stages of a school's moral development. *Religious Education, 96*(1), 105-128.

Sergiovanni, T. (1984). Leadership and excellence in schooling. *Educational Leadership, 41*, 5-13.

Sergiovanni, T. J. (2000). *The lifeworld of leadership: Creating culture, community, and personal meaning in our schools.* San Francisco: Jossey-Bass.

Sergiovanni, T. J. (2006). *The principalship: A reflective practice perspective.* Boston: Pearson Education.

Shimabukuro, G. (1998). The authentic teacher: Gestures of behavior. *Momentum, 29*, 28-31.

Snow, C., Nathan, D., & Perlmann, R. (1985). Assessing children's knowledge about book reading. In L. Galda & A. D. Pellegrini (Eds.), *Play, language, and stories: The development of children's literate behavior* (pp. 167-181). Norwood, NJ: Ablex.

Stephens, L. (1996). *Building a foundation for your child's faith.* Grand Rapids, Michigan: Zondervan.

Strickland, D. S., & Morrow, L. M. (Eds.). (1989). *Emerging literacy: Young children learn to read and write.* Newark, DE: International Reading Association.

Suhor, C. (1999). Spirituality: Letting it grow in the classroom. *Educational Leadership 56*, 12-16.

Sulzby, E. (1994). Children's emergent reading of favorite storybooks: A developmental study. In R. B. Ruddell, M. R. Ruddell, & H. Singer (Eds.), *Theoretical models and processes in reading* (4th ed., pp. 244-280). Newark, DE: International Reading Association.

Sulzby, E., & Edwards, P. A. (1993). The role of parents in supporting literacy development of young children. In B. Spodek & O. N. Saracho (Eds.), *Language and literacy in early childhood education: Yearbook in early childhood education* (Vol. 4, pp.156-177). New York: Teachers College Press.

Sulzby, E., & Teale, W. (1991). Emergent literacy. In R. Barr, M. Kamil, P. Mosenthal, & P. D. Pearson (Eds.), *Handbook of reading research* (Vol. II, pp. 727-758). New York: Longman.

Teale, W. H., & Sulzby, E. (Eds.). (1986). *Emergent literacy: Writing and reading.* Norwood, NJ: Ablex.

Teale, W., & Sulzby, E. (1996). Emergent literacy new perspectives. In R. D. Robinson, M. C. McKenna, & J. M. Wedman (Eds.), *Issues and trends in literacy education* (pp. 129-151). Boston: Allyn & Bacon.

Teur, A. W. (1896). *History of the Horn Book.* London: The Leaderhall Press.

The New American Bible (1970). New York: Thomas Nelson.

United Church of Canada. (2000, Fall). 'Seeds and Sowers" *Children, 19.* Retrieved November 3, 2006, http://www.united-church.ca/faithformation/

Unsworwth, J.M. (2000). The educating icon: Teaching wisdom and holiness in the Orthodox way. *Religious Education, 95*(4), 497-499.

U.S. Catholic Bishops. (1972). *To teach as Jesus did.* Boston: Daughters of St. Paul.

United States Conference of Catholic Bishops. (2003). National directory for catechesis. Washington, DC: Author.

Van Kaam, A., & Muto, S. A. (1978). *Am I living a spiritual life?: Questions and answers on formative spirituality.* Denville, NJ: Dimension Books.

Veverka, F. B. (2004). Practicing faith: Negotiating identity and difference in a religiously pluralistic world. *Religious Education, 99*(1), 38-56.

Wakefield, D. (2000, January-February). Soul man: My spirituality incorrect journey back to God. *Modern Maturity 43W*(1), 34-37, 74-76.

Walch, T. (2003). *Parish school: American Catholic parochial education from colonial times to the present.* Washington, DC: National Catholic Education Association.

Wallace, T. J. (1998). The faith leadership issue. *Momentum, 29,* 46-49.

Weiss, R. S. (1994). *Learning from strangers: The art and method of qualitative interview studies.* New York: Free Press.

Westerhoff, J. H., III. (1976). *Will our children have faith?* New York: Seabury Press.

Westerhoff, J. H., III. (1980). *Bringing up children in the Christian faith.* New York: Winston Press.

Westerman, W. (2005). Educating people of faith: Exploring the history of Jewish and Christian communities. *Religious Education, 100*(3), 333-336.

Wineland, R. K. (2005). Incarnation, image, and story: Toward a postmodern orthodoxy for Christian educators. *Journal of Research on Christian Education 14*(1), 7-17. Retrieved March 5, 2007, from http://www.proquest.umi.com/pqdweb?index=0&did=592655691&SrchMode=1&aid=2&Fmt=3...

Yaden, D. B., Rowe, D. W., & MacGillivray, L. (2000). Emergent literacy: A matter (polyphony) of perspectives. In M. L. Kamil, P. B. Mosenthal, P. D. Pearson, & R. Barr (Eds.), *Handbook of reading research* (Vol. III, pp. 425-454). Mahwah, NJ: Erlbaum.

Yust, K. (2004). *Real kids, real faith: Practices for nurturing children's spiritual lives.* San Francisco, CA: Jossey-Bass.

ABOUT THE AUTHOR

Sister Patricia Helene Earl, IHM is a native of Arlington, Virginia and a member of the Sister, Servants of the Immaculate Heart of Mary, Immaculata, Pennsylvania. She holds a BA from Dunbarton College of the Holy Cross, a MA from Villoanova University, and a PhD in educational leadership from George Mason University. She has been involved in Catholic education for over 35 years, having taught on the elementary and secondary level, serving as an elementary principal and an assistant superintendent of schools for the Diocese of Arlington, VA. She is currently an associate professor of education and director of the Catholic School Leadership Program at Marymount University in Arlington, VA.

Sister Patricia had given numerous presentations nationally and internationally related to faith formation of faculty in Catholic schools, including virtue and spiritually. She has published a variety of articles on this topic. She is the author of a book related to this study, *Building the Builders: Faith Formation in Virtue* (2006, National Catholic Education Association) and also has a chapter on this topic in the *International Handbook on Catholic Education* (Springer 2007)

CPSIA information can be obtained at www.ICGtesting.com
Printed in the USA
LVOW072054080413

328213LV00001B/1/P

9 781593 117146